School Management and Pupil Behaviour

Edited by

Neville Jones

The Falmer Press

(A member of the Taylor & Francis Group)
London, New York and Philadelphia

UK   The Falmer Press, Falmer House, Barcombe, Lewes,
East Sussex, BN8 5DL

USA   The Falmer Press, Taylor & Francis Inc., 242 Cherry Street,
Philadelphia, PA 19106–1906

First published 1989

British Library Cataloguing in Publication Data

School management and pupil behaviour.—(Education
  and alienation series).
  1. Great Britain. Schools. Discipline
I. Jones, Neville, *1930–*
I. Title   II. Series
371.5′0941

ISBN 1-85000-591-5
ISBN 1-85000-592-3 Pbk

**Library of Congress Cataloguing in Publication Data is available
on request**

Jacket design by Caroline Archer

Typeset in 10/12 Garamond by
Chapterhouse, The Cloisters, Formby L37 3PX

*Printed in Great Britain by
Redwood Burn Limited, Trowbridge, Wiltshire*

Contents

Contents

Editor's Foreword

Oxfordshire Disaffected Pupil Programme

The approach of the Oxfordshire Disaffected Pupil Programme (DPP) draws attention to what can and is being achieved in our schools to improve the experience of pupils who are, or who may feel, alienated in school. The positive focus of the Programme is towards the kinds of good teaching and effective management for all pupils, which in itself prevents disaffection, and which can actively engage in the processes of restitution and re-engagement for those pupils who are already alienated. This is to recognize that in spite of ideals for individual pupils, and education as a whole, such ideals cannot always be reached and regularly maintained. No matter how effective and skilled teachers are in their teaching and the management of their schools, there will always be some pupils who are more than a little disaffected with their school experience, and some who as a consequence become actively alienated.

The Programme, however, is essentially about the prevention of disaffection. This can be achieved through curriculum innovation, the ethos and values of schools — effective leadership, through teachers refining their teaching skills together with effective classroom management — all within a context of positive teacher–pupil relationships, by the involvement of parents and others from the local community — and indeed, through organizational planning within schools which can in itself so easily marginalize pupils and their learning.

Disaffection is a normal human sentiment but it has connotations that are both positive and damaging. Disaffection can be a spur to re-evaluating personal goals and a motivating force to achieve these; it can damage self-esteem, confidence and worthwhileness, when it becomes expressed in severe, complex and persisting forms. It is when pupils feel they cannot resolve their dissatisfactions, or feel they are not receiving help to do so, that they are then at risk of becoming educationally alienated. The Disaffected Pupil Programme, as part of its enquiry, liaison, and dissemination aspect, is engaged in bringing attention, through publications, to the innovatory work now being carried out throughout the Education Service in Britain. This book on *School Management and Pupil Behaviour* is part of that work.

Acknowledgements

This book was in preparation during the time the Elton Committee was in session. I would like to record my appreciation to those who contributed new material for the book, sent in copies of their evidence to the Elton Committee, and for the very positive response of contributors in dealing with the proof-reading in record time. The book was already with the printer by the time the Elton Committee reported.

Equally, I must record my grateful thanks to Christine Cox at Falmer Press, for a guiding hand in the early planning of the book, for monitoring so closely its progress and ironing out difficulties — which were few — and for adjustments in the management of production to ensure early production of the book without risk to its form, style or contents. All this was much appreciated and made the task of editing both stimulating and creative.

Neville Jones
April 1989.

Preface

As a member of the Elton Committee, I was conscious that the problems we were asked to investigate were not new. A Member of Parliament in a debate on education in Parliament at the turn of the century complained of 'urchins who could not learn and ruffians who would not learn'.

The difference was and is that we have studied the perennial issues of discipline in school and have been asked to give advice at a time of significant changes in education following the passing of the Education Act 1988. We were conscious that the desired improvements in education would not occur unless our schools were well-ordered communities in which our pupils were well motivated and had a sense of belonging. Our terms of reference confirmed this perspective:

> In view of public concern about violence and indiscipline in schools and the problems faced by the teaching profession today, to consider what action can be taken by central government, local authorities, voluntary bodies including schools, governing bodies of schools, head teachers, teachers and parents to secure the *orderly atmosphere necessary in schools for effective teaching and learning to take place*,

Immediate reaction to the Report has included criticisms that we did not keep to our brief. Some perceived our remit as being about violence in schools and not about violence and indiscipline that produces a disorderly atmosphere preventing effective learning. Our conclusions are based on a large volume and range of evidence, including the largest structured survey of teachers' perceptions of discipline in school ever carried out. This evidence presents an analysis of the problem which not only provides a good basis for our conclusions and recommendations in 1989 but gives a base line against which to monitor future developments.

We concluded that there is not a crisis in our schools but a cause for concern and need for action. The evidence suggests that we should be optimistic, that action can lead to improvement in behaviour in our schools even if we cannot totally eliminate indiscipline. While stating clearly that violent incidents should be handled firmly and victims supported and compensated, we do draw attention to a more common cause of teacher stress, namely day-to-day minor misbehaviour which is very wearing and makes teaching a very demanding job. Inappropriate management of talking out of turn, of hindering other children and jostling in the corridors can lead to an escalation into the serious incidents which make the headlines. The message is hopeful in that concerted action, which perhaps should have been the subtitle of the Report, by all concerned can lead to improvements.

As David Hargreaves notes in the Introduction which follows this Preface, the central problem is how we put well-established educational principles into effective practice in schools and lessons. While we may know too little about how school improvement works we need to ensure that the little we do know is passed on to our teachers and senior managers of schools through initial teacher training, through in-service training and through management training for heads.

A further criticism of the Report has been that it is full of bland exhortations and platitudes. We concluded that we had to in some instances restate the obvious because we found that some schools were not following what seemed to us to be obvious good practice in simple matters. Charles Handy, in his pamphlet assessing the relevance of Peters' and Waterman's *In Pursuit of Excellence* for education, comments that many of the attributes of the best companies, such as productivity through people, seem self-evident but notes that the qualities which distinguish the successful from the unsuccessful companies are the intensity and the consistency with which they pursue their good practice.

A further subtitle for the Report might have been 'Rights and Responsibilities'. The analysis of the relative rights and responsibilities of teachers, pupils and parents is very complex, particularly when one comes to consider how these are framed in the law of the land. That is why we have asked that there should be some clarification in law of the authority of the teacher and that there should be exploration of the concept of vicarious liability being extended to parents in cases of civil action.

This book comprises a useful companion reader to the Report and gives an opportunity for the reader to consider some of the evidence that was submitted to the Committee. Some of the teacher associations have already stated that the Committee has ignored all their advice and suggestions. The following list, while not being exhaustive, indicates how the Report accepts many of the recommendations of the teachers' associations. Thus the Report agrees that there should be less criticism of teachers, that there shall be better integration and resourcing of support services, that there should be more support for teachers who are victims of assault, that schools should create consistent codes of behaviour, make lessons more relevant and take firm action to exclude where appropriate, and finally that parents should give more support to schools.

Perhaps I could be permitted to complete my preface with the final words of the foreword to the Report:

> If our report does nothing else it should demonstrate that our schools do not operate in isolation. They are an integral and immensely important part of society for which we all have a responsibility at some time in our lives. We hope that its publication will lead to a practical recognition of this; to a shared and general sense of commitment to our children's education; to a realisation of the great potential latent in our schools.

Roy Atkinson
County Education Officer
Northamptonshire

Introduction

David H. Hargreaves

By the year 2000 we shall look back over the preceding decade as the age of the Education Reform Act. In ten years' time it will be much easier than it is now to assess the strengths and weaknesses of the reforms and the extent to which they have created continuities and discontinuities, progress and decline in the evolution of our school system.

The driving force behind the Education Reform Act is the government's commitment to raising standards in all aspects of education. The means of achieving this laudable end are fourfold: the introduction of the National Curriculum and the reporting of its assessment; the greater central control and greater control in the schools themselves, with a loss of power to Local Education Authorities; the greater accountability of the professionals, especially teachers, to the public; and the emphasis upon parents as consumers with greater choice within the maintained sector and an expanded private sector.

As Mary Warnock pointed out in her 1988 Ian Ramsey lecture in Oxford, the creation of an educational reform is a good time to reconsider the moral principles that lie behind educational policy and to allow the principles to shine through, illuminating and explaining what was wrong before and what will be put right in the future. Whatever the merits and demerits of the 1988 Reform Act, there is little doubt that, in comparison with the 1944 Act, it seems to lack any great moral purpose or conviction. Its underlying philosophy derives from the principles of competitive individualism and consumer rights. There is nothing to add to or enhance our view of schools as moral communities, educating the young for rational autonomy and social inter-dependence, along with academic achievement and preparation for working life.

How, then, does the work of the Elton Committee fit into the scope of the Education Reform Act? Hardly at all, one is bound to conclude. The Act devotes far more clauses to religious education and worship than to the rest of the curriculum. Moral issues are largely about the need for pupils to learn right and wrong, closely linked to religious (and notably Christian) education. Moral issues are partitioned from the rest of the curriculum and the operation of the education system. Pupil conduct and behaviour are treated as separate and distinctive issues outside the main thrust of the reforms and are, unlike almost everything else on the educational agenda, siphoned off to the old-fashioned independent committee, for the detailed consideration of Lord Elton and his colleagues.

There is here a curious discontinuity between government policy and the developments that have been taking place in our schools over recent years. In the early comprehensives there developed an unhappy divide between the pastoral and academic aspects of education, reinforced by the fact that ex-grammar school staff tended to become heads of subject departments whilst ex-secondary modern staff became heads of house or year. This was, most of us now recognise, a damaging division of labour, for staff and pupils alike, a foolish separation of the inextricably linked academic and pastoral functions. A growing understanding of personal and social education, and the development of the 'pastoral curriculum', have brought a welcome improvement.

Several contributors to this book quote a recent report by Her Majesty's Inspectors, *Secondary Schools: An Appraisal by HMI* (1988), to the effect that

> the behaviour of pupils was often extremely good and they were generally co-operative. In only a very small number of schools (5 per cent) were substantial difficulties being experienced in the classroom (paragraph 29).

In my view it is just as important to cite the words which immediately precede this important professional judgment:

> There have been moves to simplify the complex and elaborate systems of pastoral care which were established in many schools and to strengthen the place of tutorial work for the individual form or tutor group. At the same time there has been a growing recognition that pastoral care and the overseeing of pupils' academic progress are inextricably linked. Increasing prominence was given to the planned use of tutorial time for programmes which aim to promote personal and social development and there were signs of a decline in the still common view that pastoral care consisted only of coping with difficulties and reacting to crises.

HMI do not make a causal connection between these two statements; but it is perhaps implied.

Whilst this link is surely relevant to the work of the Elton Committee, it has virtually been ignored in the National Curriculum. Mr Baker has said that he believes in the importance of personal and social education, but this was after the National Curriculum proposals became law. He is, of course, preaching to the converted, for the same HMI survey shows that 60 per cent of secondary schools put some form of personal and social education within their compulsory core curriculum — far more than currently assign to the core a place for science, or the creative arts, or the humanities, or a modern language. It is earnestly to be hoped that the strange exclusion of PSE from the National Curriculum, presumably on the grounds that it is not a 'subject', will not lead schools to regress whilst they struggle to pack the compulsory subjects into the time-table.

The contributors to this book avoid the trap laid for the Elton Committee — an unwarranted separation of pupil behaviour from their academic development, and the possibility that advice and policy developments arising out of the Elton Report could reinforce such a separation. But they have to treat the basic problem posed to the Elton Committee: is there really a problem to be addressed? In several chapters of this book an attempt is made to assess the evidence that there is a problem. The evidence is confusing, partly because it is conflicting; and it is conflicting because it depends upon what one considers to be evidence. Most people will, I believe, conclude from the review of evidence that there is little to suggest that there is a major problem of pupil misconduct on a large scale in our schools or that the situation has deteriorated in recent times. Most teachers have (and always had) routine problems of classroom management and meet the occasional very difficult child who cannot easily be contained. Given the somewhat artificial nature of schools, it will probably continue to be so. It seems, then, that it is a very small number of schools, and a small number of individual teachers, who have substantial problems in relation to pupil misbehaviour.

So why is there a 'moral panic' over pupil behaviour in schools? The explanation probably lies outside the schools. Public concern over crime, and violent crime in particular, over football hooliganism, and over the national shame engendered by the alcohol-induced misbehaviour of young people in football crowds in Europe and in foreign holiday resorts, has led many to lay the blame at the door of the schools. They are, after all, a convenient scape-goat for many of society's ills, so why not blame them for this as well? Schools, we are told, must not only cure young people of their ignorance but also teach them to be good citizens. If the young do not turn out to be the model citizens we expect, then the schools are at fault. How simple it all is.

Whilst it is absurd to treat schools as the only important agency for the socialisation of the young, teachers have always accepted broad and diffuse goals as part of their task. I hope they will continue to do so. To reject the facile blaming of schools for the deviance of a minority of the young is not to be complacent. On the contrary, it is for teachers to persist in their conviction that they educate the whole person. As Jim Docking reminds us in his excellent opening chapter, good behaviour is not merely a necessary condition for teaching and learning to take place: it is an *outcome* of an effective education, and means far more than superficial classroom conformity.

This book provides a variety of analyses and a wide range of advice on this wider issue of the effectiveness of education. Interestingly, the different perspectives on analysis and advice overlap very considerably, even at times to the point of being repetitive. Perhaps it should be so. The degree of consensus among the contributors, with their very different backgrounds and experiences, is compelling. For convenience we can make a useful analytical distinction in the various contributions. At one level, the analysis and advice is directed to the *individual teacher*, whose skills in managing young people are so consequential in the life of the classroom. At the other level, the analysis and advice is directed towards the *institution as a whole*, since the general ethos, climate or philosophy of a school has its own powerful consequences. In practice, of course, the two levels must be interdependent, though it is far from clear precisely how this interaction works. But most teachers will have something to learn, as classroom teachers, about the ways in which they manage their lessons, and as members of staff within the school that generates its particular ethos.

In his chapter David Reynolds rightly advises us that good pupil behaviour may be a necessary condition for pupil achievement, but it is not a sufficient one. Good behaviour is necessary, and is of value in its own right. But pupils must also learn successfully. Wise teachers have never treated the two strands of learning and good behaviour as independent factors requiring separate treatment. Young or new teachers soon discover that without effective management of classroom behaviour very little learning will take place. Several chapters in this book provide useful and specific advice here, especially on the preventative strategies and skills that are so important. In their recent survey, *The New Teacher in School* (1988), HMI note that in 15 per cent of the lessons they observed the management of the class was unsatisfactory; and only two thirds of the new teachers considered that their initial training had prepared them well for classroom management. One wonders just how many of the small number of teachers who continue to experience significant problems of classroom control could have been made more effective had their initial training placed more emphasis on the sound acquisition of the relevant skills. Teacher trainers too have much to learn from this book. And if they can teach student teachers the more profound insight that good behaviour (however induced) does not guarantee that successful learning takes place, so much the better.

Classroom misconduct does not wholly stem from poor management skills of teachers. It can and does arise from the failure to approach the central business of teaching and learning from the right perspective. Too often secondary pupils are bored and passive; they are insufficiently engaged in, and made responsible for, their learning to resist the temptations of misconduct or, of course, to engage in that polite indifference which can so easily mask serious teaching faults. In their recent appraisal of secondary schools HMI report that:

> in many respects the nature and quality of the classroom experience of pupils seems very little changed since the 1979 survey . . . Many lessons indicated that for the majority of pupils learning and teaching, in terms of pace, content and approach, have changed little since 1979. Pupils continued to spend a large part of their time in the classroom listening or writing; in the later years of school the total volume of their written work was usually considerable. Lessons often contained little to help pupils to apply what they had learned beyond the classroom. Successive lessons frequently followed a similar sequence of activities, and this contributed a sense of sameness and predictability to the pattern of the day.

Not long ago I participated in an inspection of a school course for the Certificate of Pre-vocational Education. One young man, the teacher told me, was being very successful, despite the fact that he had been a notorious trouble-maker in the fifth year. He was clearly enjoying his work. The effects of the FE-style approach — a negotiated curriculum, negotiated teaching and learning methods, investigational and project work, active learning, work experience — were evident for all to see. If only, he told me, they had run the fifth year along similar lines. The CPVE course was a tiny, isolated course in this busy school. When I asked the head why the same principles could not be applied to the fourth and fifth years, he shrugged his shoulders and claimed that this was a different matter. But is it? The important chapters in this book by Pring, Baglin and Walker show how some schools have taken the lessons of FE practice and CPVE courses into the mainstream of secondary education. One of the most significant ways in which to improve pupil behaviour may well be through a fresh approach to styles of teaching and learning. Pupil behaviour reflects the teacher's skill in classroom management; but it also reflects the skills of engaging young people in the central purposes of their learning.

The Elton Report and the content of this book (among others) mean that teachers are not short of good advice or of good examples to follow. The central problem, as Reynolds reminds us, is how to put well-established educational principles into effective practice in the schools and classrooms where it is most needed. It is at this point that the research and the evidence fail us: we simply know too little about how school improvement works. The Elton Report may or may not assuage the moral panic about pupil misbehaviour — probably not; it may or may not satisfy ministers that they have taken public concern seriously — probably so. But if we are to make the necessary changes to make our schools more effective in all aspects of education, then research will be needed to throw more light on the successful management of innovation and change. When all is said and done about pupil behaviour, far more will be said than done until we know how to change schools.

David Hargreaves
Department of Education
Cambridge University
February 1989

Elton's Four Questions: Some General Considerations

Jim Docking

Introduction

Behaviour and discipline are important issues in education. Children and their parents need to be assured that conditions in school guarantee physical safety and psychological security; the well-being of the general community depends upon its young people accepting consensual values and acting accordingly. Effective teaching depends upon pupils respecting the teacher's authority and not inter-fering with each other's learning opportunities; teachers' stress levels are related to success in keeping class control; and a school's enrolment prospects and general reputation owe much to public perceptions of its behavioural standards. Apart from these considerations, the notions of 'good behaviour' and 'discipline' raise fundamental questions about the kinds of interpersonal relationships that are appropriate in a civilized society.

The Elton Inquiry into Discipline in Schools was concerned with an aspect of school life which is important for practical, social, educational, political, and moral reasons. In this chapter, written whilst the committee is deliberating, I wish to raise some issues related to each of the four questions for which evidence was invited, and to draw attention to some relevant research studies.

Question 1: How would you define good behaviour and discipline (and their opposites) in the school context?

The Pack Report (SED, 1977) on behaviour in Scottish schools attempted to answer part of this question:

> Discipline can best be described as the maintenance of an orderly system that creates the conditions in which learning takes place, and that allows the aims and objectives of the school to be achieved. (para. 3.1)

This formulation gives discipline an instrumental role: it is something which must be achieved before the real business of education can take place. But is discipline not also an end in itself? Whilst it is true that the term is often used simply to denote behaviour which facilitates the job of the teacher, it has other connotations in terms of mature cognition and feelings — that is, it is not just something which *allows* the school's objectives to be achieved, it is a social and educational objective in its own right.

In a recent report on standards of behaviour in English schools, HM Inspectors (1987) began with a statement reminiscent of the Pack definition of discipline but went further in suggesting that good behaviour should be qualitatively affected by the process of education:

> Good behaviour is a necessary condition for effective teaching and learning to take place, and an outcome of education which society rightly expects. (para. 1)

Unfortunately this opening paragraph failed to live up to its promise of conceptual clarification since nothing was said to explain the difference between good behaviour which is a *necessary condition* for teaching and learning to take place and that which is an *outcome* of education. Indeed nowhere in an otherwise informative and constructive report do HMI discuss what should count as *good behaviour.*

Any attempt to arrive at one all-embracing definition of good behaviour or discipline is conceptually misguided and educationally unhelpful since it ignores the variety of senses in which these terms are used and the variety of practical implications which this has for schools. I would like to suggest three different definitions of *good behaviour* and three related definitions of *discipline* which have application in the context of the school.

Definition 1: *Conforming, 'socially acceptable' behaviour*

By this I mean the kind of behaviour to which children should conform because it is regarded as minimally necessary for two related purposes in school:

  (a) to allow the school to function as a harmonious and humane community
  (b) to promote an environment which is conducive to serious learning.

In relation to this definition of good behaviour, discipline is facilitative, as the Pack Committee implied, and amounts to external control. It involves the communication and enforcement of expectations and rules (e.g. about punctuality, movement around the school, conduct in the playground and during lessons). Behavioural experiments in changing behaviour suggest that externally imposed rules are more likely to be effective if they are few in number and explicit in content (Wheldall and Merrett, 1984). However, as will be argued in response to Question 4, effective external control in schools is achieved not only through actions which are external to the process of teaching but through the way teaching itself is conducted.

Definition 2:   Self-controlled behaviour

This embraces the same kinds of behaviour as the first definition, the difference being that the rules and expectations have become internalized. Pupils will therefore behave *well* when authority figures are not around and check themselves when transgression is tempting. As far as discipline is concerned, *what* rules and expectations are decided upon and the *manner* in which they are enforced is likely to affect the pupils' willingness to develop *good behaviour* in this sense. HMI (1988) have recently observed that about 5 per cent of secondary schools are over-authoritarian, pupils resenting the staff's obsession with minutiae, and about the same proportion of schools are over-permissive because staff fear alienating pupils. Teachers thus need to be authoritative and assertive but not coercive or domineering. As HMI (1988) have put it, successful practice involves 'opportunities for pupils to practice self-discipline' and 'above all the creation of a climate of mutual respect between pupils and their teachers' (para. 283).

Definition 3:   Responsible behaviour

By this I mean behaviour which is a reflection of the pupils' understanding of and imaginative *feel* for the situation and their sense of commitment to the school as a community. It includes being sensitive to the needs of others and recognizing others' point of view, judging what needs to be done in a given situation and foreseeing the consequences of one's actions, and having the imagination both to realize what might be possible and what actions would be counterproductive. It represents qualities of human relationships which HM Inspectors (1987) should have brought out when they recognized good behaviour to be not only a 'necessary condition' for effective teaching and learning but also an 'outcome of education'.

   This kind of *good behaviour* is clearly more like acting out of a sense of moral obligation, than abiding by imposed codes of practice and internalizing the expectations of others. As in the first two definitions, discipline here is also about *orderly* behaviour, but the order is *educative* rather than *managerial* (Wilson, 1971). It involves insisting that pupils engage in experiences which enable them to develop interpersonal understanding, skills of communication, and social commitment. Pupils therefore need to participate in situations which demand planned, cooperative behaviour; they also need to be incorporated into the school's decision-making processes by being consulted about matters which affect them directly. This in turn means that staff must listen to what the pupils say and regard their perspective as valid. The Children's Legal Centre (1988) have suggested that schools draw up a Pupils' Charter, specifying not only the rights of pupils e.g. 'to participate in school decision-making', but also the responsibilities e.g. 'to show concern for the welfare of others'.

   The promotion of good behaviour in a school involves more than taking measures to reduce the incidence of disruptive behaviour. Understandably, many teachers think themselves lucky if they achieve standards of behaviour in terms of the first two definitions! But this is to miss an important point. An effective disciplinary policy does not consist of *first* reducing deviance and *then* giving pupils responsibility. If pupils are given opportunities which help them to feel empowered and significant, then they are less likely to develop feelings of alienation and of being pushed around. The third definition is thus not an optional extra, available for pupils who have passed the hurdles of the first and second definitions. When pupils feel involved in decision-making and the execution of school policy, they are more likely to want to behave in a socially acceptable way. Further, if pupil behaviour is to be qualitatively affected by experiences at school, policies must be directed at all pupils, not only those who are the most deviant.

Question 2: Is there, in your view, currently a 'discipline problem' in schools and, if so, how serious and widespread is it? What evidence leads you to reach your conclusions?

Presumably it was expected that the answer to the first part of this question is 'Yes' since the Committee's terms of reference explicitly acknowledged 'public concern about violence and indiscipline in schools and the problems faced by the teaching professions today'.

As the Children's Legal Centre (1988) has illustrated in some detail, expressions of serious concern about children's behaviour have been a feature of every age, not least the 1930s which are sometimes remembered as times of immaculate classroom order. The evidence about the incidence of disruptive behaviour and violence today comes from three kinds of sources: reports from HM Inspectors, surveys conducted by the teacher unions, and independent research studies.

1. *Evidence from HMI*

Over the last decade HMI have consistently painted an optimistic picture of pupil behaviour. Headteachers' responses to a questionnaire circulated to 384 secondary schools during the second part of the 1970s (HMI, 1979) showed that 'the very great majority [of schools] were orderly, hard working, and free from any serious troubles ... Hostility to teachers is the least of their worries' (p.251). Only just over 6 per cent of heads found indiscipline a 'considerable problem' and less than 1 per cent a 'serious one'; more specifically, less than 2 per cent found 'hostility to teachers' a 'considerable problem', and none a serious one, while over 64 per cent reported 'no' disruptive pupils.

Of course, heads do not want to impugn their professional competence and so may be 'economical with the truth' when reporting to inspectors. However, the HMI position is also based on many years of direct observation. In a review of reports published in 1983–84 (HMI, 1984), the Inspectors noted that the 'great majority' of primary schools were 'stable and well-ordered' communities (para. 13). In comprehensives the position was much the same: 'The behaviour of pupils, both in classrooms and around the school, is rarely less than satisfactory: usually it is good' (para. 33). The report, covering inspections from 1983 to 1987 (HMI, 1987), showed that opinion had not wavered:

> The overwhelming majority of schools are orderly communities in which there are good standards of behaviour and discipline: poor behaviour is unusual, and serious indiscipline a rare occurrence . . . [This] applies equally to schools in all kinds of areas. (para. 10)

Moreover the above state of affairs was held to have 'remained remarkably consistent over time'.

The recent appraisal of secondary education (HMI, 1988), based on inspections of 185 schools in England between 1982 and 1986, contained a comparable comment:

> The behaviour of pupils was often extremely good and they were generally cooperative. In only a very small number of schools (5 per cent) were substantial difficulties being experienced in the classroom. (para. 29)

Although in the same paragraph HMI added that 'in most schools there were very small numbers of pupils whose behaviour occupied a great deal of teacher time in order that acceptable standards could be achieved', the Inspectorate later made clear in bold-faced type that the position was much the same as in the late 70s:

> The National Secondary Survey found that the very great majority of schools were orderly, hard working and free from any serious troubles. This is still the case. The general picture was of civilized institutions, where most pupils conducted themselves well. (para. 281)

2. Evidence collected by the teacher unions

Recent evidence based on questionnaires to union members is presented in Table 1.1. As the unions themselves have sometimes acknowledged, the surveys are methodologically flawed in some important respects (NAS/UWT, 1985; NUT, 1988). Response rates are not always reported and estimates in these cases suggest returns of only about 4 per cent. The size of these sample is not in question, since even low returns from large memberships can yield several thousand responses; but the representativeness of the sample remains unknown and is likely to be biased since those with adverse experiences would probably have been more motivated to reply. The fact that the samples were self-selecting may help to explain the wide discrepancies in union statistics relating to verbal abuse and physical assault. The highest and probably most representative return was among head teachers, but even here the response rate was only 45 per cent (NAHT, 1988).

The wording of questions in the union surveys have sometimes been loaded and vague and therefore of doubtful validity and reliability. For instance NUT representatives were asked 'Is it the view of NUT members in your school that there

Table 1.1 Incidence of disruptive behaviour by pupils according to teacher union surveys, 1984–88

AMMA (1984) (QU from 156 schs: RR 31 per cent)	In 13 per cent of schools over half the pupils presented a 'disciplinary problem'.
NAS/UWT (1985) (QU from 3910 members: NR, ERR 4 per cent)	Experienced during previous 6 months: 1) 'Verbal abuse' on 1 + occasion by 66 per cent 2) 'Physical assault' suffered by 'over one in twenty-five'; attempted assault by 'nearly one in ten'; threats by 'almost one in four'.
PAT/Daily Express (Stewart, 1987) (QU from 1500) 67 members: NR, ERR 4 per cent)	1) 80 per cent of members subjected to offensive' verbal abuse' by pupils. 2) 32 per cent of members physically attacked by pupils, 67 per cent not, 1 per cent 'no comment'.
NAHT (1988) (QU from 1630 members in representative sample of 15 LEAs: RR 45 per cent)	Physical violence by pupils during 1987 recorded in 22 per cent of nursery, 12 per cent of infant, 12 per cent of primary, 11 per cent of middle and 45 per cent of secondary schools.
NUT (1988) (QU from 1641 NUT school reps: NR)	1) 88.3 per cent said there were 'currently significant discipline problems in school generally'. 4.9 per cent said not, 6.1 per cent 'don't know' 2) 46.1 per cent said there were 'significant discipline problems' in their own school, 41.5 per cent said not, 10.9 per cent 'don't know'.

Note:
The table does not include incidents relating to parents, pupil-to-pupil violence, or responses to questions about changes in standards of behaviour.

Key
QU = Questionnaire
RR = Response rate
NR = No response rate given, or data by which one could be calculated
ERR = Estimated response rate based on membership figure of approx. 100,000 for NAS/UWT and approx. 40,000 for PAT
NOP = National Opinion Poll

are currently significant discipline problems in schools generally?'! It is informative to compare the size of the Yes responses to this question (88.3 per cent) with that from the same question asked about the situation in the respondents' own school (46.1 per cent): behaviour is evidently almost twice as bad in other institutions! As in the above example, terms such as 'discipline problems' and 'verbal abuse' are often left undefined in questionnaires and are therefore open to different interpretations. The NAHT did define terms, but not altogether satisfactorily: for instance, 'physical violence to members of staff' included 'threatening gestures', leaving the incidence of actual attack unknown. But even if terms are defined, no questionnaire survey can allow for teachers' different levels of tolerance and perceptions of appropriate behaviour.

To compound this problem, the unions frequently asked members if they thought the situation had changed over time. (Findings based on these questions are not given in Table 1.1) The PAT/*Daily Express* questions of this kind, besides being loaded and undefined, gave no room for different levels of reply: e.g. 'Do you believe indiscipline is on the increase in schools? YES/NO/NO COMMENT' A further problem arises in the language of the reporting, which in the case of the NAS/UWT and PAT/Daily Express seems designed to elicit a response of horror rather than an impartial assessment. Because PAT used a popular national tabloid as its medium, the results were presented as a series of sensationalist statements beneath lurid headlines. The drama was continued in a letter to the Prime Minister (30.8.87), in which the union's General Secretary alleged that 'the education service faces a national crisis' and 'threatens to overwhelm the education system'. To push the point home further he warned: 'Not to put too fine a point on it, the national curriculum cannot be delivered if there is national chaos in the classroom'.

In spite of the high proportions of disruption and violence presented by the unions, not all is gloom from these organizations. In February 1988, the Legal Secretary of the Secondary Heads Association (himself a headteacher) maintained that the impression given to the public that schools are violent places is 'a travesty of the truth' (Lowe, 1988). In a letter to the Elton Committee (22.6.88), the Union's General Secretary refused to 'add to the catalogue of violence/vandalism/disruption' and instead promised to forward a list of projects which schools had developed to combat the problems positively. Even the NAHT (1988), when commenting on its statistics relating to violence, pointed out not only that the number of incidents vary enormously between LEAs but that a 'significant number' of schools in *each* authority record no cases at all. Unfortunately no figures on this point are supplied; but as regards general disruption, no increase over the year was reported by between 36 per cent and 47 per cent of schools, depending on age-phase.

3. Evidence from independent research studies

Findings from eight recent independent investigations are given in Table 1.2 on page 14.

Many of the statistics here portray a more promising picture than those in Table 1.1 perhaps because they are based on more representative samples and more tightly controlled investigative techniques. Very little serious misbehaviour was noted in those studies which used direct observation, teachers' scaled assessments over several years, or the systematic monitoring of incidents by school staff. In the 1988 National Opinion Poll conducted for the NUT but not confined to the union's members, 55 per cent of the teachers said that 'indiscipline' was either 'no problem' or 'rare', whereas in the NUT's own poll of its school representatives almost 14 per cent fewer said there were no 'significant discipline problems' in their school. In both the Primary and Secondary surveys conducted by the Centre of

Child Study at Birmingham University (Wheldall and Merrett, 1988 and Houghton *et al*. 1988) it was frequent minor offences which concerned teachers, only 1 per cent reporting physical aggression or verbal abuse as a frequent problem.

The response rates for questionnaire returns in the independent studies were way above those achieved by the union surveys: the lowest was 53 per cent and two were above 90 per cent. In the case of the Dierenfield and NOP surveys responses were also more finely graded than those supplied by the unions, though problems of definition and levels of perception still remain, with terms such as 'disruption', 'indiscipline' and 'verbal abuse' undefined. However, the questionnaire used in the recent Wheldall, Merrett and Houghton, *et al*. studies were carefully piloted and respondents were provided with examples of categories of 'troublesome' behaviours.

Perhaps the most interesting finding that emerges is contained in the study of Primary schools by Lawrence and Steed (1986). Local education authorities were asked to nominate schools in which the behaviour of pupils admitted was assessed as potentially 'difficult', 'average' and 'easy'. Within each of these categories a wide range of experiences were reported by heads: among schools with difficult intakes, for instance, the proportion of pupils perceived as 'disruptive or difficult' varied from 0.5 per cent to 40 per cent. It seems unlikely that discrepancies of this magnitude can be explained away by differences in respondents' tolerance levels, and more likely that they reflect different rates of success on the part of the schools. This suggests that the impact of the school is very important.

There is no way in which research on disruptive behaviour and verbal abuse can eliminate subjective opinion and reveal objective reality since these concepts are necessarily based on personal perceptions of the problem. We should not use these difficulties, however, to explain away reported incidents of serious misconduct or to adopt an attitude of complacency. Granted that, when speaking to their union, teachers may exaggerate their troubles to make their case, the NOP (1988) data suggests that rather over one-third believe standards of behaviour are declining. Such a view is not a unique state of affairs historically and, on the NOP evidence, it by no means reflects the position of all teachers; but the nature of some of the incidents reported by all the unions, and the early age at which disruption is reported, give grounds for concern.

From the independent surveys, it seems that the daily stress-inducing problems that confront most teachers are more to do with fairly trivial but regular incidents of misbehaviour, such as talking and mucking around, than with serious offences such as violence and verbal abuse. Moreover since it also appears that in *all* kinds of behaviour there are wide variations between schools with similar intakes, the right question to ask is not so much 'Is there a problem?' but '*Where* is there a problem and *where* is there not, and therefore *is there something we can learn about 'good practice' from the schools which are not experiencing serious indiscipline?*'. It is this issue which will provide the focus of the next two sections.

Table 1.2   Incidence of disruptive behaviour by pupils according to independent surveys, 1982–88

DIERENFIELD (1982) (QU from 465 teachers and heads in 41 LEAs in England: RR 53 per cent)	'Classroom disruption totally out of control': 0 per cent: 'a severe situation': 3.6 per cent; 'possible to cope': 67.8 per cent; 'only a mild difficulty': 19.3 per cent; 'not really a problem': 7.7 per cent
DENSCOMBE (1984) (OB in 2 London compr. schs. (over 4 yrs + 67 interviews with teachers)	1 serious incident against a teacher; a number of mild assaults on teachers, but mainly confined to 1 teacher. Routine disruption not violence the main concern of teachers.
LAWRENCE & STEED (1986) ((1) QU from 85 heads of Primary schs in England: RR 71 per cent (2) Staff monitoring of incidents in 77 schs)	(1) Pupils 'disruptive or difficult' in schools assessed by LEAs as having an intake potentially 'difficult': 0.5–40 per cent; 'average': 0.5–9 per cent; 'easy': 0–17 per cent. (2) Number of disruptive incidents per 100 pupils during one day in schools assessed by LEAs as having an intake potentially 'difficult': 0–18 per cent; 'average': 0–3.3 per cent; 'easy': 0–2.5 per cent.
BLATCHFORD *et al.* (1987) (OB in reception classes of 33 London infant schs)	'Off task' behaviour: 9 per cent — mostly inattention; disruption and aggression: <1 per cent
DAWSON (1987) (QU from teachers in random sample of 9 sec and 22 pr schs in Barnsley: RR 91 per cent)	Children causing 'an unusually high degree of concern' re conduct: 1.5 per cent.
MORTIMORE *et al.* (1988) (Class teachers' structured assessment in 50 London junior schools)	'Disobedient' pupils: 10 per cent; 'cooperative' pupils: >75 per cent.
WHELDALL & MERRETT (1988) (QU from 198 teachers in 25 per cent random sample of Primary schs in a West Midlands LEA: RR 93 per cent)	1) 51 per cent said Yes to 'Do you think that you spend more time on problems of order and control than you ought' 2) 'Troublesome' pupils: 16 per cent 3) Most troublesome (T) and frequent (F) behaviours identified by teachers: 'talking out of turn' (T47 per cent; F55 per cent) and 'hindering other children': (T25 per cent; F21 per cent). 4) 'Physical aggression': T5 per cent; F1 per cent.
HOUGHTON *et al.* (1988) (QU from 251 teachers in 30 per cent stratified random sample of sec schs in a West Midlands LEA: RR 62 per cent)	1) 55 per cent said Yes to 'Do you think that you spend more time on problems of order and control than you ought' 2) 'Troublesome' pupils: 20 per cent 3) Most troublesome (T) and frequent (F) behaviours identified by teachers: 'talking out of turn' (T50 per cent; F49 per cent), 'hindering other children' (T17 per cent; F13 per cent) and 'idleness/slowness' (T13 per cent; F18 per cent) 4) 'Physical aggression': T5 per cent; F1 per cent 5) 'Verbal abuse': T1 per cent; F1 per cent.

Table 1.2   Continued

NOP (1988) for NUT (National poll of 484 teachers [not confined to NUT members])	In respondent's school 'in the last year': 1) 16 per cent said 'indiscipline' was a 'regular' feature, 28 per cent 'frequent', 46 per cent 'rare', 9 per cent 'no problem', 1 per cent 'don't know'. 2) 36 per cent had been subjected to 'serious interruptions' to teaching. 64 per cent not. 3) 18 per cent alleged 'violence against teachers' in their school, 74 per cent did not, 6 per cent 'don't know'. 4) 5 per cent had been personally 'physically assaulted or threatened', 93 per cent had not. 5) 24 per cent had been 'verbally abused', 72 per cent had not.

Key
OB = Structured observation
QU = Questionnaire
RR = Response rate.

Question 3:   What, in your view, are the principal causes of disruptive incidents and misbehaviour by pupils? What evidence is there to substantiate any causal connections that you may be suggesting?

The notion of cause in human conduct is not a simple one. Behaviour is the product of many interacting factors, and for any one person the make-up of such factors and the relative weight which can be attached to each is unique.

Undoubtedly there are important influences on children's behaviour which lie outside the immediate control of the school. The main factors (see Docking, 1987, for a brief review) include:

— temperamental and other constitutional factors in the child;
— inconsistent or inappropriate standards set by parents and permissive or punitive child-rearing practices;
— stress generated by such factors as poverty, sub-standard living conditions and homelessness, long-term unemployment, family discord;
— elements of violence and other antisocial behaviour in society and its portrayal in the media;
— dietary deficiencies.

Most of the research evidence, however, relates to clinically diagnosed conduct disorders and evidence of criminal delinquency rather than to classroom misbehaviour as such.

Recent evidence suggests that teachers' explanations of pupils' difficulties, including conduct problems, tend to be dominated by assumptions relating to the child or to factors within the home environment (Croll and Moses, 1985; Dawson, 1987). In some circumstances teachers may find it reassuring to explain their lack of success by using attributional terms such as 'maladjusted' or 'disturbed', which suggest temperamental disorders among their pupils and therefore the inevitability of anti-social behaviour. In other circumstances teachers may prefer to explain their lack of success by attributing intentionality to pupils' unacceptable behaviour, since the pupils can legitimately then be blamed for not controlling themselves (Rohrkemper and Brophy, 1983). As regards attributions to the home, teachers have no doubt been influenced by the prominence which was given to parental influence on achievement in well-publicized reports and research during the 60s and 70s.

Whilst each of these explanations has some foundation in fact, the behaviour of any human being at any particular time is materially affected by the context in which she or he is placed. For pupils in school this means the relationships of the classroom and general school environment. In short, 'good' and 'bad' behaviour should be recognized as a joint product of the pupil and the situation. The main factors which predispose many children to behave unacceptably may lie outside the immediate control of the school, but the extent to which a child realizes any tendency to behave badly will depend upon the quality of life experienced at school. Children who experience a high level of stress due to disharmony in the home, for instance, may or may not use the school to vent their frustration, depending on their perception of what is expected of them at school and how they believe they are valued in the school community.

Of course, *some* children will misbehave even when the school staff do everything which seems humanly possible to alleviate the situation. Nonetheless, evidence from a number of studies suggest that it is a gross over-simplification to attribute the *cause* of *in*-school behaviour only to factors *outside* the school. The influence of schools and teachers are very important.

This conclusion is suggested by two sorts of findings. The first comes from studies which demonstrate that pupil behaviour can vary markedly between schools with comparable intakes. At the secondary age phase, much of the evidence belongs to the 70s, in particular Reynolds (1976) and Rutter *et al.*, (1979). In the latter study, for instance, no significant association was found between pupil behaviour scores in twelve London comprehensive schools and the proportion of pupils admitted from areas of high delinquency. Further, the very great differences in pupil behaviour between schools was only very weakly associated with behaviour in primary school. More recently, there is evidence to suggest that variations in school suspension and exclusion rates cannot be attributed to features of the catchment area (Galloway *et al.*, 1982 re: Sheffield; ILEA, 1984 re: London; McManus, 1987 re: Leeds).

At the primary level, the study by Lawrence and Steed (1986), referred to in the previous section, revealed wide variations in reported misbehaviour between schools admitting children of potentially similar behavioural difficulty. The effect of background factors was more directly examined in the London Junior School Project (Mortimore *et al.*, 1988). Although the percentage of the variance in school behaviour which could be uniquely attributed to the school was somewhat lower than that which could be attributed to background factors such as sex and age (10 v.

13 per cent), behaviour scores were found to differ substantially between the most and least effective schools, even when carefully controlling for a wide range of background variables.

The second sort of finding which points to the influence of schools and individual teachers over pupils' behaviour relates to particular features of school organization or classroom practice. Examples of the former include: exacerbating the risk of pupil-stereotyping and consequent behaviour problems through certain methods of grouping children (Hargreaves, 1967; Ball, 1981; Wright, 1985); generating pro-social behaviour through the involvement of pupils and their parents in the organization of the school (McPartland *et al.*, 1971; Reynolds and Sullivan 1979; Epstein, 1981); and reducing the risk of alienation by giving thought to the number of school rules, the manner in which they are enforced, and the extent to which they are perceived as legitimate by most pupils (Wertham, 1963; Reynolds and Sullivan, 1979). Giving form tutors a positive role in pastoral care and avoiding the escalation of trivial incidents into serious confrontations brought about by a system whereby deviant pupils are automatically referred upwards to senior staff (Galloway *et al.*, 1982; McManus, 1987), and ensuring pleasant working conditions (Rutter *et al.*, 1979) are further features of school organization affecting pupil behaviour.

Examples of particular classroom practices which should maximize the chances of good pupil behaviour include: the avoidance of negative labelling and the provacation of confrontation (Hargreaves *et al.*, 1975; Beynon, 1985), avoiding jokes that have racial overtones (Wright, 1985); taking account of pupils' perceptions of good teaching (review in Docking, 1987); understanding the dynamics of classroom management (Kounin, 1970; Doyle and Carter, 1987); praising for good behaviour as well as academic achievement (e.g. Merrett, 1985); and promoting a work-centred environment (Rutter *et al.*, 1979; Mortimore *et al.*, 1988).

It seems, however, that behaviour is more strongly related to *combinations* of factors rather than any one alone (Rutter *et al.*, 1979) and that the impact made by one teacher is more or less affected by the stance being taken by other teachers (Mortimore *et al.*, 1988). These findings bring out the importance of staff working together within the framework of a common policy. Another complication concerns the sensitivity with which any particular strategy is used. For instance, rewards can undermine intrinsic interest in curriculum activities (see Lepper, 1983) and praise in certain circumstances can be ineffective and even counterproductive (Brophy, 1981; Schwieso and Hastings, 1987).

In spite of these caveats, the general picture which emerges from these studies is that the general atmosphere and practices of schools and individual teachers can and does make a substantial difference to pupil behaviour. If this is the case, then it is clearly important that our knowledge about effective and ineffective practices are put to the benefit of all schools. This consideration suggests possible responses to the fourth question posed by the Elton Committee.

> Question 4: What action could be taken by relevant organizations and
> individuals (e.g. teachers, parents, local education authorities, the
> Government) to promote an orderly atmosphere in schools? What
> evidence is there to suggest that such action would be effective?

The action to be taken to promote an orderly atmosphere in schools should presumably reflect the causes of pupil misbehaviour outlined in response to the previous question. Hence a three-pronged attack could be envisaged, directed at features of the child's general social and physical environment, the home, and the school. Of these I wish to concentrate on the last two.

As regards the home environment, it is one thing to acknowledge that parental practices influence children's behaviour in school and another to *blame* parents for poor standards of classroom conduct. Of course some parents do deserve to be admonished for over-permissive or punitive methods in the handling of their children. But the root of the problem may be less to do with moral failings and more to do with feelings of ambivalence about the values which should be passed on to children today, stress generated by social and economic pressures, and poor understanding of parenting skills. In the Lawrence and Steed (1986) inquiry involving eighty-five primary schools, about two-thirds of the heads stated that children are becoming more difficult to handle at an earlier age. However, the schools were not seeking to find fault with parents, but to provide support through more effective liaison. When heads were asked to identify directions in which schools could work to reduce disruptive behaviour, parental liaison was identified as the most effective. Reactive measures such as harsher penalties by the courts are unlikely to improve the general quality of parenting. To achieve this, the emphasis must be on approaches which help parents to acquire parenting skills, which give them a greater sense of control over their children's development, which involve them in the general life of the school, and which encourage them to be partners in their children's education.

There is certainly evidence of specific ways in which schools and parents, by working together, can improve the quality of pupil behaviour:

1. The London Junior School Study (Mortimore *et al.*, 1986) noted that schools in which there was better behaviour tended to be those in which the head was always available to see parents at particular times during the week without appointment. This strategy presumably facilitated parent–teacher relationships in general and created the opportunity for behaviour problems to be discussed before they became serious.

2. Children's motivation towards learning seems to improve in Primary schools which have developed reading projects involving parents (e.g. Tizard *et al.*, 1982; Hannon and Jackson, 1987). By listening to their children read for a short time each day and by entering into a dialogue with class teachers, these projects seem to facilitate a constructive triangular relationship between parents, teachers and children.

3. Home-based reinforcement experiments have been widely practised in the

United States to induce more conformist behaviour in adolescents (Leach and Byrne, 1986), and the West Norfolk Psychological Service has shown how parents can be helped to manage referred children more effectively (Long, 1988). These schemes work on behavioural principles, the parents rewarding their children according to daily reports from the school. In the West Norfolk scheme, success or partial success has been claimed in 82 per cent of cases during the course of one year.

4. Lickona (1988) has described four ways in which some American schools have collaborated with the local communities to help children develop social values and skills. The first involves articulating an agreed core of values. Apart from generating mutual understanding, the consensus encourages parents to be more certain about what to teach their children. In the second strategy, help is given whereby the community can regain a sense of cohesiveness through small parent support groups. These meet in school or in a parent's home to discuss matters of common concern such as measures to stop alcohol and drug abuse or excessive exposure to violence on television. Thirdly, Lickona describes examples of school-sponsored family projects to promote prosocial values; these might involve families watching and discussing a film with a moral theme. Lastly, illustrations are given of parental involvement in the school's personal and social development programme; for instance the school might suggest ways in which parents could follow-up lessons on interpersonal relations. In terms of the three definitions of *good behaviour* set out earlier in this chapter, these ideas do more than teach pupils to be compliant and to develop self-control, for they show how a partnership between families and schools can help to promote responsible behaviour based on greater understanding, concern and sensitivity.

Apart from building up better relations with parents, what else can schools do? Again, reactive strategies which do not come into operation until *after* pupils have been deviant at best help to contain the problem but at worst exacerbate it. Indeed they may even make things worse. Punishment, for instance, has the propensity to deter, to reinforce the importance of school rules and teacher expectations, and to prompt culprits to see error of their ways. But unless administered sensitively it can alienate, reinforce attention-seeking behaviour, encourage avoidance tactics, induce feelings of rejection, and, if severe, expose pupils to inappropriate adult models whose aggression might be imitated. (For a review of the moral arguments and empirical evidence, see Docking, 1987).

Strategies which remove the worst culprits and place them in special units are also problematic. Off-site units may help pupils with a history of learning problems to achieve success and bring about better relationships with adults in authority (Mortimore *et al.*, 1983); and of course they relieve schools of responsibility for the *disruptive influence*. Yet the evidence shows that the cost incurred is high, problems arise over referral procedures, curriculum opportunities are restricted, the pupils do not necessarily benefit, reintegration rates into mainstream schooling are low, and, for those readmitted to school, the problem behaviour is quite likely to reoccur (review in Docking, 1987). In any case the units can only deal with the worst cases and so do nothing to help teachers cope with the general run of behaviour problems. Increasing the number of places in special units, as the NAHT (1988) have recommended, would therefore seem an inefficient and educationally unsound way of meeting the problem. There is, however, a case for units which are for short stays and a specific task (Coulby and Harper, 1985).

All schools must have the means to deal effectively with pupils who regularly misbehave. But the *emphasis* should not be on reactive measures but on policies and strategies which minimize the risk of disruption in the first place and make it more likely that pupils will *want* to behave well. This course of action is more about prevention and early intervention than punishment or cure. The approach is based on the assumption that behaviour is context-related, that it emanates from particular personal interactions and relationships, and that even those categorized as the 'disruptive pupils' do not behave badly all the time or with every teacher.

Preventative strategies can be considered at both school and classroom levels. At the *school level*, the importance of the head's management style and school ethos cannot be overestimated. In its review of comments on school behaviour contained in recent reports, HMI (1987) stated that effective leadership 'is the most consistent feature of those schools where pupils behave well' (para. 15). The head needs to give a clear sense of direction and transmit high expectations to staff and pupils whilst also involving all teachers in the determination of policy. The role given to senior pupils is also important. The work of Epstein (1981) and MacPartland *et al.*, (1971) shows that, provided that it is not just cosmetic, pupil involvement in decision-making improves staff–pupil relationships and generates feelings of commitment and responsibility.

Part of the trouble in secondary schools may stem from an examination system which emphasises, covertly if not overtly, cognitive–developmental skills and individual achievement at the expense of the expressive arts and community-orientated studies: as Hargreaves (1982) has argued, this destroys the dignity of many pupils and renders them inferior and powerless. But other matters which can precipitate bad behaviour are more easily within the control of the school. Two factors seem crucial in promoting a positive school ethos. The first is the extent to which a climate of justice permeates all aspects of school life. It is not just a matter of ensuring that the rules and expectations are clear and communicated effectively, but also that most pupils perceive them as reasonable, fair and not needlessly infringing their freedom (Children's Legal Centre, 1988). Nor is it just a matter of ensuring that rules are enforced consistently but that teachers save their reprimands for things that matter, avoid making an issue out of unimportant incidents, and do not demand polite behaviour while demonstrating bad manners themselves (Reynolds, 1976; Davies, 1984).

The second factor associated with a positive school ethos is the extent to which the staff is introspective, reviewing and being prepared to adapt teaching arrangements, organization and policies. Systematically assembling information on behavioural incidents, examining the reasons for them and agreeing appropriate strategies provides a structured means of developing a constructive whole-school policy (see Watkins and Wagner, 1987). This gets away from drawing up do's and don'ts with associated penalties, and instead involves staff in a programme of action research. The kinds of issues which emerge from such efforts will vary according to the school's circumstances and the data generated: indeed, the strength of the approach is its capacity to deal with individual school situations. Examples of questions which have arisen are: Do first year secondary pupils have so many teachers that they cannot develop stable relationships with adults in authority? Should the school do more to emphasize praise rather than punishment? Would a reallocation of rooms and timetable arrangements be conducive to more orderly behaviour? Is the pastoral system suffering from too many pupils being referred to senior staff for minor disciplinary infringements, and could it work harder to generate feelings of interpersonal concern?

At *classroom level*, the problem evolves around teaching styles, relationships with pupils, and classroom management. Essentially the skills are about engendering integrative class behaviour and an atmosphere of purposefulness. A class is not just a collection of individuals with individual needs but a group with collective needs. As Roberts (1971) has shown in her study of American urban classrooms, integrative group behaviour is more likely when the teacher refrains from assuming all the leadership roles and gives the pupils a sense of agency and a feeling that their perspective is valid. The collective needs of a class include opportunities to assume responsibility, give feedback, express feelings, voice opinions, evaluate the ideas of other pupils, make suggestions for courses of action, and test the feasibility of group suggestions.

In his study of a third year class renowned for its disruptive tendencies and lack of response to ordinary sanctions, Raymond (1987) has shown the value of listening to the perceptions of pupils when reviewing teaching strategies. Pupils' inclination to disrupt a lesson appeared to be materially affected by the degree to which teachers were prepared to explain when pupils were not understanding and to provide plenty of opportunity for discussion. The class expected teachers to *interact with* them rather than to talk *at* them. Eliciting pupils' views about what is going on can, Raymond argues, provide early warning signals about potential disturbances.

The pioneering work of Kounin (1970) in the United States and follow-up studies there (e.g. Doyle and Carter, 1987) and in this country (e.g. Wragg and Dooley, 1984) have shown how teachers who generate an atmosphere of purposefulness are not those who concentrate on what to do *after* a pupil has misbehaved. Rather they are those who *reduce the opportunities* for disruption by focusing on ways of organizing classroom activities more effectively and developing more constructive relationships with the pupils. Examples of good practice here involve (a) variety of content, type of work and mode of presentation, (b) activities which are motivating because they are neither too difficult nor too easy but moderately challenging, (c) time spent giving feedback on work and talking about problems of understanding, (d) making pupils accountable for what they do, (e) praising children for their successes and, through the way praise remarks are phrased, helping children to develop feelings of competence and worth, (f) reprimanding the right child on time but not disrupting the rhythm and momentum of the lesson by making an issue out of matters that can wait, (g) reorganizing seating arrangements to fit the nature of the activity.

Perhaps most important of all is the refusal to assume that it is the pupil who must change while the teacher remains the same. Where change in the pupil is clearly required, then the role of the social education is important. Behaviour is sometimes rude and malicious because pupils lack competence in dealing with adults. Some interesting work has been done by Goddard and Cross (1988) in training such children to acquire social skills. Through discussion, modelling, role-play and the use of video feedback pupils can be taught to avoid confrontation and relate to others more effectively.

A selection of books which develop aspects of classroom management are listed at the end of this chapter. Many writers to a greater or lesser extent adopt a behavioural approach: that is, they emphasize that teachers will be more successful if they attend to what the child does rather than speculate about underlying causative factors, and if they remember that good behaviour can be learned and bad behaviour unlearned by changing the context in which misbehaviour occurs and is maintained. Wheldall and Merrett (1984) argue that this approach needs to be distinguished from the crude excesses of behaviour modification such as the token economy. They emphasize strategies based on the principles of negotiating easily understood rules with a class, ignoring contraventions of those rules unless they are serious, and praising pupils when they keep to the rules. Other writers, such as Watkins and Wagner (1987), place more emphasis on curricular considerations and school ethos. Chazan *et al.* (1983) are among those who assume that success in changing a child's behaviour depends on influencing the child's thinking which controls that behaviour. For instance in their problem-solving approach with young children, teachers are shown how to adopt a daily routine which encourages children who have been aggressive to formulate alternative pro-social ways of resolving their interpersonal problems.

In summary, teachers are more or less successful at keeping order not so much because some are better than others in dealing with trouble when it arises but because some are more skilled at preventing it. Such strategies, of course, benefit *all* pupils, and not only those who, in a less favourable environment, would be disruptive. Moreover, the more successful teachers change their strategies when pupils fail to respond. Their less successful and more stressful colleagues doggedly persist with the same approach (such as getting angry or using sarcasm) even when it is not yielding the intended effect (Lewis and Lovegrove, 1987)!

The accreditation arrangements for pre-service training programmes provide scope for ensuring that student teachers are given the means to develop the skills of managing pupils effectively. The current official emphasis on subject studies must not be at the expense of sound training in pedagogy. This then needs to be supplemented by measures which help schools to analyze their teaching arrangements and strategies for managing pupils. The work in Tower Hamlets, recently described by Coulby and Harper (1985), is an example of what can be done by a local authority peripatetic support team when disruptive behaviour is regarded less as a handicap requiring separate provision, and more as a special educational need that requires an analysis of class management strategies in regular school settings.

There are many inner-city schools whose teachers have found the means, individually and collaboratively, to secure high standards of pupil behaviour. Given the support and the resources, our knowledge about *good practice* can be utilized by all.

Some recent books on discipline which deal with preventative strategies and whole-school policies

BULL, S. (1987) *Classroom Management: Principles to Practice*, Beckenham, Croom Helm.

CHAZAN, M., LAING, A.F., JONES, J., HARPER, G. and BOLTON, J. (1983) *Helping Young Children with Behavioural Difficulties*, Beckenham, Croom Helm.

CHISHOLM, B., *et al.* (1986) *Preventive Approaches to Disruption: Developing Teaching Skills*, London, Macmillan.

COHEN, L. and COHEN, A. (1987) *Disruptive Behaviour: A Source Book for Teachers*, London, Harper and Row/Paul Chapman.

COULBY, D. and HARPER, T. (1985) *Preventing Classroom Disruption*, Beckenham, Croom Helm.

DOCKING, J.W. (1987) *Control and Discipline in Schools: Perspective and Approaches* (2nd edition), London, Harper and Row/Paul Chapman.

GRAY, J. and RICHER, J. (1988) *Classroom Responses to Disruptive Behaviour*, London, Macmillan.

LASLETT, R. and SMITH, C. (1983) *Effective Classroom Management*, London, Croom Helm.

ROBERTS, T. (1983) *Child Management in the Primary School*, London, Allen and Unwin.

ROBERTSON, J. (1981) *Effective Classroom Control*, London, Hodder and Stoughton.

SCHERER, M. and GERSCH, I. (1987) *Disruptive Behaviour: Assessment, Intervention, Partnerships*, London, Macmillan.

TWEDDLE, D. (1987) *Preventive Approaches to Disruption: Developing Teaching Skills*, London, Macmillan.

WATKINS, C. and WAGNER, P. (1987) *School Discipline: A Whole-School Approach*, Oxford, Blackwell.

WHELDALL, K. and MERRETT, F. (1984) *Positive Teaching: The Behavioural Approach*, London, Allen and Unwin.

WRAGG, E.C. (ed.) (1984) *Classroom Teaching Skills*, Beckenham, Croom Helm.

References

ASSISTANT MASTERS AND MISTRESSES ASSOCIATION (1984) *The Reception Class Today*, London, AMMA.

BALL, S.J. (1981) *Beechside Comprehensive*, Cambridge, Cambridge University Press.

BEYNON, J. (1975) *Initial Encounters in the Secondary School*, Lewes, Falmer Press.

BLATCHFORD, P., BURKE, J., FARQUHAR, C., PLEWIS, I. and TIZARD, B. (1987) 'A systematic observation study of children's behaviour at infant school', *Research Papers in Education*, **2**, pp. 47–61.

BROPHY, J.E. (1981) 'Teacher praise: a functional analysis', *Review of Educational Research*, **51**, pp. 5–32.

CHAZAN, M., LAING, A.F., JONES, J., HARPER, G. and BOLTON, J. (1983) *Helping Young Children with Behavioural Difficulties*, Beckenham, Croom Helm.

CHILDREN'S LEGAL CENTRE (1988) *Evidence to the Department of Education and Science Committee of Enquiry into Discipline in Schools*, London, CLC.

COULBY, D. and HARPER, T. (1985) *Preventing Classroom Disruption*, Beckenham, Croom Helm.

CROLL, P. and MOSES, D. (1985) *One in Five*, London, Routledge and Kegan Paul.

DAVIES, L. (1984) *Pupil Power: Deviance and Gender in School*, Lewes, Falmer Press.

DAWSON, R. (1987) 'What concerns teachers about their pupils?, in: HASTINGS, N. and SCHWIESO, J. (Eds) *New Directions in Educational Psychology: 2 — Behaviour and Motivation in the Classroom*, Lewes, Falmer Press.

DENSCOMBE, M. (1984) 'Control, controversy and the comprehensive school', in: BALL, S. (Ed.) *Comprehensive Schooling*, Lewes, Falmer Press.

DIERENFIELD, R. (1982) 'All you need to know about disruption', *Times Educational Supplement*, 29 January.

DOCKING, J.W. (1987) *Control and Discipline in Schools: Perspectives and Approaches*, (2nd edn), London, Paul Chapman Publishing.

DOYLE, W. and CARTER, K. (1987) 'How order is achieved in classrooms', in: HASTINGS, N. and SCHWIESO, J. (Eds) *New Directions in Educational Psychology: 2 — Behaviour and Motivation in the Classroom*, Lewes, Falmer Press.

EPSTEIN, J.L. (Ed.) (1981) *The Quality of School Life*, Toronto, Lexington Books.

GALLOWAY, D., BALL, T., BLOOMFIELD, D. and SEYED, R. (1982) *Schools and Disruptive Pupils*, London, Longman.

GODDARD, S. and CROSS, J. (1988) 'Social skills training in the ordinary school setting', *Educational Psychology in Practice*, **4**, pp. 24–8.

HANNON, P. and JACKSON, A. (1987) *The Belfield Reading Project: Final Report*, London, National Children's Bureau.

HARGREAVES, D.H. (1967) *Social Relations in a Secondary School*, London, Routledge and Kegan Paul.

HARGREAVES, D.H. (1982) *The Challenge for the Comprehensive School*, London, Routledge & Kegan Paul.

HARGREAVES, D.H., HESTER, S.K. and MELLOR, F.J. (1975) *Deviance in Classrooms*, London, Routledge and Kegan Paul.

HER MAJESTY'S INSPECTORATE (1979) *Aspects of Secondary Education in England*, London HMSO.

HER MAJESTY'S INSPECTORATE (1984) *Education Observed 2*, London, Department of Education and Science.

HER MAJESTY'S INSPECTORATE, (1987) *Good Behaviour and Discipline in Schools* (Education Observed 5), London, Department of Education and Science.

HER MAJESTY'S INSPECTORATE (1988) *Secondary Schools — An Appraisal by HMI*, London, HMSO.

HOUGHTON, S., WHELDALL, K. and MERRETT, F. (1988) 'Classroom behaviours which secondary school teachers say they find most troublesome'. *British Education Research Journal*, **14**, pp. 295–310.

INNER LONDON EDUCATION AUTHORITY (1984) *Improving Secondary Schools* (Hargreaves Report), London, ILEA.

KOUNIN, J. (1970) *Discipline and Group Management in Classrooms*, New York, Holt, Winehart and Winston.

LAWRENCE, J. and STEED, D. (1986) 'Primary school perception of disruptive behaviour', *Educational Studies*, 12, pp. 147–57.

LEACH, D.J. and BYRNE, M.K. (1986) 'Some spill-over effects of a home-based reinforcement programme in a secondary school', *Educational Psychology*, 6, pp. 265–75.

LEPPER, M. (1983) 'Extrinsic reward and instrinsic motivation: implications for classroom practice', in: LEVINE, J.M. and WANG, M.C. (Eds.) *Teacher and Student Perceptions: Implications for Learning*, Hillsdale, NJ: Erlbaum.

LEWIS, R. and LOVEGROVE, M.N. (1987) 'What students think of students' classroom control technique', in: HASTINGS, N. and SCHWIESO, J. (Eds.) *New Directions in Educational Psychology: 2 — Behaviour and Motivation in the Classroom*, Basingstoke, Falmer Press.

LICKONA, T. (1988) 'How parents and schools can work together to raise moral children', *Educational Leadership*, May, pp. 36–38.

LONG, M. (1988) 'Goodbye behaviour units, hello support services', *Educational Psychology in Practice*, 4, pp. 17–23.

LOWE, C. (1988) Speech to the Institute for the Study and Treatment of Delinquency, February.

MCMANUS, M. (1987) 'Suspension and exclusion from high schools: the association with catchment and school variables', *School Organization*, 7, pp. 261–71.

MCPARTLAND, J.M. *et al.* (1971) *Student Participation in High School Decisions: A Study of 14 Urban High Schools*, Baltimore, John Hopkins University Center for Social Organization of Schools.

MERRETT, F.E. (1985) *Encouragement Works Better than Punishment*, Birmingham, Positive Products.

MORTIMORE, P., DAVIES, J., VARLAAM, A. and WEST, A. (1983) *Behaviour Problems in Schools*, Beckenham, Croom Helm.

MORTIMORE, P., SAMMONS, P., STOLL, L., LEWIS, D. and ECOB, R. (1986) *The Junior School Project*, London, ILEA Research & Statistics Branch.

MORTIMORE, P., SAMMONS, P., STOLL, L., LEWIS, D. and ECOB, R. (1988) *School Matters: The Junior Years*, Wells, Open Books.

NATIONAL ASSOCIATION OF HEAD TEACHERS (1988) *The Evidence of the National Association of Head Teachers to the Committee of Enquiry into Discipline in Schools*, Haywards Heath, NAHT.

NATIONAL ASSOCIATION OF SCHOOLMASTERS/UNION OF WOMEN TEACHERS (1985) *Pupil Violence and Disorder in Schools*, Birmingham, NAS/UWT.

NATIONAL OPINION POLL (1988) Discipline NOP poll, *Teacher*, 13 June.

NATIONAL UNION OF TEACHERS (1988) *Written Submission to the Enquiry into Discipline in Schools*, London, NUT.

RAYMOND, J. (1987) 'An educational psychologist's intervention with a class of disruptive pupils using pupil perceptions', *Educational Psychology in Practice*, July, pp. 16–22.

REYNOLDS, D. (1976) 'The delinquent school', in: HAMMERSLEY, M. and WOODS, P. (eds.) *The Process of Schooling*, London, Routledge and Kegan Paul/Open University Press.

REYNOLDS, D. and SULLIVAN, M. (1979) 'Bringing schools back in', in: BARTON, L. and MEIGHAN, R. (eds.) *Schools, Pupils and Deviance*, Nafferton, Nafferton Books.

ROBERTS, J.I. (1971) *Scene of the Battle: Group Behaviour in the Urban Classrooms*, New York, Anchor Books.

ROHRKEMPER, M. and BROPHY, J.E. (1983) 'Teachers' thinking about problem students', in: LEVINE, J.M. and WANG, M.C. (eds.) *Teacher and Student Perceptions: Implications for Learning*, Hillsdale, New Jersey, Lawrence Erlbaum.

RUTTER, M., MAUGHAN, B., MORTIMORE, P., and OUSTON, J. (1979) *Fifteen Thousand Hours: Secondary Schools and their Effects on Children*, London, Open Books.

SCHWIESO, J. and HASTINGS, N. (1987) Teachers' use of approval, in: HASTINGS, N. and SCHWIESO, J. (eds.) *New Directions in Educational Psychology: 2 — Behaviour and Motivation in the Classroom*, Basingstoke, Falmer Press.

SCOTTISH, EDUCATION DEPARTMENT (1977) *Truancy and Indiscipline in Schools* (Pack Report), London, HMSO.

STEWART, W. (1977) 'Violence in class: The full, appalling facts', *Daily Express*, 25 and 26 November. [Professional Association of Teachers survey results.].

TIZARD, J., SCHOFIELD, W.N. and HEWISON, J. (1982) 'Collaboration between teachers and parents in assisting children's reading', *British Journal of Educational Psychology*, **52**, pp. 1–15.

WATKINS, C. and WAGNER, P. (1987) *School Discipline: A Whole School Approach*, Oxford, Basil Blackwell.

WERTHAM, C. (1963) 'Delinquents in school: test of the legitimacy and authority', in: COSIN, B.R. *et al.* (eds.) *School and Society*, Routledge and Kegan Paul/Open University Press.

WHELDALL, K. and MERRETT, F.E. (1984) *Positive Teaching: The Behavioural Approach*, London, Allen and Unwin.

WHELDALL, K. and MERRETT, F. (1988) 'What classroom behaviours do Primary school teachers say they find most troublesome?', *Educational Review*, **40**, pp. 13–28.

WILSON, P.S. (1971) *Interest and Discipline in Education*, London, Routledge and Kegan Paul.

WRAGG, E.C. and DOOLEY, P.A. (1984) 'Classroom management during teaching practice', in WRAGG, E.C. (ed.) *Classroom Management and Control*, London, Macmillan.

WRIGHT, C. (1985) 'Opportunities of children of West Indian origin', *I and II Multicultural Teaching*, **4**, pp. 11–22.

Part I
Pupil Behaviour and School Discipline

1
Effective Schools and Pupil Behaviour

David Reynolds

Introduction

In the last decade the research literature on effective schools and their characteristics
has increased dramatically. In both the United States and Britain there now exists a
substantial body of knowledge, and in other countries such as Australia, the
Netherlands and Sweden there are rapidly developing research programmes in this
area. Increasingly this activity is not generated only by academics or researchers —
in Britain, for example, local education authorities, like the Inner London
Education Authority, have developed schemes of monitoring, evaluation and direct
advice-giving that attempt to identify ineffective or under-performing schools and
then place professional advisers in them to improve their functioning. In the
United States, literally thousands of schools are attempting school effectiveness
evaluations or improvement schemes based directly on the effective schools research
literature.

With all this international activity, it would be understandable for the reader
to think that the question 'What factors make up the school which generates well
behaved children?' is close to being answered. However, as is the case with any new
area of research activity, the number of questions to be answered and the number of
issues to be resolved greatly exceeds those areas where there is firm substantive
agreement amongst researchers and practitioners. Outlining these areas of agreement and disagreement is the first aim of this chapter, which will then be followed
by an attempt to outline the educational policy implications of the knowledge that
we have.

It is important to realise firstly that the number of studies which have looked at
school effectiveness in terms of pupil *behaviour* is still very small, since the great
majority of the research has looked predominantly at pupils' academic achievement
or examination passes as the criteria for the effectiveness of schools. This near obsession with academic development is particularly marked in the United States,
where only the pioneering studies of Brookover (1979) and his colleagues have
attempted to look at the factors that also make for effective *social* outcomes from
schools. In Britain, whilst there have been some research studies that have looked at

behavioural and academic effectiveness (Rutter *et al.*, 1979; Reynolds *et al.*, 1987; Mortimore *et al.*, 1988), the great majority of work has also looked at the academic effectiveness of schools (Gray, McPherson and Raffe, 1983; Cox and Marks, 1983, Department of Education and Science, 1984).

Our problems in drawing conclusions about effective schools and how they influence pupils' behaviour are magnified secondly by the fact that many of the British studies into school effectiveness do not have *any* systematic information on the processes within the schools that may be making them effective or ineffective with their pupils. The work of Gray and his colleagues from Sheffield (Gray, *et al;*. 1984) is an example, as is the early work of researchers in Scotland (Willms and Cuttance, 1985).

Our last problem is that the category of pupil behaviour covers a wide variety of meanings. It is often used in research to mean antisocial behaviour such as delinquency, vandalism, truancy, disruption in class and the like. Sometimes, though, it is used to refer to pro-social behaviour such as involvement in school and non-sexist or non-racist behaviour. Sometimes studies have used measures of pupils' *attitudes* rather than of their *behaviour*, with questionnaires that have covered views of teachers, pupils' perceptions of school and similar areas of educational life. Sometimes studies have just used school rates of suspension or referral to outside units as their indices of pupil behaviour in school, even though schools may differ considerably in their definitions of what constitutes problem behaviour that is worthy of suspension. Given these different ways in which various studies have defined behaviour, this variability from study to study, and the other two factors above, must be kept in mind during our discussions below, since the quality and variability of the research literature may affect some of the confidence which can be placed in our conclusions.

How large is the school's influence on pupils' behaviour?

Early work by Power (1967) in London, by Gath (1977) in Oxford and from our Welsh research (Reynolds, 1976) suggested that schools had a very large effect upon the behaviour of their pupils. Power found a twenty-fold difference in delinquency rates between secondary schools in Tower Hamlets, differences which he argued were independent of the sorts of pupils entering the schools. Both Gath and Reynolds also argued for their schools' levels of problematic behaviour and delinquency to be virtually independent of the social quality of their catchment areas, with the latter using census data on social class composition of school catchment areas in an attempt to prove the case.

Because of doubts about the extent to which these three studies had in reality measured enough characteristics of their school's catchment areas to be completely sure that their more effective schools were not just taking more educable pupils at age eleven, it was perhaps the well known *Fifteen Thousand Hours* study of Rutter and his colleagues (1979) that generated more convincing evidence that the school can have a substantial role in generating problem behaviour amongst its pupils.

Rutter found that the variation in the behaviour of the pupils in their secondary schools (measured by extensive use of observational scales) was almost completely due to the effects of the school environment itself, since there was virtually a non-existent relationship between the academic and social characteristics of the pupils on *entry* to the school and their *later* behaviour within the school (the Pearson correlations were very low and ranged from .19 to − .01). Furthermore, Rutter found that of forty-six process variables that looked at the school environment, twenty-three were significantly linked with the school's levels of behaviour, which amounted to more than for any of the other three outcome measures that were used. Also, the researchers found that the strength of these links between school environments and behaviour increased more during pupils' school lifetime than for any of the other outcome measures. More recent evidence has also found large differences in the behaviour of pupils at different schools and has suggested that these differences are mostly due to the effects of schools themselves. Galloway *et al.*, (1985) found that suspension rates for disruptive behaviour varied greatly between schools and that these rates were completely independent of twenty-two measures of the social quality of these schools' catchment areas.

Recently Mortimore (1988) and his colleagues looked at junior schools and have supported the thesis of large school effects when they found large differences in children's behaviour: after taking into account the effects on behaviour of such factors as the ability, social class and sex of the pupil, the impact of the school explained more of pupil's levels of behaviour than it did of their levels of self conception, levels of attendance, or reading ability.

Are schools effective in promoting good behaviour effective in other areas also?

Evidence on this issue is more limited than that which shows the substantial size of school effects. Early work by ourselves (Reynolds *et al.*, 1976, 1979) and by Rutter *et al.*, (1979) suggested that schools tended to be equally effective or ineffective on *all* the various areas of pupil development such as the production of high examination success, low truancy levels, low delinquency levels and positive pupil behaviour within the school. The good school, then, was always *good* in these studies.

More recently, though, has come evidence that shows schools as not necessarily being consistent across the whole range of outcomes but as being potentially good in some areas and bad in others. In Galloway's (1983) work, one of his four schools with exceptionally low levels of disruptive behaviour also had exceptionally poor levels of examination results, the result perhaps of the school adopting a policy of minimal demands upon its pupils. Effectiveness in behavioural areas may be a necessary, but not a sufficient, condition for academic effectiveness, Galloway argued.

Likewise, a school that is academically very effective may obtain this effectiveness by high levels of academic pressure upon its children, thus also producing the high levels of rebellion, disruption and poor behaviour within the school as shown by our study of comprehensive schools (Reynolds *et al.*, 1987). The potential *independence* of a school's effectiveness in preventing poor behaviour and its academic success in promoting pupil attainment is shown even more recently by the results of the Mortimore *et al.*, (1988) study in the Inner London Education Authority, where schools which were positive in their effects upon non-cognitive areas like behaviour or attendance were not necessarily positive in their effects upon academic achievements. In this study, in fact, there was no systematic relationship between success in the two areas.

Are schools consistently effective in generating good behaviour?

Information on the *consistency* with which some schools prevent problem behaviour over a period of time is even more sparse than on the other issues above. Rutter *et al.*, (1979) and our own studies (Reynolds *et al.*, 1976, 1979) note the consistency with which some schools produce poor levels of attendance and high levels of problems such as delinquency but more recently we have evidence (Blakey and Heath, 1989) that schools' *academic* effectiveness can fluctuate quite markedly from year to year and a school which is effective one year may not be so the next. Whether — as I strongly suspect — the same may be true for schools that are effective/ineffective in terms of pupil behaviour remains to be confirmed.

Are effective schools effective for all types of pupil within them?

Early work in the field (Reynolds *et al.*, 1976; 1979; Rutter *et al.*, 1979) argued that schools had something of a *steampress* effect and that the effective or ineffective schools had their effects *consistently* on all types of pupil, whether they were boys/girls, high ability/low ability, high social class/low social class or white/ethnic minority children. More recently, studies which have concentrated upon academic attainment as their criteria of effectiveness have found that schools may be *differentially* effective for the various sub groups of pupils within them. Cuttance (1989) noted that schools have much greater effects upon their low ability pupils than on others and McPherson and Willms (1988) argue that the change towards comprehensive schools in Scotland had much greater benefits upon lower social class children than upon others. If these findings on academic attainment can be further confirmed by work into pupil behaviour, the whole notion of the effective school as being something that exists and which benefits all children in a school may need urgent re-examination.

What factors make some schools effective in promoting positive pupil bahaviour?

We noted at the beginning of this chapter that the great majority of the North American research has looked at schools' effectiveness defined only in academic terms. British work, though, has also looked in detail at those factors associated with effectiveness in terms of pupil behaviour and suggests the following factors to be important in determining the school experiences that may prevent the development of behaviour problems (see reviews in Reynolds, 1982; Rutter, 1983; Mortimore *et al.*, 1988):

(i) High levels of pupil involvement in academic activities (e.g. a lesson monitor) and in the wider life of the school (e.g. a prefect or a society organizer or a sports team monitor).

(ii) A positive climate of high expectations of pupils in terms of academic work and behaviour, where teachers evoke a positive response from pupils from the way that they interact with them, in the classroom, both verbally and non-verbally. Such academic competence that this produces on the part of pupils is likely to give the sort of self esteem that will prevent behavioural problems.

(iii) An *incorporative* rather than *coercive* disciplinary system, which attempts to socially control pupils by means of using relationships with them and by means of the creation of a *truce* on the enforcement of certain rules which may make those relationships more difficult to maintain as pupils get older.

(iv) A headteacher who can combine leadership, clear goal setting and a motivational role with respect to his or her staff whilst at the same time involving staff in decision making within the school.

(v) Good school/parent relationships, both in the formal sense of organized school/parent interactions like a Parent Teacher Association but also at the informal level of being open and accessible to parents at other times for non-formal contact.

(vi) A reward based rather than punishment orientated school ethos, which rewards good behaviour and attitudes and which particularly avoids whole group sanctions and any forms of physical punishment.

The above characteristics of a school which is likely to be generating positive behaviour amongst its pupils reflects the findings of researchers, but it is interesting in this context to compare this research description with that of the Inspectorate, produced on the basis of their experience of visiting schools during regular inspections (HMI, 1987). Interestingly, these practitioner accounts of what makes for effective practice are quite similar to those derived from the research data above (the list below has been edited slightly from the original):

> The focus of such policies is the development of a positive climate for the whole school; this is based on a quiet yet firm insistence on high standards of behaviour at all times, and draws its strength from community of purpose, consistent practice and constant vigilance.

> This climate is affected by all the school's activities. Within a well-planned curriculum there is a high quality of teaching and learning, in which purposes are clear to all involved; pupils as well as being intellectu-

ally challenged have opportunities for taking initiatives and for accepting responsibility for their progress. Such learning is supported by a range of activities outside the classroom which also contribute to pupil's personal and social development.

There is a range of rewards and privileges, with due emphasis on well-merited praise; their use outweighs that of the sanctions available. The sanctions relate to defensible principles; they are applied with flexibility and discrimination. In using them to improve pupils' behaviour schools also offer teachers support and the opportunity to improve their expertise.

The school's leadership sets a good example, with clear aims and high expectations which are matched by constant vigilance and a willingness to provide support, to identify in-service training needs and take action to meet them, and to encourage the professional development necessary for the maintenance of high standards.

The ethos of the school is grounded in the quality of relationships at all levels: between teachers, between teachers and pupils, and between pupils. Such relationships are characterized by mutual respect, by the valuing of pupils, by a willingness to listen and understand, and by a positive view of teachers as professionals and pupils as learners. Through good models of adult behaviour, there is constant encouragement to develop self-esteem, self-discipline and autonomous adherence to high standards.

The school makes full use of the strengths available to it through the wider partnership: its links with parents, with the local community and with the various supporting agencies are all used to enhance the quality of the school as a community, and to help maintain high expectations.

Much other research undertaken outside the specific area of school effectiveness studies but within areas such as the sociology of the school, points also in the same general direction as the school effectiveness research and the practitioner accounts. Hargreaves (1985) and his colleagues note the adverse effects on behaviour of the enforcement of rules which pupils believe to be illegitimate, and of confront-ational, deviance provocative behaviour by teachers. Overly authoritarian teachers in other studies (Finlayson and Loughran, 1976) have the same negative effects on behaviour. Streaming practices which encourage the 'labelling' of certain groups of pupils as more prone to poor behaviour are also frequently argued (Ball, 1981; Hargreaves, 1967) to be likely to produce that same poor behaviour.

From all this evidence, though, it would be very unwise to conclude that we definitely have some kind of 'recipe' that will make for the generation of better pupil behaviour if it were to be applied through schools. We have hints from American work that the effective school may be a different kind of institution in poorer areas than in more socially advantaged areas. Brookover *et al.*, (1979) noted that their high achieving schools in both advantaged and disadvantaged areas had positive views of students, high expectations and gave students a sense of control over their environment. However, the *application* of these school organizational principles was very different in the two types of catchment area, with the principal emphasizing a role as instructional leader in the advantaged school and as an administrative leader in the disadvantaged school. There was also evidence that the advantaged white school stressed academic achievement over discipline and that the disadvantaged black school stressed discipline over academic matters. In no way were the two types of equally effective schools similar institutions.

Further evidence that should lead us to doubt whether any recipe for effectiveness exists independently of the characteristics of the precise local background of each school comes from Galloway (1983). In his study of four local head teachers with exceptionally low rates of disruptive behaviour, two were autocratic, one democratic in style and one could be called mixed. The important thing determining effectiveness was that the head teachers were successful in gaining support for their philosophies and practices from their staff, which they did in *different* ways that were appropriate to their own personalities and the dynamics of their local settings.

It follows from our discussions so far that the early certainties generated by research in the area of school effectiveness and behaviour amongst pupils have been replaced by a wide range of areas where considerable controversy and doubts now exist. Although it is clear that individual schools have larger effects upon behaviour than upon other aspects of pupil development, it is possible and perhaps even likely that:

(i) schools may not be consistently effective or ineffective in their impact upon behaviour over time,

(ii) the same school may have a positive effect upon the behaviour of some groups of pupils and negative effects upon others,

(iii) schools which have a positive impact upon pupil behaviour may not have a positive impact upon other areas of pupil development,

(iv) the factors which make schools effective may be somewhat different in different local contexts.

It must be clear, then, that we need much more research into the issues noted here and that such research also needs to advance into areas of school practice where school effectiveness studies have been thus far reluctant to venture. In some fascinating findings from New Zealand, Ramsey *et al.*, (1982) found that the curriculum itself differed in the effective schools, with the successful schools incorporating elements of Maori and Pacific Island culture across the curriculum to make it more relevant to the lives of pupils. As well as studying the curriculum itself, British research needs to look in detail at the actual classroom behaviour of teachers in different kinds of school, since this important area has also not received the attention it deserves. How do teachers in the effective schools actually stop potentially troublesome incidents from escalating? What supports do teachers have in the effective schools that are absent for their colleagues in ineffective schools? Do effective classroom teachers together create an effective school in behavioural terms or is it the case, as I suspect, that an effective school's ethos and environment actually creates the incident-free classroom settings? Is it enough for pupils to gain positive academic experiences to prevent behavioural problems, or conversely, is it more effective for pupils to be firstly encouraged to be well behaved on the assumption that academic achievement will follow naturally from this? All these — and many other — areas would all repay urgent investigation.

From school effectiveness to school improvement

The array of questions that currently await answers in order to improve our knowledge as to how schools can act to create or to reduce pupil problem behaviour pale into insignificance when it comes to the even more complex issue of how to apply knowledge about the characteristics of *good schools* in order to make other schools *good*. Overall, it must be said that the translation of school effectiveness work into programmes of detailed school change, using those factors identified above from the various research studies, has been pitifully poor; and the take up of knowledge by practitioners has been very limited indeed, with the exception of specific ILEA initiatives associated with the Inspectors Based in Schools Initiative.

In part, this may be because school effectiveness research in Britain has been heavily academically dominated, unlike the United States where practitioners have undertaken most of the research and where the school effectiveness *movement*, as they call themselves, was launched by a Black American school board superintendent, Ron Edmonds. As one might expect, take up of research insights is therefore much greater in North America than in the United Kingdom. To some, it is the actual character of the research itself that has probably contributed to poor levels of implementation by practitioners and policy makers — there are high levels of abstraction and a lack of detail in some of the concepts like *academic press* or *positive teacher expectations*. Practitioners are still heavily content or curriculum orientated whereas school effectiveness work has not been concerned with the curriculum but mostly about the organization of the school. Research is strong on school ethos, climate or environment but weak on the precise curricular and organizational arrangements that are the *means* to attain effective environments.

The problems relating to the nature of the research that has been undertaken have been magnified in their effects because, also, the academic study of school improvement, school review and school change has been a very separate discipline, with a distinctively different set of traditions. School improvement in Britain probably began with the teacher researcher movement (Elliott, 1977, 1981), moved into school self evaluation and review (Clift and Nuttall, 1987) and later attempted to ensure that the review process was linked to an improvement policy, as with the Hargreaves report on *Improving Secondary Schools* (1984), the GRIDS scheme of McMahon *et al* (1984) and the International School Improvement Project of Bollen and Hopkins (1987).

Overall the school improvement researchers have continued to be concerned

more with individuals than with the organization of schools, and have rarely em-
pirically evaluated the effect of changes in their schools. They have often indeed
been more concerned with the journey of undertaking school improvement than
with the particular destination, and have often celebrated practitioner knowledge
whether it is itself a valid improvement strategy or not, leading to a futile re-
invention of the wheel in each project. The sociology of education has been particularly good at the latter (Woods and Pollard, 1987). The lack of *mesh* between the
school effectiveness and school improvement communities — seen for example in
numerous disparaging comments about school effectiveness work by the school im-
provers Holly and Hopkins (Reid *et al.*, 1986) — has clearly reduced the potential
practitioner impact of school effectiveness work (see Reynolds, 1988, for elaboration
on this theme).

The lack of knowledge about school change strategies within the school effectiveness community has probably, with other factors mentioned above, also been
responsible for the rather disappointing results that have occurred when school
effectiveness researchers have themselves attempted directly to change schools. The
London research team of Rutter and his colleagues attempted to bring their knowledge about effective practice derived from research into some of their original
sample of schools (Ouston and Maughan, 1989), yet generated rather disappointing effects on pupil outcomes probably because of the *top-down* knowledge
transfer process, the lack of technological applicability in their research data, and
the neglect of the important *headteacher factor* in the original study. In Wales, we
tried a consultancy based method of bringing the results of school effectiveness
work to schools, in which the school staff owned the change process which was itself
bottom-up in orientation. This too has rather disappointing results (Reynolds,
1987).

More recently, (Davie *et al.*, forthcoming), there are occasional examples of
the successful translation of school effectiveness work into school change programmes, as in our study where teachers attending in-service training as school
change agents generated over six major organizational changes per person, over 80
per cent of which had survived in a six-year follow-up study. Overall, though,
school effectiveness research has had much to say about what makes a *good* school
rather than about how to make schools *good*. An improvement in knowledge and
appreciation of the practical issues of how to improve schools would seem to be an
urgent necessity.

School effectiveness and contemporary educational policies

Whilst researchers attempt to unravel the complexities of the relationship between
the characteristics of a school and the behaviour of its pupils, educational policies
that attempt to deal with the problems caused by pupil behaviour continue of
course to move independently and rapidly. Concern about the issues of discipline in
schools, vandalism, delinquency, truancy and any other instances of pupil maladjustment or antisocial behaviour, often appear as a kind of moral panic, where

logical and rational thinking about the nature, scale and causes of the particular problems are prevented by the need for instantaneous policy reactions to the emotional and irrational political climate within which the problems are discussed.

Such reactions in the past have led to a whole host of policies that aimed to *treat* or deal with problem behaviour, yet virtually all of them attempted to deal only with the problem pupils rather than the schools which may have been causing pupils' problems. Within schools guidance and counselling and school-based social workers all attempted to deal with the individual not the system (Reynolds and Jones, 1978). Educational welfare officers and juvenile courts routinely *individualized* the explanations of truancy in their reports on truants but rarely considered if truancy simply indicated not defective family dynamics but defective schooling. Educational psychologists, perhaps because of the influence of the abnormal psychologists such as Freud, explained problems as due to outside school influences (Reynolds, 1984). A whole array of specialist off site provision like *sin bins*, disruptive pupil units, child guidance clinics, intermediate treatment centres and special schools have been built to take children with behavioural problems out of their schools for the supposed benefit of the school's other clients and the child him/herself (Topping, 1983).

As opinion has turned against such approaches because of their manifest ineffectiveness and high costs, and as educational professionals and practitioners have become aware of the evidence that many forms of problem behaviour from pupils may be caused by the existence of various deficiencies in their schools, so enthusiasm has turned towards policies which attempt *whole-school* change and towards policies that aim to change those features of schools that may be causing children's behavioural problems. Yet this new emphasis upon changing schools that is now in the forefront of political and professional thinking (Ramasut, 1989) is itself beset with difficulties and problems.

In the past one could hope that the arrival of a new head teacher at a school would give the chance of improvement, yet nowadays the drop in child numbers and the large number of premature retirements mean that there is now little turnover in the number of heads. Likewise, the hope of changing schools by changing personnel at senior or junior level has also substantially vanished with the lack of teacher vacancies. Even at ineffective schools, there is no hope that the staff will *turn over* by 10 per cent or 20 per cent per annum as they did in the mid 1970's. All change attempts, then, must deal with the existing ineffective schools and presumably ineffective personnel as they are. The participants in schools have to be transformed since they cannot be replaced.

There is no doubt that a large variety of current *whole-school* policies to uncover and change ineffective schools, or schools performing below the levels that we would expect from their pupil intakes, are an inefficient waste of time and resources. Taken in turn, it is clear that conventional in-service training is not the answer. Threatened or insecure staff groups are, in my experience, the least likely to take up any form of in-service exercise. The LEA advisory services are also highly unlikely to be able to change the ineffective school. They have been conventionally involved in curriculum development, not in the organizational or management areas which they have regarded as the province of the individual school head-teacher. Many of them have no experience of comprehensive schools, or of management other than as a head of a department on the academic side of a school. Publishing school examination results as practised after the 1981 Education Act is likely to be ineffective, since these are not weighted or adjusted to take account of the catchment areas, or the intakes into schools, but are merely published in a *raw* form. Schools that are apparently highly effective in these raw terms may not be if we allow for their intakes. The Inspectorate, too, are unlikely to be able to change poorly performing schools. They are often shrewd in their judgments of internal school processes, management competence and school ethos or atmosphere, yet recent evidence (Gray and Hannon, 1986) suggests that they make no systematic attempt to allow for variations in the pupil raw material that schools are getting. Comparisons of individual schools are often against national or LEA or other schools' standards, which is meaningless unless one allows for variations in the pupils that the individual school is getting.

Most important of all, there is no evidence that the recent changes in educational policy following the Education Reform Act of 1988 will in any way deal with the problem of those schools which may be generating problem behaviour amongst their pupils. Only examination data and the results of the assessment of pupils' academic abilities will be available and published about primary and secondary schools: data upon behaviour, attendance, delinquency, vandalism and child guidance referral is not to be included. The academic data will be published set against the context of the characteristics of the schools' local catchment areas, yet there will be no *systematic* attempt to adjust raw performance data to take account of the kinds of intakes schools are getting and no attempt to *predict* what different schools should, given their catchment areas, be obtaining by way of test scores. Also, no breakdown of the pupils into different categories has been proposed, for example, into low ability/high ability, since only aggregate data has been referred to thus far in the policy proposals on national testing.

There is of course some activity currently into the design of performance indicators that will cover the more behavioural outcomes of schooling. The Coopers and Lybrand report (DES, 1988) on financial management of schools, the Public Finance Foundation programmes of research into American educational indicators and the trialling of indicators that is proceeding in some British local education authorities are all indications that measures of pupil behaviour *may* come to be included in the information available to educational consumers that exists to inform and advise them on the relative performance of their children's potential schools. However, even if these indicators of behaviour were to be introduced, there are no indications that the assessment of schools on the basis of their success or failure in producing good pupil behaviour will be any more valid than the assessments to be made of school academic quality. What approaches would be needed to generate a more valid system for school behavioural assessment?

The main data requirement is that each school would need to examine and measure the quality of its intake and the academic and behavioural quality of its output of pupils, generating *expected* levels of academic and behavioural success to compare with the *actual* levels. These measurements of each school's pupils' behaviour should be as multi-dimensional as possible, covering within-lesson behaviour, delinquency, attendance and referral to specialist outside provision, and also tapping pupil attitudes which may be important in determining behaviour such as self esteem, sense of personal control, self conception and sense of personal efficacy. The data must also be collected on whole cohorts of pupils as they progress through their schools, to compare like with like, and must be collected on individuals to permit the whole pupil group to be broken down into component parts. Such a data set is simply light years away from the ludicrously simple quality and performance system proposed by the government.

Does the government really care about pupil behaviour?

The ideal approach to evaluating school effectiveness outlined above is, of course, unlikely to become part of the national assessment system by which school quality is to be assessed. Indeed, there is a strange hypocrisy in governmental thinking about pupil behaviour problems, since the stated govenmental concern about tackling the problem that led to the report of Lord Elton's committee is clearly in no way matched by any development of information systems to help inform policy or to help in the remediation of ineffective schools.

We can perhaps explain the discontinuity and conflict between governmental expressed concern and its lack of specific action to combat the problems of pupil behaviour as perhaps symptomatic of a deeper conflict that has been brought about by recent legislation. Many comprehensive schools nationally and in our local research community have explicitly attempted to reorientate themselves towards serving their lower ability pupils, who have often generated their behavioural problems, by eroding some of their traditional grammar school ethos, by modifying their academic curriculum and by concentrating more heavily on social as well as narrowly academic goals. In most accounts (see review in Reynolds *et al.*, 1987) it is clear that schools in the 1980's have been changing in an attempt to deliberately reduce some of the levels of behavioural problems that they had been producing in the 1970's. Paradoxically, government policy now is to bring back exactly those school organizational forms and philosophies which comprehensives were moving away from, because the schools believed that they were generating behavioural problems.

The legislative pressures in this direction are formidable and are explained in more detail elsewhere (Hargreaves and Reynolds, 1989). To summarize, it is clear that:

(i) The 1981 Education Act required schools to publish their examination results, which is likely to have led to a renewed concentration upon those pupils of higher ability who will give the greatest 'return' on any investment of school human and financial resources.

(ii) The same Act's requirement that only academic — and not social — outcomes be published is likely to encourage the comprehensives to devalue their more recent preoccupation with social goals.

(iii) Increasing parental power over schools through giving parents the right to express a preference for their chosen school and giving increased parental power on governing bodies in the 1986 Education Act is likely to push schools towards a greater involvement with higher ability pupils, because they are likely to have parents who lobby on their behalf, and towards academic rather than social goals, because parents are likely to hold instrumental views about the goals of education.

(iv) The Education Act 1988 increased the probability of schools competing against each other for children through its provisions allowing popular schools to increase in numbers through open enrolment. Such competition will again intensify the pressure on schools to concentrate on those pupils who can deliver examination result passes that will make the schools attractive in the eyes of the parents.

(v) Many have voiced fears that proposals to allow state schools to *opt-out* of local education authority control will lead to a neglect of lower ability or special educational needs children because of an opted-out schools' likely concentration on other parts of the ability range.

(vi) The proposed core curriculum is predominantly academic in character, with traditional subjects and proposing clearly demarcated subject boundaries which threaten new subjects, the emphasis on social development and the integrated approach to teaching increasingly found in schools. The small time allocation allowed for all the non-core or foundation subjects — 20 per cent in the present estimate — suggests that they will have to struggle for status in the future.

It is interesting to speculate, then, that these recent educational policies towards comprehensive schools — involving returning them to concentrate more on academic outcomes and concentrating them more on the needs of higher ability pupils — may paradoxically have been because they *were* beginning to succeed in generating authentic comprehensive education, not because they were *not*. The school's increasing concentration upon the bottom two-thirds of the ability range may have adversely affected the top third of the ability range and also the traditional sixth formers — this is clearly shown by the small rise in the proportion of the ability range getting 'A' levels and the more rapidly rising proportion acquiring lower level 'O' and CSE qualifications (Rutter, 1980). The schools' increased concern with social goals, even more marked in other societies with the *common school* such as Sweden or the United States, was perhaps threatening to open the curriculum and the schooling experience to forms of discourse and interaction much more suited to the expressive culture of lower social class pupils (Bernstein, 1959). The widening of the curriculum to include more relevant or 'new' knowledge may well have been a powerful spur to the learning of those of lower ability who had come to be labelled as culturally disadvantaged because of their non-possession of the *cultural capital* (Bordieu *et al.*, 1977) necessary to perform well in acquiring the old, traditional curriculum. The hegemony of this traditional, subject centred curriculum is being emphasized to reinforce the advantages of those pupils who can acquire it easily, even though this may generate problems for the pupils not so equipped.

It would be wrong to attempt to make judgments as to whether present educational policies are *right* or *wrong* — that is a value question for others than educational researchers to decide upon. All one can do in this context is to note that present policies may well generate *grammar school-like* comprehensive schools which may generate the same range of pupils behavioural problems that have been so notable in the past, problems which the schools themselves deliberately changed to try to avoid. The more relevant curriculum, the increased concern for social goals and the increased concern for the lower ability child were all intended to avoid the problems that conventional comprehensive schooling had been generating. Policies that are likely to eradicate such organizational features of schooling may well bring back the pupil behaviour problems that generated those organizational features in the first place. If the government really cares about pupil problem behaviour, it would be proceeding in very different ways to these.

References

BALL, S.J. (1981) *Beachside Comprehensive*, Cambridge, Cambridge University Press.

BERNSTEIN, B. (1959) 'A public language: Some sociological determinants of linguistic form', in: *British Journal of Sociology*, **10**, 4.

BLAKEY, L. and HEATH, A. (1989) 'Differences between comprehensive schools: Some preliminary findings', in: REYNOLDS, D. and CUTTANCE, P. (Eds.) *School Environments and Child Development*, (in press).

BOLLEN, R. and HOPKINS, D. (1987) *School Based Review: Towards a Praxis* Leuven, Belgium ACCO Publishing.

BOURDIEU, P. and PASSERON, J.C. (1977) *Reproduction: in Education, Society and Culture*, London, Sage.

BROOKOVER, W.B., BEADY, C., FLOOD, P., SCHWEITZER, J. and WISENBAKER, J. (1979) *School Social Systems and Student Achievement*, New York, Praeger.

CLIFT, P. and NUTTALL, D. (Eds) (1987) *Studies in School Self Evaluation*, Lewes, Falmer Press.

COX, C. and MARKS, J. (1983) *Standards in English Schools: First Report*, London, National Council for Educational Standards.

CUTTANCE, P. (1989) 'Assessing the effectiveness of Schools', in: REYNOLDS, D. and CUTTANCE, P. (Eds.) *School Environments and Child Development*, (in Press).

DAVIE, R., REYNOLDS, D. and PHILLIPS, D. (forthcoming) *Changing A School*, Lewes, Falmer Press.

DEPARTMENT OF EDUCATION AND SCIENCE, (1984) *School Standards and Spending: Statistical Analysis. A Further Appreciation*, London, HMSO.

DEPARTMENT OF EDUCATION AND SCIENCE, (1988) *Local Management of Schools*, (Coopers and Lybrand Report), London, HMSO.

ELLIOTT, J. (1977) 'Evaluating in-service activities: from above or below?' *Insight*, Nov.

ELLIOTT, J. (1981) *School Accountability*, London, Grant McLatyre.

FINLAYSON, D. and LOUGHRAN, J.L. (1976) 'Pupils' perceptions in high and low delinquency schools', *Educational Research*, **18**, 2.

GALLOWAY, D. (1983) 'Disruptive Pupils and Effective Pastoral Care' *School Organisation*, **13**, pp. 245–54.

GALLOWAY, D., MARTIN, R. and WILCOX, B. (1985) 'Persistent absence from school and exclusion from school: the predictive power of school and community variables', *Bristol Educational Research Journal*, **11**, pp. 51–61.

GATH, D. (1977) *Child Guidance and Delinquency in a London Borough*, London, Oxford University Press.

GRAY, J. and HANNON, V. (1986) 'HMI's interpretations of schools examination results', *Journal of Education Policy*, **1**, 1.

GRAY, J., JESSON, D., and JONES, B. (1984) 'Predicting differences in examination results between Local Education Authorities: does school organisation matter?' *Oxford Review of Education*, **10**, 1, pp. 45–68.

GRAY, J., MCPHERSON, A. and RAFFE, D. (1983) *Reconstructions of Secondary Education*, London, Routledge and Kegan Paul.

HARGREAVES, A. and REYNOLDS, D. (1989) *Education Policy: Controversies and Critiques*, Lewes, Falmer Press.

HARGREAVES, D.H. (1967) *Social Relations in a Secondary School*, London, Routledge and Kegan Paul.

HARGREAVES, D. (1984) *Improving Secondary Schools*, Report of the committee in the curriculum and organisation of secondary schools, London, ILEA.

HARGREAVES, D., HESTER, S.K. and MELLOR, F.J. (1985) *Deviance in Classrooms*, London, Routledge and Kegan Paul.

HER MAJESTYS INSPECTORATE (1987) *Education Observed 5: Good Behaviour and Discipline in Schools*, London, HMSO.

MCMAHON, A., BOLAM, R., ABBOTT, R. and HOLLY, P. (1984) *Guidelines for Review and Development in Schools*, Primary and Secondary Handbooks, York, Longman.

MCPHERSON, A. and WILLMS, D. (1987) 'Equalisation and improvement: Some effects of comprehensive reorganisation in Scotland', *Sociology*, **21**, 4, pp. 509–40.

MORTIMORE, P., SAMMONS, P., ECOB, R. and STOLL, L. (1988) *School Matters: The Junior Years*, Salisbury, Open Books.

OUSTON, J. and MAUGHAN, B., (1989) 'Innovation and change in Secondary schools', in: REYNOLDS, D. and CUTTANCE, P. (Eds.) *School Environments and Child Development*, (in press).

POWER, M.J., ALDERSON, M.R., PHILLIPSON, C.M., SCHOENBURG, E. and MORRIS, J. (1967) 'Delinquent Schools?' *New Society*, **10**, pp. 542–3.

RAMASUT, A. (1989) *Whole School Approaches*, Lewes, Falmer Press.

RAMSAY, P.D.K., SNEDDON, D.G., GRENFELL, J. and FORD, Y. (1982) 'Successful and unsuccessful schools: a South Auckland Study', *Australia and New Zealand Journal of Sociology*, **19**, 1.

REID, K., HOPKINS, D. and HOLLY, P. (1986) *Towards the Effective School*, Oxford, Blackwell.

REYNOLDS, D. (1976) 'The Delinquent School', in WOODS, P. (Ed.) *The Process of Schooling*, London, Routledge and Kegan Paul.

REYNOLDS, D. (1982) 'The Search for effective schools', *School Organisation*, **2**, 3, pp. 215–37.

REYNOLDS, D. (1984) 'Creative conflict: The implications of recent educational research for those concerned with children', *Maladjustment and Therapeutic Education*, Spring 1984, pp. 14–23.

REYNOLDS, D. (1987) 'The consultant sociologist: A method for linking sociology of education and teachers', in WOODS, P. and POLLARD, A. (Eds) *Where The Action Is: A New Challenge For the Sociology of Education*, Beckenham, Croom Helm.

REYNOLDS, D. (1988) 'British school improvement research; The contribution of qualitative studies', *International Journal of Qualitative Studies in Education*, 1, 2.

REYNOLDS, D. and JONES, D. (1978) 'Education and the prevention of juvenile delinquency', in TUTT, N.S. (Ed.) *Coping With Crime*, Oxford, Basil Blackwell and Martin Robertson.

REYNOLDS, D. and SULLIVAN, M. (1979) 'Bringing schools back in', in BARTON, L. (Ed.) *Schools Pupils and Deviance*, Driffield, Nafferton.

REYNOLDS, D., SULLIVAN, M. and MURGATROYD, S.J. (1987) *The Comprehensive Experiment*, Lewes, Falmer Press.

RUTTER, M. (1980) *Changing Youth in a Changing Society*, Oxford, Nuffield Provincial Hospitals Trust.

RUTTER, M. (1983) 'School effects on pupils progress — Findings and policy implications', *Child Development*, 54, 1, pp. 1–29.

RUTTER, M., MAUGHAN, B., MORTIMORE, P. and OUSTEN, J. (1979) *Fifteen Thousand Hours*, London, Open Books.

TOPPING, K. (1983) *Educational Systems For Disruptive Adolescents*, Beckenham, Croom Helm.

WILLMS, D. and CUTTANCE, P. (1985) 'School effects in Scottish secondary schools', *British Journal of Sociology of Education*, 6, 3, pp. 289–305.

WOODS, P. and POLLARD, A. (Eds) (1987) *Sociology and Teaching*, Beckenham, Croom Helm.

2
Discipline: The Teacher's Dilemma

Ken Reid

In this chapter, I will focus on four aspects relating to school discipline. First, I shall outline some of my own experience as a teacher and draw on this to suggest some practical guidelines for combating and preventing outbreaks of ill discipline in the classroom. Second, I will try to examine discipline from the pupils' point of view. Third, I will question the appropriateness of teachers' initial and in-service training for the tasks they undertake in school in relation to maintaining school and classroom discipline. The evidence presented here is drawn from my own research into teacher education and my experience as a teacher educator. Finally, I will make some suggestions as to how individual teachers and their schools can improve their own disciplinary records and on ways the DES and Welsh Office can facilitate them.

The novice years

Most new teachers intuitively know when they begin their teaching careers that their ability to maintain order in the classroom will either make or break them. I was no different from anyone else in this respect. However, it came as a real surprise to me on my first day in a secondary modern school that I should enter 3.11 at nine-fifteen to a chorus of *boos*. Apparently, the class were upset about the fact that they had been given a new form tutor rather than keeping Mr Phillips, their previous incumbent. For a few seconds, I froze. No one had told me what to do in this situation!

Eventually, I coped. The position immediately improved on the first Wednesday afternoon of term when I took 3.10 to 3.14 for games (soccer). My form contained several members of their age group school team and most of the boys were feverishly interested in football, particularly the fortunes of Swindon Town and Oxford United. I deliberately selected two teams, one containing all the good footballers in my form, and then played on the opposite side. Apart from refereeing I marked Joe Bugden, a supposedly fearsome *skinhead* who played centre forward for the school team and was the self-appointed leader and *wag* of 3.11. To their dismay, the boys in my form lost. Worse, *Sir* scored the winning goal which, seemingly, according to the debates which followed, *was not fair*. Moreover, Bugden was marked out of the game — something he was not used to. His fan club were soon blaming his poor performance for their defeat.

The boys changed and returned to class. The next day a group of the boys arrived at the staff room door at morning break. My name was called out. I went to meet the deputation. They wanted to know whether I would take their school team for practices and matches that year; I agreed. The boys did well throughout the year playing one or two matches a week and only losing two all season. Several of their number had county and other trials. I never had any further problems with the form or in the school. Bugden was elected form prefect and was always first to volunteer to clean the board. He played in every match throughout the season and in games lessons, by mutual agreement, we also played on the same side.

About half-way through the year an incident occurred in the playground when I was on duty. I walked across the yard to find out what was going on. I need not have bothered. When I got there, I discovered that Bugden and others had already broken up the dispute. It seemed that whenever I was on duty Bugden and his *crowd* took it upon themselves to ensure that there was no trouble in the playground. It was their way of ensuring that I continued to organize their sporting activities for them.

When I left the school following promotion to a Scale 2 (remember those days?) in a very large comprehensive, Bugden, now a little older and wiser, presented me with a gift. He made a little speech. He told me that he had done a deal with his peers on pain of death that they behave in my lessons *or else*. He also said that he knew if anything went wrong, I would mark him on the football field again!

At my second school, I initially took up an appointment as the teacher in charge of courses for the raising of the school leaving age (ROSLA). No one at the school could understand why I had abandoned history for fourth and fifth year work with lower ability pupils only. Neither could they understand why I seemed to enjoy the challenge of working with known difficult and disruptive elements in the school. Later, my success with this work brought me early promotion as head of the fourth year.

Looking back, I can now see there were several reasons for my action. First, I strongly felt that all pupils were equal irrespective of ability or background. Consequently, I treated them all the same. I soon learnt that this was not the case amongst a large proportion of my colleagues, many of whom dreaded working with lower ability, difficult pupils and, accordingly, lowered their own interest and performance levels. For instance, on a Monday afternoon, when the fourth year had a key lecture/film as part of their English syllabus, I used to have to go along to the lecture theatre to gain order and to introduce the subject matter even though it was not my responsibility. Usually, only one or two of the department stayed in the lecture theatre for the duration. The rest took it as a free afternoon. I lost count of the number of times I was summoned back to the lecture theatre from my office to quell disturbances which ranged from communal smoking to the taking over of the projection room.

Second, I derived more satisfaction when one of my ROSLA group achieved success than I ever did when able pupils achieved their expected academic success. I came to define success in a broad sense. Explicitly, I was very pleased when one of the pupils gained a place as a trainee apprentice with a well known motor racing team. I was delighted when one of our pupils unexpectedly achieved a Grade One C.S.E. Mode 3 Social Studies pass on the recommendation of the moderator or when one of the boys was signed on as a professional footballer. It was equally gratifying when an aggressive, disruptive girl, who had been transferred to the school from an Inner London Borough, calmed down to the point that her social worker and probation officer described her as being unrecognizable from the person they had previously known. The message to me was clear. If you treat pupils with appropriate respect, empathy and concern they will reciprocate. When you don't, they will respond in kind. Therefore, teachers' attitudes are a key variable in classroom control.

What did I learn practically from those early years? The answer is quite a lot. Therefore, what I will now do is to list a number of essential points.

1. Bad behaviour in classrooms is associated with poor teaching strategies such as not treating pupils with respect, applying rules in classrooms inconsistently, bartering, poor or non-teaching, not preparing lessons properly. Poor behaviour in schools is often related to school organization and school policies — running down the corridor, not wearing school uniform, talking in assemblies.

2. Bad behaviour is associated with individual teacher performance. Pupils who behave well with one teacher will behave badly with another. Teachers' expectations of pupils' academic levels can also adversely or favourably influence pupil performance. Explicitly, a teacher who enthuses about maths and causes the pupils to enjoy her lessons is likely to achieve a better performance and standard of behaviour in the subject than another colleague who bores the class to tears and is unable to maintain order.

3. Schools take too little notice of possible problems caused by their own decision-making. For example, changing subject or form teachers often has greater consequences upon individual pupils' and classes' behaviour and learning than many school managers appreciate. Teachers who expect less get less. Teachers who cannot control classes find they have to combat more misbehaviour than others — ask any good head of year or deputy. Teachers who expect negative outcomes probably influence those outcomes. Classroom interaction is all important. Teaching is far more than standing up in front of a class relating facts to pupils. Teaching is also about understanding individuals and groups of pupils. Therefore, however difficult time-wise, teachers need to devote attention to finding out what makes their pupils tick as people. They need to be able to communicate with their pupils at an interest level as well as at an academic one. Such discussion time is well spent and will repay them fully by improving pupils' classroom attitudes, effort and performance. Failure to take an interest in pupils

makes the latter feel that their teachers do not care. Hence, understanding is likely to lead to empathy. In turn, this will lead to better pupil–teacher relationships, better lessons, less need for overt control which, in their turn, all lead to a reduction in the possible number of opportunities for disruptive conduct to occur.

4. Successful schools contain a majority of staff who:

Are able to keep control at all times (most important);
Are able to 'have a laugh' with pupils; a sense of humour is important in a teacher;
Foster warm, empathetic relationships with pupils;
Like and understand children;
Enjoy and teach their subjects well, with enthusiasm and in interesting ways;
Teach all the time rather than indulging in aimless activities;
Are consistent and fair;
Treat children with respect and as equals;
Create a sense of 'freedom' and 'purpose' in class;
Do not adversely 'label' disaffected or disruptive pupils for life;
Are prepared to give deviant pupils a second chance.

Pupils' perspectives

Pupils have to be remarkably sophisticated in responding to individual teachers in schools. In an eight-lesson day, pupils have to behave differently with their teachers on eight occasions. In one lesson they can keep their coats on. In another, they can't. With one teacher they have to put their hands up. With another they are encouraged to talk. One teacher doesn't mind if they eat sweets in class. Another does. From pupils' perspectives where is the norm?

Worse, with one teacher one day they can talk freely in class. With the same teacher the next day they can't. For three weeks Mr H gives them large amounts of homework. For the next three weeks he gives them none. Mrs Johnson praises Carole for her performances at netball. The next day she sends her to the Head of Year for failing to wear school uniform.

My experience suggests that many pupils have legitimate complaints when they are singled out or punished. Why should Adam be punished because his science teacher cannot maintain order? The previous year with a different science teacher his behaviour was exemplary.

Pupils appear to dislike the following traits in teachers:

Teachers who are 'inhuman' and interpret their role too literally. These kind of practitioners are regarded by pupils as being *a load of rubbish*. Stand-offish approaches are unlikely to work with pupils;
Teachers who treat pupils anonymously. Despite current teacher ratios, it is vital that pupils are treated as individuals;

Teachers who are soft and/or inconsistent. This includes teachers who do not teach to goals forcing their pupils to underperform or underachieve. Teachers who barter for good classroom order are particularly at risk;

Teachers who are unfair, make unreasonable demands on pupils, are insensitive at times of illness or with, for example, pupils' learning problems, as well as those who bully pupils and/or hold grudges as a result of past misdemeanours.

When pupils regard their schools as having a lot of staff in these categories, it is likely that they will manifest their displeasure by rebelling. Consequently, schools with higher than average numbers of disaffected pupils (with all this implies in terms of violence, vandalism, confrontation and large doses of teacher stress) might well be advised to examine their own professional laurels as well as other factors. Whilst social class and catchment area might be two mitigating circumstances, they are not the cause *per se*. There are well ordered, purposeful schools in deprived areas, albeit fewer than those in favourable catchment areas. Hence, as we shall see later, having appropriate school policies are a very important part of the behavioural equation.

Initial teacher education

The relationship between initial teacher education and classroom management is a complex, under researched area. Between 1979 and 1983, Gerald Bernbaum, Helen Patrick and myself took part in a large-scale DES sponsored study into The Structure and Process of Initial Teacher Education Within Universities in England and Wales (SPITE) (Patrick *et al.*, 1982; Bernbaum, Patrick and Reid, 1985). The project used questionnaire, interview and diary techniques with 4,350 graduate student-teachers in their initial and probationary years including in-depth studies with two structured sub-samples from seven university departments of education. In addition, we carried out a staff survey and selection of interviews with approximately 1200 teacher educators in the same thirty university departments of education.

Space precludes me from writing about all the relevant issues here. What I will try to do is to provide a summary of those key findings which are related to classroom management and pupils' behaviour.

1. On pedagogical (theory) courses within the UDE's, issues like truancy, discipline, slow-learning children and behavioural techniques were then covered by few departments. Much depended on the interests and expertise of departmental tutors. Student-teachers were left therefore to glean what they could from their method (subject) tutors and much of this work was of the *tips for teachers* kind. Furthermore, a large proportion of teacher educators have never themselves worked in, for example, a comprehensive school such has been the scale of changes over the years. Thus, approximately one in five students thought that their PGCE courses gave

them considerable insight into classroom discipline. Conversely, half thought they had only been given some insight and 29 per cent little or no insight into the topic of classroom discipline. By contrast, of those students who had followed courses on classroom management and organization, and control and discipline in the classroom, over four-fifths had found the topic(s) helpful on their teaching practice.

2. The analysis of the data on students' problems on teaching practice found that a majority of them had major or some problems with only one item on teaching practice: being unable to control difficult classes. However, almost half admitted having some or major problems with difficult classes.

3. The interview and diary data showed that the student-teachers believed discipline was the one item which could make or break them on teaching practice and in their subsequent teaching experience. In some of the diary accounts there was evidence of personal anguish over this matter which appeared to be out of proportion to all aspects of their training. There were indications that some students who were experiencing disciplinary problems kept matters to themselves and/or received little help from their teacher mentors or departmental supervisor/s.

4. Owing to the crucial importance of these findings, the variable on the difficulties which the students experienced in maintaining classroom discipline on teaching practice was subsequently broken down into ten separate items for further investigation. In order of importance, the results showed that students' problems were linked with:

Not being sufficiently firm at the beginning of teaching practice (50.4 per cent);
Having different standards of teaching from those of the regular teachers (39.8 per cent);
Attempting to be too friendly with the pupils (38.9 per cent);
Taking over classes from weak teachers (29.6 per cent);
Teaching topic/subjects with which they were not sufficiently familiar (28.9 per cent);
Being inadequately prepared for the problems of discipline (28.7 per cent);
Being unable to spot potentially difficult situations (23.9 per cent);
Not being familiar with the type of children in the school(s) (22.4 per cent);
Lack of support/help from school staff (14.8 per cent);
Being placed in a particularly difficult school (11.5 per cent);

5. More men than women admitted having serious problems with discipline on teaching practice.

6. More maths and science students than arts or modern language students experienced problems which is probably related to the gender finding above as more men than women train to be maths and science specialists and vice versa with arts and modern languages. Interestingly HMI (1988), in *The New Teacher In School*, reported more weaknesses amongst maths

and PE teachers (the latter rather surprisingly) than in other subject disciplines.

Induction and probationary year programmes

In our research project we followed up the student-teachers into their probationary year (Reid, 1985b). We found that help given to new staff by schools varied considerably and was often of the informal and ad hoc kind rather then pre-planned and well structured. As you will now see, our findings suggest that schools could do a great deal more to help their new colleagues through properly prepared induction and probationary year programmes.

Help during probationary year

Table 1 shows the people from whom the probationers received help in schools during their first year of training. It should be noted that the totals are taken as a percentage of 2397 respondents — the number of probationary teachers who were employed. The total percentage is greater than 100 because many respondents received help from more than one person.

Table 2.1   Distribution of people from whom probationers reveived help

	N	%
Nobody	132	5.5
Headteacher	420	17.5
Deputy Headteacher(s)	843	35.2
Head(s) of Department	1750	73.0
Pastoral Head(s) of year	652	27.2
Other Teacher(s)	1693	70.6
Local education authority (LEA) adviser(s)	530	22.1
Her Majesty's Inspectorate of Education (HMI)	81	3.4
Someone else	204	8.5

Not surprisingly, new teachers were most likely to say that they had received help during their probationary year from heads of departments and from other teachers. Over 70 per cent had received help from each of these categories, while over a third had been helped by a deputy headteacher. Only 5.5 per cent said that nobody had helped them. Those teaching science subjects and physical education (P.E.) were least likely to have had no help, while those teaching in independent schools and in colleges of further or higher education were among those most likely to have had no help. To some extent the people from whom new teachers received help varied according to the type of school in which they taught. Those working in primary and middle schools tended to get help from the head or deputy headteachers, while those in comprehensive schools, grammar schools and sixth form colleges were more likely to have been helped by heads of department. LEA advisers seemed most often to have been of help to P.E. and primary teachers.

Respondents were also asked whether they had attended any induction or in-service courses for probationary teachers in those pre-GRIST days. Nearly half (47.6 per cent) had done so. Those teaching P.E. and primary and middle school subjects were most likely to have done so, as were those teaching in primary, middle and comprehensive schools. Teachers in independent schools and colleges of further and higher education were less likely than their colleagues elsewhere to have had the benefit of such courses. Many respondents gave no specific details of the courses they attended, noting only that they consisted of general discussions or talks organized by an LEA adviser. Courses on individual teaching subjects tended to be taken by those teaching the relevant subjects. Apart from specific subjects, other topics on which courses were attended by relatively high numbers of probationers included counselling and pastoral care; the use and management of resources; remedial education; assessment; the organization and administration of the education system; discipline; the role of the teacher; language; teaching methods; visits to other schools and to places other than schools; the teacher and the law; and safety. Courses in remedial education tended to be taken by English and maths teachers, while those on safety were attended almost exclusively by science teachers.

The probationary teachers were also asked whether their schools made any special arrangements for the induction of new teachers. Just over two fifths (41.6 per cent) said that they did. Those teaching primary and middle school subjects and those teaching in independent schools were less likely than other groups to report that special arrangements were made. Such arrangements took a variety of forms, the most commonly mentioned being a senior member of staff with responsibility for all probationers in the school. Many probationers attended meetings specially arranged for new teachers. Some had fewer teaching periods than other members of staff or were relieved of tasks such as playground duty. Other arrangements mentioned were short courses in the school before the term began to introduce new teachers; opportunities to observe other teachers at work; and a requirement to submit lesson plans to the head of department or other senior teacher.

As they neared the end of their first year of teaching, the probationary teachers were also asked whether there were any topics on which they would now like a course. In all, 975 (40 per cent) of those employed as teachers noted at least one area on which they would like a course. Most wanted a course on some aspect of their own teaching subject or on some closely related subject. English teachers, for example, might want a course on drama; mathematicians on computing; and primary teachers on reading. Beyond this, the topics most commonly mentioned, in order of frequency, were remedial education (including the teaching of slow learners, under-achieving pupils and the less able); discipline and control; pastoral care; assessment; mixed ability teaching; the organization and administration of education; various teaching methods; the use of resources (including audio-visual aids and libraries); the role of the teacher; sixth form teaching; multicultural education; and first aid.

Probationary year problems

The SPITE probationers were asked to indicate which, from a list of ten items, had caused them some or major problems during their first year of teaching. Table 2.2 shows that the issue which caused problems to more teachers than any other was difficulty in controlling individual pupils; 63.5 per cent had some problems with this, and 14.0 per cent had major problems. This was followed by difficulty in controlling classes, with which 57.0 per cent had some problems and 7.6 per cent had major problems. 63.0 per cent had some or major problems with the amount of marking required.

Table 2.2   Distribution of beginning teachers' problems

	None %	Some %	Major %	N/A %
Problem				
— Teaching subjects for which your training has not equipped you	33.0	36.4	4.2	26.4
— Amount of marking required	34.7	53.7	9.3	2.3
— Lack of non-teaching time	47.7	40.8	8.8	2.7
— Lesson preparation	41.8	50.6	7.0	0.6
— Difficulty in controlling individual pupils	21.8	63.5	14.0	0.6
— Difficulty in controlling classes	34.4	57.0	7.6	7.0
— The administrative tasks associated with teaching	58.1	35.8	3.7	2.4
— Inadequate school textbooks	33.4	42.4	20.2	4.0
— Inadequate audio-visual resources	49.3	30.8	13.6	6.4
— Lack of clear direction from established staff	46.2	39.2	11.8	2.8

Although only 42.4 per cent said that inadequate textbooks had caused some problems, 20.2 per cent said that this had caused them major problems — a higher percentage than for any other item on the list. There were few differences between the sexes with regard to the problems thay had encountered, but the women were slightly more likely to have difficulty in controlling both individual pupils and classes, and the men were slightly more likely to have difficulty with the administrative tasks associated with teaching.

Not unexpectedly, teachers of different subjects tended to encounter different problems. Relatively few modern linguists had problems arising from teaching subjects for which their training had not equipped them, but this did cause problems for relatively high numbers of primary teachers, as did a lack of non-teaching time. Primary teachers, however, were less likely than their colleagues in other subjects to have problems arising out of most of the other items on the list. The amount of marking caused problems for teachers of arts subjects, while the social scientists suffered from the problems of teaching subjects for which their training had not equipped them; a lack of non-teaching time, inadequate audio-visual resources; and a lack of clear direction from established staff. On most items the science teachers did not seem particularly prone to problems. They were slightly more likely than were teachers of other subjects to have problems in controlling classes, but comparatively few had problems with regard to inadequate audio-visual resources or the lack of clear direction from established staff. P.E. staff were also relatively fortunate, being less likely than their colleagues in other subjects to have problems with the amount of marking required; lesson preparation; controlling individual pupils or classes; inadequate textbooks; or audio-visual resources. They did have problems, however, with the administrative tasks associated with teaching and with a lack of clear direction from established staff.

Teachers working in different types of schools faced, to some extent, different problems. As might be expected from the preceding paragraph, those teaching in primary and middle schools were more likely than their peers in other schools to have problems because of teaching subjects for which their training had not equipped them and because of a lack of non-teaching time, but comparatively few had problems in the other areas listed. Those working in comprehensive and secondary modern schools were among those most likely to face problems because of difficulty in controlling individual pupils, difficulty in controlling classes, and inadequate school textbooks, while a higher proportion of those in secondary modern schools than in any other type of school or college suffered from a lack of clear direction from established staff. Those teaching in grammar schools tended to have problems because of audio-visual resources but, apart from this, teachers in grammar schools, sixth form colleges and independent schools were no more likely than their colleagues elsewhere to have problems with most of the items listed, and were comparatively unlikely to have problems with regard to lack of non-teaching time, and controlling classes and individual pupils. Relatively small proportions of those working in independent schools faced problems because of the administrative tasks associated with teaching, inadequate school textbooks or inadequate audio-visual resources.

Apart from this, other key findings revealed:

1. 80.1 per cent and 76.9 per cent of the cohort considered advice given by tutors on control and management to have been useful on teaching practice. These items were ranked fifth and sixth respectively from a list of thirty behind lesson preparation, the skills involved in questioning pupils in class, the preparation of materials for teaching, varied methods of teaching your subject and the use of the blackboard;
2. Probationary teachers regarded control and discipline in the classroom as the third most useful topic covered in their PGCE courses for their probationary year when compared with other important issues from a list of thirty items. Classroom management and organization came fifth;
3. 65.5 per cent of the probationers thought they should have spent more time on classroom management and control on their PGCE courses; 71.8 per cent felt the same way about control and discipline in the classroom. These items were ranked eighth and second respectively from a list of the same thirty items on this variable.

The research also indicated that induction and probationary year programmes varied considerably between LEAs and schools. Some schools and some LEAs took these programmes very seriously. Others virtually ignored them.

Present-day evidence shows a similar trend with in-service training programmes. Courses for coping with difficult and/or disruptive pupils are notoriously absent in some regions. With the demise of long courses since GRIST, this tendency has increased. Moreover, there is growing evidence that in some LEAs teachers' needs for improving their performance with lower ability and/or difficult pupils are not being met despite the demand.

Improving teacher education

The attempt to turn academic subject specialists into teachers in a maximum of thirty-five weeks has long been recognized as extremely difficult, if not impossible, by those who have gone through the process as much as by teacher educators themselves. This was a matter on which there was a general consensus from the SPITE data. There has long been a feeling within the profession that one-year PGCE-trained teachers have been disadvantaged when compared with their four-year trained BEd counterparts. Of course, this is extremely difficult to prove. There is no comparable research. Moreover, until recently, most PGCE-trained teachers have been secondary-orientated while the majority of their BEd colleagues have been primary trained. Nevertheless, this has never prevented invidious comparisons from being made by many within the profession itself.

What does all this mean? By and large secondary teachers have felt reasonably confident to cope with any educable, well-behaved and highly-motivated pupils. They have felt uncomfortable with such pupils as the less-able, difficult and disruptive and those who are less highly motivated than their able peers. The problem is that this excludes a very high proportion of pupils in many schools from being involved in well-constructed and controlled lessons taught by the best qualified, able and experienced teachers. In far too many schools, staff who find themselves with a majority of difficult classes to teach cope on a day-to-day basis as best they can with their limited training and knowledge.

In my own research programmes with persistent absentees, it has become increasingly obvious that the weakest pupils get some of the poorest teachers and vice versa. It is equally apparent that some staff teach able pupils extremely well but appear to put very little effort into their work with lower-ability pupils. National homework patterns aptly illustrate this point.

So this brings us full circle back to the start of the chapter where I described my own first experiences. Like most teachers I was forced to think on my feet, learn *on the job*. What therefore can be done to improve the situation?

School improvement

The notion of school improvement and pupil behaviour requires a chapter in its own right and I am forced to be brief. What follows, therefore, is a list of ideas and suggestions. Some of these ideas can be considered further by reading relevant parts of some of my other books (Reid, 1985a; 1986; 1987; 1989a,b; Reid, Hopkins and Holly, 1987; O'Sullivan, Jones and Reid, 1988).

First, new and better initial and induction teacher education programmes are required. These should be devised along some kind of *sandwich* model. Proper regard should be given to the practical and theoretical needs of trainees (apprentice teachers) as well as utilizing the respective skills of teacher educators and teacher tutors alike. New recruits need more grassroots practical help with issues like classroom control and management.

Second, each secondary school should have a specific member of staff designated and trained to provide the back-up expertise on discipline. This person could be used to help and train colleagues as part of in-house in-service or staff development events. The idea is not dissimilar to the *master* teacher concept which is growing and developing in parts of the United States.

Traditionally, the disciplinary function has been part of the managerial functions of the senior management team. Often, therefore, it has been left undone. This in unsatisfactory. The topic of school discipline has become too important to be allowed to drift as the setting up of the Elton Committee in 1988 implied. The subject should be given priority for GRIST funding on an annual basis. Until the topic is taken seriously, far too many teachers will remain ignorant of the processes (trigger points, escalation) involved in managing disruptive pupils in classrooms, of relevant research on successful classroom management, teacher–pupil interaction and school practice. Without this information, no teacher is properly equipped to combat, cope and eradicate possible and actual misconduct in the classroom. Consequently, teachers will continue to do the best they can without having a firm basis for their actions. Hence, some actions taken by teachers in schools today tend to exacerbate rather than reduce conflict situations. This is no basis on which a profession or professionals should operate.

Courses for training the expert practitioner on discipline in schools will need to be carefully planned. This will also be no easy task as ideally practical approaches will be at least as important as the theoretical. Pedagogically, courses will need to consider relevant aspects of psychology and counselling practice above everything else.

At the grassroots, practical level, there is a great deal of contrasting opinion in the literature about the best ways for teachers to cope with dissatisfied and troublesome pupils in the classroom. The following represent some ideas.

1. A key factor in maintaining control in the classroom is to provide plenty of work and vary the activities and tasks. With difficult groups early control is essential. It is often a good idea to start the lesson with a short piece of desk work — perhaps something from the blackboard or from pre-prepared work sheets. This avoids unnecessary movement and minimizes opportunities for disturbance.

   In earlier times, many teachers used to sharpen classes up by giving them five minutes or so of mental arithmetic or spelling or other quick tests under examination conditions which sufficed for more than one purpose.

These measures ensured that all the pupils sat in their places with their books and materials, thus minimizing later opportunities for disturbance. Nowadays, in mixed-ability situations, there is often a need to keep the momentum going throughout a lesson, especially with the most able (fast finishers) or those who cannot cope with the theme of the main lesson. Sometimes flexible or alternative worksheets, text books, schemes of work or additional tasks for early finishers need to be resorted to and all have their merits in particular circumstances. Hard work is what all children need and actually like although this is not always apparent from their comments or teachers' lesson plans.

2. It is very important that commands in class are given clearly and precisely. Transitions need to be kept as brief as possible. At the outset of a lesson it is sometimes helpful to summarize a lesson's content so that the moans and groans are overcome straight away.

   Class rules and teachers' expectations of the pupils should be consistently applied and made explicit. If an exception is made, a clear and fair reason for the exemption should be stated. As in soccer, once a yellow card is shown, teachers, like referees, must respond positively in similar circumstances. Failure to do so can escalate disturbances. Pupils need to know where they stand at all times. Teachers should take opportunities to praise good classroom performances as well as highlighting naughtiness. Generally speaking, just as animals like to please their owners so children prefer to please their teachers given a free choice.

3. Within the classroom, teachers need to be vigilant at all times and show that they are in control and aware of what is going on by developing their intuition and powers of perception (eyes in the back as well as the front of their heads). My own view is that banishing children from the classroom should always be avoided except as a last resort. Banishment merely reinforces the fact that a teacher has failed. It also reduces pupils' self-worth and hardens their attitudes against teachers.

4. During unpleasant confrontations it is important that teachers restrain their tongues and keep their innermost thoughts to themselves. Otherwise, a difficult situation is likely to be made worse. Teachers must never lose their tempers with or in front of pupils. Teachers have to learn to 'manage' and overcome difficult situations rather than over-reacting, passing the buck to someone else or liberally handing out punishment. To be effective the latter should always be used sparingly as a last resort. Once again, consistency is all important. Children find great difficulty in rationalizing love and rejection, empathy and abuse, encouragement and criticism, pleasantness and nastiness from the same teacher.

   Amongst other qualities which teachers need for coping with disaffected and underachieving pupils, those most frequently mentioned include: stability, compassion, sensitivity, intelligence, resilience, humour, maturity, stamina, patience, empathy and flexibility. Who said that teaching is easy?

A disproportionate number of behavioural problems occur in lower ability forms or with lower ability or underachieving pupils. Therefore, teachers and schools should have clear policies for their lower ability and underachieving pupils.

According to Mortimore (1982), teachers can best help in the following ways:

Monitor the progress of all groups of pupils so that differences in achievement can be identified early, and appropriate remedial action be taken.

Consciously strive to raise teachers' expectations of the achievement of pupils from working-class homes, of girls in some subjects and of ethnic minorities, in order to reduce the influence of negative stereotypes.

Select books and learning materials which are suitable for *all* pupils.

Critically evaluate classroom practices so that any unintended biases can be eliminated.

Achieve closer co-operation between specialist and remedial teachers so that joint approaches to learning problems can be developed.

Draw on the new technology to provide individual learning programmes where these seem appropriate.

Capitalize on parental influence by showing how pupils can be helped at home.

Provide extra learning opportunities such as homework clubs and revision courses to help pupils who have poor facilities for study at home.

With regard to sex differences:

1. implement a school policy on equal opportunities;
2. include at least one physical science in the compulsory core of fourth- and fifth-year work;
3. hold special parents' evenings, prior to option choices, in order to focus on the importance of maths, science and technology for girls.

With regard to ethnic groups:

1. have a language policy that caters for individual needs and takes account of the literacy heritage of other cultures;
2. accept and build upon the diversity of culture in the school;
3. have an agreed school policy on racism. Provide a forum for discussion of this difficult subject for older pupils within the security of the school.

Mortimore considers that these changes will not eliminate underachievement. They will, however, make school life more profitable and acceptable for many pupils and, indirectly, make life more worthwhile for many teachers. Like Hargreaves (1984), Mortimore believes that the real educational answer to underachievement lies in the reform of the curriculum, the examination system and the internal organization of secondary schools. The latter aspect is often forgotten. Few secondary schools, for example, provide pupils with an opportunity to *catch up* once they fall behind with their class work either because of illness, personal difficulties or for any number of other reasons. Quite often, once a pupil begins to fall behind, he or she tends to fall further and further behind his or her peers and may give up altogether.

School management and pupils' behaviour

The exact relationship between school systems and disruptive and disaffected behaviour is a complex subject because schools vary so much. There is some evidence which shows that disruptive behaviour is more likely to happen in long lessons, at the end of a school day when teachers and pupils are tired and comparatively minor incidents can erupt, in mid-week, mid-term and mid-year especially, November, February and March (York, *et al.*, 1972; Lawrence, *et al.*, 1981; Galloway, *et al.*, 1982).

The Pack Committee (SED, 1977) took the view that difficulties in schools could be related to the raising of the school leaving age; the maturation of pupils earlier than in previous generations; pupil confusion and unsettlement arising from a period of rapid educational change in schools; disenchantment and apathy with the curriculum and the kind of secondary education provided, especially amongst non-academic groups; teacher shortages and/or high rates of staff turnover; and poor and weak teaching in some cases. Undoubtedly today, unfavourable or uncertain employment prospects can be added to this list.

There appears to be a measure of agreement between writers on the need for schools to introduce coherent staff policies on organizational matters if they are to combat disaffection and disruption. There is, however, some disagreement on the best way of introducing these schemes and the kind of detail which is required.

Hastings (1981) suggests that many schools need to change radically their timetabling structure so as to reduce the *slack* time when vandalism and conflicts between children, and children and teachers tend to occur. Effective measures include use of staggered lunch-breaks and reducing the number of pupils out of class at any one time, so making for easier control and less pressure on open space.

Gillham (1984) suggests that institutions need to develop their own guidelines for policy and practice based on general agreement amongst staff which aim at reducing opportunities for deviant behaviour to take place. To this end, he began some experimental work in a Nottingham comprehensive school which minimized opportunities for teacher–pupil confrontations to occur. As a result of his deliberations with staff the following practical scheme emerged. Staff agreed to a new managerial system based on four governing principles. These were: enforcing a minimum number of indispensable school rules; careful planning and manipulation of the timetable; providing an adequate system of remedial education and ensuring good lesson plans and classroom management. The logic behind Gillham's scheme should be fully understood as it has considerable potential for adoption by other schools.

1. Reduce school rules so that those which are left are both necessary and enforceable. Maintaining a large number of unnecessary and/or unworkable

school rules is one of the functions that puts teachers most at risk of confrontation. When a rule is unreasonable, unnecessary or incapable of enforcement, then the vulnerability it creates for the teacher is unwarranted. In order to ensure that pupils understand the reasons for implementing rules, it makes good practical common sense to give them every opportunity to get to know the school rules well. When pupils are unaware of school rules they will either fall foul of them unwittingly or test out limits to find what behaviour is acceptable to staff. Gillham suggests that providing 'home-base' tuition on institutional practice in the first year is essential. This should include a substantial amount of form-tutor time to ensure that pupils entering the secondary school have a gradual induction into the rule system and prepare themselves accordingly. It also provides a means of form tutors and pupils 'breaking the ice'.

2. Like Hastings, Gillham suggests that timetabling is important in two respects. It can be used as a means of avoiding too much free time when there are not clearly defined activities. It can also be used to ensure an even distribution of lessons throughout the week and between and across years so that some pupils are not coping with the most demanding subjects on top of one another when their peers are engaged in day-long non-academic work; to ensure that pupils are not involved in key work at times of the day or week when their motivation is low, such as double English last thing on a Friday afternoon.

3. An adequate system of remedial provision is very important to ensure that pupils are not faced with work demands they cannot meet. Dissemination of appropriate information to subject staff is vital in this process, especially for those engaged in mixed-ability work. Detailed support from specialist teachers through the provision of alternative work materials being devised for use with retarded or underachieving pupils is also very important.

4. Good well-planned lessons and classroom organization are fundamental, especially with less able groups or in academically demanding situations. Staff who participated in Gillham's experiment felt these goals could be achieved by the implementation of the following policies:

Ensure the work is suitable to all levels of ability in the group;

Have clear rules and routines in class that pupils get to know quickly and understand. Pay particular attention to organization at the beginning and end of lessons to avoid confusion. Specify seating arrangements to keep mutually provocative children apart and so prevent unseemly scrambles for seats;

Ensure that less able children experience success in terms of short-term and well-defined objectives;

Avoid shouting or 'gunning' for pupils. This is likely to be provocative. The occasional confrontation between teachers and pupil can be worthwhile when followed by a constructive action. Sometimes misdemeanours can be more successfully dealt with privately after the lesson rather than immediately — after the situation has calmed down and rational processes are at work.

Gillham points out that staff saw the management of confrontation situations largely as a function of individual teacher's skills. He suggests that there are two main procedures for dealing with confrontation: de-escalating the process and/or getting the child out of the classroom and away from potential peer support. This avoids potential *loss of face* situations on both sides. Not all educationalists will agree with this latter suggestion since in one sense removing a pupil from a classroom is by itself an admission of failure.

Mortimore (1980), based on the findings from the book *Fifteen Thousand Hours* (Rutter *et al.*, 1979), suggests that schools have it within their own means to improve their levels of academic achievement and reduce their levels of misbehaviour by following five particular guidelines. These are:

1. Instigate a common staff plan on pupil behaviour to foster consistent policies and overcome erratic, unfair and idiosyncratic sanctions. Such unity of purpose limits the number of chances for spontaneous disruption to occur in response to teachers' actions.
2. Place an emphasis on academic achievement for *all* pupils in the school irrespective of ability. This means that all pupils should receive homework, have their work marked in detail and be expected to achieve to their maximum potential. Careful lesson preparation is also associated with better pupil behaviour.
3. Ensure conscientious behaviour on the part of teachers in starting and finishing lessons on time. It is often forgotten that teachers have a legal duty to start classes at the designated time. Moreover, such promptness avoids the slack time between lessons when pupil confrontations occur and spirits rise. It also reduces the amount of time needed to re-control classes. Finally, it suggests to pupils that their teachers take their work seriously, care for their academic progress and mean to complete their syllabuses.
4. Make use of effective rewards. Regular praise for the recognition of good behaviour, work and achievement are strongly associated with high-achievement schools.
5. Promote pleasant working conditions in schools, with pupils encouraged to take an active part in the daily life of the institution. Mortimore suggests that this includes ensuring the physical conditions within the schools are as pleasant as possible, giving pupils opportunities to assume responsibility through monitor and prefect schemes and for looking after resources and equipment, as well as encouraging their participation in meetings and assemblies.

Lawrence, Steed and Young (1984) argue that teachers too often feel ashamed at their failure to cope with disruptive children in class. They believe that teachers should be more honest and open about their difficulties and not regard them as a sign of professional incompetence. Case studies taken from their work show that

most experienced teachers make mistakes in their handling of classroom
based on staff notes kept at two London comprehensives, they found that
were seventy-seven incidents at the first school (1250 pupils) in a week,
ranging from fighting in class and insolence, to talking, whistling and eating sandwiches during lessons; a ratio of one incident per 15.6 pupils. About half the incidents were reported by the teachers to more senior staff.

The authors' advice to teachers is:

Nip the incident in the bud. If a problem is brewing up, try warning the child
off or take practical action such as ordering him to switch seats;

Take account of group dynamics in class. Look for leaders or troublemakers.
Find ways of changing the group layout. Stand in a different place at different times throughout lessons;

Do not accuse groups of troublemaking when only one or two pupils are
involved;

Talk to individual troublemakers outside lesson time, especially when a pupil
is becoming a persistent nuisance over several lessons;

Give children the benefit of the doubt if they make excuses which cannot be
checked — such as a stomach-ache;

Defuse potentially dangerous situations by cracking a joke;

Think carefully before getting too angry about pupils eating in class;

Avoid becoming personally involved. Be alert to your feelings and state of
mind. A teacher who is in a bad mood may over-react;

If you do decide to have a confrontation, do it on your own ground and on
your own terms. Never be rushed into events. Know exactly what you are
going to say.

Lawrence *et al.*, indicate that schools themselves can help to cut down on disruptive behaviour by changing their timetables, curricula or internal organization.
They suggest spacing out periods with the same class, cutting down the length of
time a group of pupils is together, finding efficient means of making changeovers
between lessons as smooth as possible and avoiding over-rigid sanctions for minor
misbehaviour.

Finally, staff of schools should remember that parents can be great allies when
sorting out pupils' behavioural problems. Evidence from research indicates that
pupils fear the involvement of their parent/s more than any other single factor
(Reid, 1986). Sometimes, when dealing with the most difficult of disruptive pupils,
teachers need all the help they can get!

References

BERNBAUM, G., PATRICK, H. and REID, K. (1985) 'Postgraduate initial teacher education in
England and Wales: Perspectives from the SPITE Project', in: HOPKINS, D. and REID,
K., *Rethinking Teacher Education*, Beckenham, Croom Helm.

GALLOWAY, D., BALL, T., BLOMFIELD, D. and SEYD, R. (1982) *Schools and Disruptive Pupils*, London, Longmans.

GILLHAM, B. (1984) 'School organization and the control of disruptive pupils', in FRUDE, N. and GAULT, H. (Eds) *Disruptive Behaviour in Schools*, Chichester, John Wiley.

HARGREAVES, D. (1984) *Improving Secondary Schools*, (Report of the Committee on the Curriculum and Organization of Secondary Schools), London, ILEA.

HASTINGS, D.J. (1981) 'One school's experience', in: GILLHAM, B. (Ed.) *Problem Behaviour in the Secondary School*, Beckenham, Croom Helm.

HER MAJESTY'S INSPECTORATE, (1988) *The New Teacher in School*, London, DES.

LAWRENCE, J., STEED, D. and YOUNG, P. with HILTON, G. (1981) *Dialogue on Disruptive Behaviour: A Study of A Secondary School*, London, PJP Press.

LAWRENCE, J., STEED, D. and YOUNG, P. (1984) *Disruptive Children: Disruptive Schools*, Beckenham, Croom Helm.

MORTIMORE, P. (1980) 'Misbehaviour in Schools', in UPTON, G. and GOBELL, A. (Eds) *Behaviour Problems in the Comprehensive School*, Cardiff, Faculty of Education, University College Cardiff.

MORTIMORE, P. (1982) 'Underachievement: A framework for debate', *Secondary Education Journal*, **12**, 3, pp. 3–6.

PATRICK, H., BERNBAUM, G. and REID, K. (1982) *The Structure and Process of Initial Teacher Education in Universities in England and Wales*, Leicester, Leicester School of Education.

REID, K. (1985a) *Truancy and School Absenteeism*, London, Hodder and Stoughton.

REID, K. (1985b) 'The Postgraduate Certificate of Education: Teaching practice and the probationary year', in: HOPKINS, D. and REID, K. *Rethinking Teacher Education*, Beckenham, Croom Helm.

REID, K. (1986) *Disaffection From School*, London, Methuen.

REID, K. (1987) *Combating School Absenteeism*, London, Hodder and Stoughton.

REID, K. (1989a) *Helping Troubled Pupils in Secondary Schools, Vol. 1.* Oxford, Basil Blackwell.

REID, K. (1989b) *Helping Troubled Pupils in Secondary Schools, Vol. 2*, Oxford, Basil Blackwell.

REID, K., HOPKINS, D. and HOLLY, P. (1987) *Towards The Effective School*, Oxford, Basil Blackwell.

RUTTER, M., MAUGHAN, B., MORTIMORE, P. and OUSTEN, J. (1979) *Fifteen Thousand Hours*, London, Open Books.

SCOTTISH EDUCATION DEPARTMENT (1977) *Truancy and Indiscipline in Scotland*, (The Pack Report), Edinburgh, SED.

YORK, R., HERON, J. and WOLFF, S. (1972) 'Exclusion from school', *Journal of Child Psychology and Psychiatry*, **13**, pp. 259–266.

3
Alternative Approaches to Disruptive Behaviour

Delwyn P. Tattum

Introduction

Deviant behaviour is a fact of organizational life and indiscipline an inevitable outcome of compulsory schooling. The questions we face are whether the incidence of disruptive behaviour is on the increase and how best we should cope with the problem when it occurs. Attempting to answer reliably the question of incidence is beset with problems mainly because our identification of indiscipline as a major concern for research is recent so we lack hard data that will present a baseline for comparative purposes. In an attempt to provide a recent historical perspective on indiscipline in maintained schools Furlong (1985) was obliged to turn to less conventional sources, such as, oral histories, diaries, biographies and semi-fictional accounts of schooling.

> Whether such evidence gives a 'true picture of disruption and truancy in earlier periods is impossible to say. All that can be said with any certainty is that challenging behaviour at schools is nothing new . . . it has a history as long as mass education itself (Furlong, 1985).

Furlong also concludes that the most distinctive feature of the last two decades has been the continuing expression of public concern. The *moral panic* has found regular expression in the mass media, provoked questions in parliament, initiated a government enquiry (The Elton Enquiry into Discipline in Schools, 1988), preoccupied teacher union conferences, and spawned a vast body of educational literature on the subject. In Tattum (1982) it was observed that the education service was in danger of creating a self-fulfilling prophecy in this field by convincing itself that a major problem existed and events of the subsequent years have done little to dispel this concern. In fact, the last twelve months have seen a major hype of the issue so that we are in danger as a profession of talking ourselves or society into the belief that a *blackboard jungle* exists in our schools.

Research and surveys

In Tattum (1989a) a detailed review and critique of the available major research is made covering surveys by teacher unions, government and local authorities, and individual and local surveys. Therefore, in this section, I shall summarize the main problems associated with research into indiscipline and consider some of the more recent surveys. Data gathering difficulties arise, firstly, from lack of agreement about what constitutes disruptive behaviour, and secondly, from the associated factor that some teachers are more tolerant than others. There is also evidence of reluctance on the part of local authorities, schools and individual teachers to admit that they are experiencing a problem. When one examines surveys conducted by teacher unions there are problems associated with very low return rates so that the teachers who do respond are not necessarily representative of the profession but a biased group. In addition to the statistical problems, two other concerns emerge, namely, that the research projects are very different in style and form which prevents data comparison with any great confidence, and secondly, the government does not gather national figures on suspensions, exclusions, or pupils sent to special units, so that we even lack a reliable national data of extreme disciplinary cases.

In considering recent surveys we can highlight some of the problems noted in the previous paragraphs and also observed evidence of conflicting findings. The DES (1979) survey of a 10 per cent sample of maintained secondary schools in England asked the headteachers of the 384 schools visited by Inspectors to assess the extent of pupil behaviour problems in their own school. The overwhelming majority of schools indicated nothing worse than some minor problems of indiscipline, in fact, 64 per cent reported that they had no disruptive pupils and 13 per cent estimated that they had 10 or more. This general picture is supported by the Inspectors' report on 'Good Behaviour and Discipline in Schools' (1987). The report is based on evidence gained from inspections since January 1983 and supplemented from special attention given to behaviour and discipline during visits to schools in the summer term of 1986.

> The general picture of behaviour within schools which emerges from these publications is that the overwhelming majority of schools are orderly communities in which there are good standards of behaviour and discipline; poor behaviour is unusual, and serious indiscipline a rare occurrence (DES, 1987).

A more detailed review of recent inspections appears in the HMI (1988) report on 'Secondary Schools' based on 185 maintained schools visited during 1982–86. This is an important document because it provides us with the best, available, comparative data between the late 1970s and the mid 1980s, and on discipline the data does not indicate any serious deterioration in secondary schools.

> Notwithstanding the difficulties in attempting to sum up behaviour in any school, classroom behaviour was assessed as good in 61 per cent of schools and in another 34 per cent satisfactory or better, with only 5 per

cent where there were substantial difficulties. Outside the classroom, 10 per cent of schools had examples of behaviour that was less than satisfactory but 52 per cent where behaviour was good and other 38 per cent where it was at least satisfactory. (HMI, 1988).

In Autumn 1987, the *Daily Express* inserted a questionnaire in the professional journal of PAT and from the responses of 1,500 teachers to the question, 'Have you ever been subjected to a physical attack by a pupil?' a disturbing 32 per cent answered in the affirmative. A similarly worded question was included in a NOP survey of a controlled sample of nearly 500 NUT members but only 5 per cent said that they had been physically assaulted or threatened (Teacher, 1988). Consideration of the wide discrepancy in the percentages highlights the research problems. The NUT figure was produced from a randomly selected sample of the membership whilst the PAT result came from a self-selecting sample of 1,500 teachers from a total membership of 43,000. The question is whether the sample is representative of PAT members and whether these figures can be confidently generalized to the whole membership and to the profession?

Finally, in this brief consideration of disruption as a problem two cautionary points need to be made. Firstly, from research carried out by the AMMA (1984), Lawrence *et al.*, (1986), Laing and Chazan (1986) there is growing concern that the prevalence of behaviour problems is increasing in infant and junior schools. Secondly, most surveys indicate that teachers perceive the problem as getting worse, and whether the statistical evidence supports their views is of secondary importance because they are the people who have to face the difficult pupils. And as the W.J. Thomas dictum alerts us — if teachers perceive an increase in frequency and intensity then they will procede to conduct themselves in accordance with that perception.

Alternative approaches

The approach a school or teacher may adopt in coping with disruptive behaviour will depend to a considerable extent on whether they regard the causes of the behaviour as being outside the school's sphere of control, that is, that they are innate or the results of adverse familial or societal influences, or whether they regard the school or their own behaviour as being contributory factors. Maxwell (1987), in a study of teacher's attitudes towards disruptive behaviour in six secondary schools in Scotland, hypothesized that

> teaching staffs who believe that important factors determining the occurrence of disruptive behaviour in schools are within the control of the schools themselves should be those who are most effective in tackling the problem. Schools in which it is generally believed that disruption is caused by factors outwith the schools' control may develop an insti-

tutional version of learned helplessness and thus be inhibited from taking constructive action.

Consequently, schools' and teachers' attitudes towards indiscipline will determine whether they adopt a crisis-management, interventionist or preventative approach to problem behaviour. A crisis approach is reactive in its policy and locates the problem in the child; an interventionist approach is also relative in that it responds to problems as they arise but it also looks beyond the child for understanding and aims to construct more beneficial relationships and structures; finally, a preventative approach aims to develop structures and processes which are geared to reducing problems and anticipating crises within the school itself. In the following sections we shall examine in detail each of the three approaches.

a. A crisis-management approach

This approach focuses mainly on the individual child *seeking both cause and cure within the sphere of the pupil's individual psychology* (Frude, 1984), and is referred to as the medical model. It is a way of looking at social deviance and abnormality as a form of illness, thus the focus of the approach is the individual in whom the signs or symptoms are manifest, and an appropriate form of treatment is prescribed as necessary to bring about a recovery. In a conceptualization of the problem an analogy between physical and mental health is closely drawn.

> The solution is therefore to extract problem pupils and transfer them to a special place where they will receive medical or pseudo-medical treatment. But concentration on the social pathology of the individual permits us to ignore deficiencies in the system. To look beyond the pupil takes us into the school and classroom, and requires us to consider whether the nature of the organization places constraints and controls on the pupil which are themselves problematic. What is more, the attitudes and expectations of teachers can create confrontational situations for pupils who lack the social skills to *please teacher*. If this is the case, then the handicap is social and not medical, and though recognizing that children behave badly the approach also concentrates our attention on the context and relationships in which they display their inappropriate behaviour (Tattum, 1985).

Ford *et al.*, (1982) are, amongst others, highly critical of the medical model on the grounds that *it has simply not worked*. They also identify other criticisms which are elaborated on under the following four headings:

(a) The problem of expert control

As the approach is supported by the medical profession, psychiatrists and psychologists, it cultivates in teachers and others an attitude of unquestioning acceptance. It also enables teachers to accept that transfer to a special school is for *the good of the child*, without in any way questioning their professional position in the process of selection, categorization and segregation.

(b) Medical social control

Expert intervention places the stamp of professional legitimacy on the procedures. Despite our commitment to the ideal of comprehensivization LEAs have expanded their special provision to exclude more and more pupils from mainstream schooling, and even, recently, identified a new category in the disrupter.

(c) The individualization of social problems

To some extent this point had already been covered, but additionally, individualization prevents us from considering wider issues of which deviant behaviour may be symptomatic, for example, social class, sex and race.

(d) The depoliticization of deviant behaviour

By individualizing the problem we take the focus of attention away from the system and the nature of experiences it provides for children. Deviance is seen simply in terms of action engaged in by the individual and not a process of interaction between active participants in the social context (Tattum, 1985).

The major crisis-management response to disruptive behaviour has been the establishment of a new type of educational provision, namely, the special unit. They have proliferated throughout the United Kingdom and are known by various labels, such as school support unit, adjustment unit, pupil placement unit or exclusion unit — more emotive names are *sin bins* or *mini borstals*. In some cases they are attached to a school and pupils may be placed there for all or some of their lessons. Off-site units usually serve a number of schools; they may be physically and administratively independent, and pupils may attend them on a part-time or full-time basis. In most instances the pupils remain on the roll of their school. Many questions about the benefits and disadvantages of units have not been adequately addressed; the most detailed evaluative study was by the ILEA (Mortimore *et al.*, 1983), whilst other reviews may be found in Lloyd-Smith (1984), Topping (1983).

The peak year for setting up of special units was 1974, and in a DES survey it was found that in 1977 as many as sixty-nine of the ninety-six English LEAs had one or more units, giving a total of 239 units providing 3962 pupil places (HMI, 1978). Evidence of further expansion in the 1970s was provided by ACE (1980) in a survey which indicated the existence of units in Scotland, Wales, the Isle of Man and the Channel Islands. The total number was markedly increased in 1979 when ILEA approved 240 support centres to accommodate 2280 pupils; and the latest national survey by the Social Education Research Project (Ling and Davies, 1984), found that there had been a further increase of 140 per cent in off-site units compared with the DES figures (HMI, 1978). In a survey of European countries, Lawrence *et al.*, (1986) found that few countries had adopted segregation as a solution to school behaviour problems. Most had initiated schemes to tackle the problem where it occurs, in the school and classroom.

In an analysis of the characteristics of pupils in ILEA centres West *et al.*, (1986) found that the majority were in the 14–16 age group (60 per cent); boys out-numbered girls by a 2:1 ratio; children classified as Caribbean were disproportionately represented, as were pupils whose parents were in semi-skilled or unskilled occupations. The research team also expressed concern about the quality of the curriculum and the difficulties associated with reintegrating pupils into mainstream schools. Following a review of its off-site provision, ILEA (5042 and 5141) recommended that there should be a reduction in their numbers and that they should be larger so that they could offer a broader curriculum and reduce the feeling of professional isolation experienced by many staff. Even more constructively, it was recommended that there was a need to change the concept of where units actually fit into a local authority's provision for children with special needs, so that larger units could become centres of alternative education which would offer pupils something in educational terms.

In Tattum (1985) three critical questions are asked about the social control function of special units.

1. Who benefits from the transfer?
   In most cases the interests of other pupils and teachers are probably given priority concern, which runs contrary to the entire philosophy of children with special needs where the interests of the child are paramount.
2. Who decides and on the basis of what information?
   Local authorities have widely varying admission procedures, from a multi-disciplinary team to a single person (Tattum, 1982). Behavioural criteria are problematic because of their subjectivity, and the measurement schedules available only describe behaviour, concentrate on negative aspects, and focus on the individual pupils without taking teacher–pupil interaction into account.
3. What are the functions of units?
   Their functions have been variously described as diagnostic and therapeutic, but negative elements of containment and punishment are implicit in their place in the system. Units must have an educative function, but the quality of physical provision and education is unacceptable in many cases (HMI, 1978; Dawson, 1980: Topping, 1983).

Units conform to a crisis-management approach to disruptive behaviour in that they can only cope in a negative and reactive way with a small number of extreme cases. For this reason they will continue, and as a result of the abolition of corporal punishment in 1987 the pressure will increase for their proliferation. Finally, if we are to adopt the crisis-management approach there are many sound educational reasons in support of on-site units in preference to off-site.

1. The transfer should not be too disturbing for the child, with the resulting problem of re-introduction into mainstream schooling as with a detached unit.

2. Movement in and out of the main school provides for special lessons and examination tuition for older pupils.
3. The school is able to provide a wide range of experiences and facilities, e.g. school field, gymnasium, specialist rooms.
4. The staff in the unit benefit from contact with the rest of the teaching staff — they do not feel isolated.
5. Information about a pupil can be exchanged, and teachers can brief each other before a pupil moves into the unit and then later back into the school. Communication is a major problem for staff in a detached unit.
6. Extreme behaviour is less likely to be accepted as the norm — as can happen in an off-site unit (Tattum, 1982).

1b. Interventionist approaches

Whilst units will continue to cater for a minority of disruptive pupils, alternative approaches which focus less on the individual pupil and more on the context and interaction need to be developed. Intervention in a school or classroom may be carried out by individuals. Topping (1986) considers the strengths and handicaps of consultancy by educational psychologists, local authority advisors, peripatetic support teachers, and higher education teachers, and advocates the *problem-solving model* of problem specification, data collection, objective setting, intervention and evaluation. The objective is to work with schools to initiate person and/or organizational change.

The individual change agent approach has been extended into a peripatetic team approach by a number of local authorities. Griffiths (1981) described how a *Special Education Team* operates on an itinerant casework basis with disruptive pupils in twenty-three comprehensive schools in a northern LEA. The team consists of six teachers who are invited to work within schools, sometimes on a one-to-one basis with a particular pupil, or to negotiate a strategy with a teacher or group of teachers. Because each problem is different, the emphasis is on flexibility in the process of problem analysis and negotiated intervention. Similar teams exist in a number of other authorities, but the best documented operations are the two *Schools Support Teams* in ILEA. Coulby and Harper (1985) describe in detail the development of one team's objectives and procedures from its 1979 date of operation. When at full strength it consisted of a teacher-in-charge, twelve scale three teachers, an educational psychologist, a clerical officer, and a senior educational welfare officer. One teacher was responsible for running a small class of secondary pupils at the Centre. In all, the team catered for the eighty primary schools and fifteen secondary schools in the Borough. The area is divided into *patches*, so that two or three team members are responsible for working in all the primary and secondary schools in that patch. This means that during a given week a support teacher would work in a range of settings — schools, classrooms, pupils' homes, other agencies; work with a number of different teachers, other adults, and pupils; and face a multiplicity of presenting problems. The role is a challenging and stressful one, and 'team teachers need not only training and supervision, but support and advice. These are provided through the processes of induction, consultation, and in-service training' (Coulby and Harper, 1985). The team also has a five stage model — referral, assessment, formulation, intervention, and evaluation, which can be applied at different levels — pupil, classroom, school, and LEA and, as such, can take account of how change at one level may affect others.

Describing similar operations in the other support team, Lane (1986) subscribes strongly to an interactionist approach to behaviour problems:

> Deviance in schools is not a product of specific deficits in the child or the school; it is an interactive, dynamic process'. It is that interaction which is the main focus of attention and therefore the success of the team's interventionist programmes depend upon 'the combined efforts of the schools, the children, the families, other agencies, and the centre, in pooling resources and skills to meet complex problems and the use of validated techniques of analysis and intervention. The importance of that partnership has been established at the experimental, theoretical, and practical level' (Lane, 1986).

Regardless of the level or nature of the intervention specific principles should be followed and Lane (1986) provides an excellent framework for application:

1. No intervention can be predetermined in advance of the situation and the construction of a formulation which explains why the behaviour occurs in a given context. An intervention has to be based on the formulation;
2. As far as possible, interventions should take place in the context in which difficulties were reported;
3. The principle is maintained that any action taken should be aimed at the minimum level of intervention necessary to achieve agreed objectives in the setting;
4. The range of response offered should be flexible, to ensure rapid movement between levels of intervention, as necessary.

c. Prevention — whole-school approaches

The two previous sections on coping strategies are reactive, in that they are a response to a problem. How much better for a school to create policies which are proactive, that is, they initiate practices which are anticipatory and so reduce the incidence of indiscipline throughout the pupil body. Therefore, the recommendation in this section is the adoption of a *whole-school approach* to discipline (Watkins and Wagner, 1987; Tattum, 1989b). In working towards a whole-school approach the aim is to create an ethos of good order supported by a system of monitoring pupil behaviour and progress. Ethos has both content and process (Purkey and Smith, 1982). Content refers to policy, structure and curriculum, and process refers to the school culture, quality of social relationships, and channels of communication.

In addition to experiencing problems of social control, schools are also caring communities and as relatively closed communities they have a measure of control over internal variables such as those discussed in this section. A preventative approach has to be school-wide,

> it must be integral to the ethos of the school, emanating from its structures and processes, and evident in the attitudes and behaviour of teachers. Schools spend a great deal of time and energy discussing academic matters and no self-respecting head would be without a curriculum policy (Tattum, 1988b).

Schools cannot function without order and control and therefore the recommendation must be that schools review and develop their discipline policy as an integral part of their total organization. A whole-school approach to discipline is therefore predicated on the belief that good order and a positive learning environment are created when *all* members of staff accept responsibility for the behaviour of *all* pupils, not only in their own classrooms, but as they move about the school. Behaviour expresses itself on a continuum with major disruptive acts at the negative pole but teachers experience a series of minor disturbances which interrupt their teaching and frustrate their professional expectations. That is why it is necessary to look at discipline in an expansive way and regard it as integral to the entire teaching function. There is a close relationship between behaviour in the corridor and behaviour in the classroom — and vice versa.

In their study of twelve inner London comprehensive schools Rutter *et al.*, (1979) found considerable variation between schools on both behaviour and attainment outcomes. What did emerge was that the more successful schools had an identifiable *ethos* which Mortimore (1980), one of the co-authors, summarized under five general headings:

1. A common staff policy on behaviour to encourage consistency.
2. Positive staff attitudes towards pupils' academic progress were reflected in improved behaviour.
3. Teachers presented themselves as good models in the way they prepared and conducted their lessons.
4. The use of effective praise and rewards was strongly related to good behaviour.
5. There was less misbehaviour where conditions were pleasant and pupils were encouraged to take on responsibilities and participate in school activities.

Finally, in this general examination of a whole-school approach to discipline we would do well to consider elements identified in the report, Secondary Schools: An appraisal by HMI (1988), which summarizes their findings based on the inspection of 185 maintained and voluntary secondary schools in England during the years 1982–86. They record that the general ethos of a school was evident in the ways pupils behaved both in lessons and outside the classroom, and where a reasonably balanced and effective regime existed a number of factors could be identified:

1. clarity of expectations;
2. an atmosphere conducive to effective learning with pupils adhering to a sensible and fully understood code of behaviour as a matter of course;
3. a successful combination of firmness and kindness together with the expectation of courtesy;
4. warmth and humour in relationships;
5. support which helped to combat the problems of a difficult environment, where such existed;
6. a general demonstration of sensitivity.

In further development of a whole-school approach to discipline the following sections will concentrate on aspects of school organization and leave consideration of the curriculum, the place of external examinations, teaching styles and learning methods and wider social issues to other contributions. Three aspects will be dealt with, namely, consistency management and school rules, rewards and incentives, and the role of the pastoral form tutor.

(i) Consistency management and school rules

The disruptive pupils who formed the basis of research in Tattum (1982) were highly critical of inconsistent behaviour between teachers and by the same teacher. They claimed that they were singled out by teachers; and whilst they admitted that they were not passive recipients they complained that inconsistencies in the way rules were applied bred a sense of grievance and precipitated confrontations. In addition, they were unlike their more conformist peers in that they were unwilling to acquiesce to boredom, abuse or injustices. In their efforts to preserve their self-identity they returned verbal, physical and organizational assaults on their persons with similar abuse and violence. 'If a teacher bawls at me I bawl right back at her' (Tattum, 1982).

Schools are rule-governed organizations and it is conceivable that every move a pupil makes is covered by one rule or another — and if no rule exists then teachers have the authority and discretion to create one. Individual teacher inconsistencies occur when they respond differently towards different pupils for the same mis-behaviour.

Teachers should be seen to be fair, neither having favourites nor picking on individuals, but there is evidence that preferential treatment is given to certain pupils because of their social or academic status (Lufler, 1979; Hollingsworth *et al.*, 1984). Not all pupils are treated the same by teachers, for there is the human practice of rewarding those who conform most closely to the ideal pupil role as a teacher perceives it, and punishing those who deviate most prominently from perceived expectations. Differential treatment based on reputation or organizational labelling is amply recorded (Hargreaves, 1967; Lacey, 1970). Inconsistencies among teachers are most evident as the teachers display variable commitment to the enforcement of school rules as they move about the building. Many teachers concentrate on maintaining good discipline in their own classrooms, and hold to the view that about-school discipline is the responsibility of the headteacher and other senior colleagues. Unfortunately, this differential response to good order results in different treatment for the same offence (Tattum, 1986).

Rules are the fabric of school life; together with regulations, ritual and routine they are the main mechanisms used to achieve and maintain good order. In discussion with teachers, Duke (1986) found that many admitted to being inconsistent and justified their behaviour on the grounds there were too many school rules for any individual to enforce effectively. Hargreaves *et al.*, (1975) also were *depressed by the sheer quantity and complexity* of rules encountered in their study of deviant behaviour in classrooms. Similarly, the writer has found very few instances when teachers could report that their school had engaged in a general discussion of their rule system in order to devise a school-wide policy on good discipline. If teachers are uncertain in this area of management then it is not surprising that inconsistencies occur and pupils for their part exploit the varying interpretations applied by teachers. A function of rules is to give structure to social interaction by reducing uncertainty, confusion, and ambiguity, but if they are not shared by staff and communicated to pupils and parents then problems will occur.

In an attempt to understand the complexity of school rules the following five fold categorization was drawn up (Tattum, 1982). It should be noted that the categories are not intended to be discrete as school organization and teacher–pupil relations are interrelated.

1.   Legal/quasi-legal rules
2.   Organizational rules
3.   Contextual rules
4.   Personal rules
5.   Relational rules

Effective management at both school and classroom levels aims to pre-empt disciplinary problems and therefore, alongside consistency, which refers to putting into operation agreed goals and procedures, there is also the need for coherence, which applies to the ways in which plans and policies are formulated and articulated to all parties.

> The *atmosphere* of any particular school will be greatly influenced by the degree to which it functions as a coherent whole, with agreed ways of doing things which are consistent throughout school and which have the general support of all staff (Rutter *et al.*, 1979).

In the next section a two stage process of policy formulation and enunciation will be briefly discussed as they apply to both school and classroom. School-wide disciplinary problems are different from those experienced in a classroom for many reasons. There is uncertainty about the rule system as already commented on, teachers' willingness to involve themselves in school discipline varies from person to person, and teachers hold differing expectations and tolerance levels regarding acceptable behaviour. In a classroom pupils see one authority figure but around the school they encounter teachers with different designations, dining room and playground attendants, secretaries, prefects, and others, all with some degree of authority and different methods of enforcement. The sheer number and diversity of persons adds to the problems of inconsistency.

(i.i) School management and consistency

Five recommendations are offered which will contribute to the achievement of greater consistency in the application of rules and consequences (Tattum, 1986).

1. Teachers and pupils should be closely involved in the creation and review of rules. A more open discussion will bring about a better understanding of their purpose and the problems they create for both parties.
2. Rules are of little value if they are not communicated to members of the organization, as order is based on the supposition that knowledge of the rules exists. Therefore, it is important that they are communicated to teachers, pupils, parents, and other involved adults.
3. Teachers should communicate through their own behaviour the standards which they hold for the pupils. 'Teachers must give respect if they want to receive it, they must expect success if they want pupils to achieve, they must present good models in their own behaviour and dress if they want to influence pupil behaviour positively' (Tattum, 1986).
4. Schools should keep accurate, up-to-date records of pupils' levels of attainment and behaviour.
5. Rules are an important ingredient of the hidden curriculum as they give substance and expression to values; for whilst values are vague and general rules are specific and situational. And so, when a school reviews its control practices it will also examine what forms of behaviour teachers deem worthwhile and desirable.

(i.ii) Classroom management and consistency

Classroom management includes the allocation of time and space, the distribution of materials, careful record-keeping, as well as coping with pupil behaviour. Kounin (1970), in his investigation into the disciplinary techniques of effective and ineffective teachers found that the significant difference lay not in their ability to cope with indiscipline once it occurred but in their ability to prevent it from happening in the first place. Successful teachers employed management techniques which reduced unwanted behaviour, for example, being well prepared and organized, coping effectively with competing and overlapping events, moving smoothly from one activity to another, maintaining pace and momentum, and displaying class awareness. Wragg (1984) also emphasizes *first encounters*, most especially at the beginning of a school year. Established teachers saw these initial encounters as management rituals when they established rules and routines, and lay down the patterns of acceptable behaviour for subsequent lessons.

A review of the literature into effective classroom management presents four broad themes.

1. The first few lessons require detailed planning and preparation, which can be both short-term and long-term. It extends beyond subject matter, activities and materials, and gives due attention to pupil groups, basic rules and procedures, appropriate consequences, whole-class rather than group exercises, and assignments that promote success and involvement. Stanford *et al.*, (1983) found that not only were new teachers and ineffective teachers unaware of the amount of detailed planning necessary at the beginning of the year, but they did not know what to plan for.

2. Effective classroom managers introduce consistency into their lessons by carefully teaching rules and procedures. They take time to present, explain, and even discuss the rationales, some rehearse them with pupils, whilst others write them out and post them on a noticeboard. Rules need to cover general classroom behaviour: entering and leaving the room, talking and shouting out, movement, the distribution and collection of materials and so on — and work habits, that is, the manner in which learning activities are carried out — neatness, sharing, setting out work, and so on.

3. One of Kounin's off-beat words is *withitness*, that is, frequent monitoring of pupils' behaviour to prevent problems from arising. In early encounters consistency by teacher enables pupils to learn that their actions will result in consequences, in other words, they will, if detected, invoke a response from teacher.

4. Alongside teachers' consistency of behaviour is coherent communication of instructions and information. Directions, objectives and routines governing class activities and assignments need to be clearly stated in a step-by-step way so that pupils understand their tasks and know how to go about completing them. The establishment of a climate of learning also means that a teacher circulates amongst the pupils, makes individual contact with as many of the class as possible, and so communicates involvement and awareness.

(ii) Rewards and incentives

In the fifth in the series of Education Observed (HMI, 1987), HMI looked at *good behaviour and discipline in schools*. The review draws on evidence from a number of specific visits to schools where high standards of behaviour were known to exist, and one of the features of good practice observed was a positive approach to rewards and praise.

> The balance between rewards and sanctions, in both policy and practice, is a useful touchstone of a school's approach to maintaining good standards of behaviour. The best results are found where schools lay particular emphasis on rewards. Pupils appear to achieve more, to be better motivated, and to behave better, when teachers commend and reward their successes and emphasize their potential rather than focusing on their failures and shortcomings. In many schools, however, the guidelines for staff contain much on sanctions and punishments, and very little on praise and rewards. Yet the results of a positive approach are clear (HMI, 1987).

It is the case that schools in general have concentrated more on the negative aspects of discipline than on a more positive approach of rewards and incentives. According to the second secondary schools survey covering inspections during the years 1982–86, Her Majesty's Inspectors indicated some evidence of an 'increasing awareness in schools of the need to offer rewards as well as punishments' (HMI, 1988). From their review the most successful practice involved:

(i) a good balance between rewards and punishment;
(ii) clear systems understood by staff and pupils;
(iii) a prompt response to problems;
(iv) opportunities for pupils as individuals;
(v) staff treating pupils as individuals;
(vi) a willingness on the part of staff to find approaches which worked with individuals (a 'contract' system to develop a pupil's concentration span at the suggestion of pastoral staff, for example);
(vii) teachers praising the day-to-day work and behaviour of pupils, giving equal attention to all;
(viii) above all, the creation of a climate of mutual respect between pupils and teachers, (HMI, 1988).

Research into this area of school management is sparse and Withey (1979) provides an early classification of rewards:

(i) Material rewards — prizes, trophies and badges.
(ii) Symbolic rewards — title, status or housepoints.
(iii) Assessment — marks, grades, stars and similar devices.
(iv) Teacher reactions — as in praise, encouragement, approval and recognition.

Thus a reward system is seen to fulfil a number of functions for a school. It may promote the institutional aims of a school and provide a mechanism for competition; offer an incentive and reinforcement of approved behaviour; and finally, reward and confirm a pupil's achievement. The range of rewards and incentives available to schools is extensive, ranging from a word of approval to public acknowledgement, stars, badges and certificates. The National Association of Head Teachers (1984) provides a comprehensive list.

The first systematic study of rewards and punishment conducted in this country was by Highfield and Pinsent (1952) and their work was replicated by Burns (1978) who found that few changes had occurred in the intervening twenty-four years. From their combined evidence there are discernible differences between pupils and teachers; the former preferring rewards which indicate successful personal achievement, such as, a favourable report home, doing well in a test, winning a prize, obtaining good marks, whilst the latter ranked highly, rewards representing adult approval, such as, public praise, good marks, and election to positions of leadership.

Also, research indicates that rewards are much more effective in producing desirable behaviour than sanctions (Brophy, 1981; Galloway *et al.*, 1982), and that a carefully considered whole-school policy on rewards can be built into teacher–pupil relationships (Richards, 1983; Boxer *et al.*, 1987). There is also a high degree of consistency in their findings of pupils' perceptions of the relative merits of various rewards and punishments, which do not always coincide with the perception of teachers. Sharp *et al.*, (1987) found that their sample of 396 secondary school pupils generally perceived praise and rewards as appropriate and desirable, whilst Boxer *et al.*, (1987) revealed no marked differences over preferred rewards between boys and girls, or across the 11–16 years age range of their sample in three secondary schools. On the other hand, the latter did find some discrepancies in the perceptions of staff compared with pupils and summarized them accordingly:

(i) School social events were strongly favoured by pupils but not by teachers;
(ii) A Certificate of Merit was favoured more by older pupils than by teachers;
(iii) Praise by other pupils and non-verbal praise was favoured more by staff than by older pupils.

All research emphasizes a whole-school approach of consultation and implementation: '. . . the success of any scheme is directly related to the planning that precedes implementation allied to the enthusiasm and commitment of staff' (Milburn, 1980). In the light of the research evidence on differing perceptions, schools would be well advised to include pupils in their consultative process. Richards' (1983) work is interesting because he describes in detail how he, as deputy headteacher of a large comprehensive school, successfully negotiated and introduced a merit awards system for good work and behaviour throughout the first five years. The scheme fully utilized the House System so that the accumulated merits culminate in a House Merit cup being awarded at the end of the year, and as pupils gain personal awards they are privately and publicly praised by senior staff and a letter of commendation is sent to the parents. Richards also confirms other researchers' findings in noting that the formal reward system was perceived as being of less incentive by staff than by pupils and the latter favoured awards of a credit or certificate of merit for good work or behaviour.

(iii) The role of the pastoral form tutor

Disruptive pupils, more than any other group, challenge the philosophy and practice of pastoral care. By their behaviour they distract specialist pastoral staff from their positive, caring role into more disciplinary and administrative functions associated with control. These conflicting priorities were noted by Johnson *et al.*, (1980) as they confirmed that pastoral staff spent a disproportionate amount of time and energy coping with a few difficult pupils, whilst 'few resources are dedicated to drawing out and encouraging quiet pupils'. One of the historical weaknesses of the system is that responsibility for pastoral work has been centralized in a middle management team with the consequences that they become overwhelmed with crisis-management cases to the neglect of a more constructive role and, also, the role of the form tutor has not been developed or given meaningful status.

With these concerns in mind a consideration of a developmental approach to pastoral care and a preventative role for form tutors will be examined within the concept of a whole-school approach to discipline.

> As is the case with all organizations schools have objectives, structures and processes, and in their pastoral system they have declared their objectives in prospectuses and other documents, erected elaborate structures, but the processes of what is actually experienced by pupils is far removed from the rhetoric of words and symbols, such that a credibility gap exists between what is said and what is done' (Tattum, 1988b).

What is offered below is a seven stage model which has been discussed in full in Tattum (1989b).

1. In order to gain the commitment of staff to the idea of a wider, more integrated function for pastoral care, an agreed policy needs to be formulated as to its objectives, structures, processes and roles. Schools spend a great deal of time discussing academic and curriculum policy, it is not unreasonable to expect that the same drive, energy and commitment be devoted to the personal and social development of pupils.
2. A school will need to consider the nature of the support it wishes to give all pupils in their personal, social, educational and vocational development. A number of tutorial packages are available but schools would do well to construct their own programme and materials.
3. Coincidental with the production of a pastoral curriculum must be the negotiation of tutorial time so that tutors may carry out guidance and counselling in a meaningful way.
4. Once a pastoral programme has been designed and time allocated consideration can be given to the effective management and organization of the pastoral tutor's role. Given the time and opportunity to work with a tutorial group, a tutor will be able to establish the quality of relationships associated with the role expected by the pupils. Preventative work not only means early identification and intervention in crisis cases but improved pupil self-confidence and the enhancement of each pupil's self-image.

5. The next step is to bring about consistency in the management of pupils. This requires effective channels of communication with particular reference to channels of referral and the recording of behaviour. Ultimately, a whole-school approach is as effective as a staff's commitment to its concept and practices.

6. One of the intended outcomes of a preventive approach is that improved tutor–pupil relationships will be able to flourish as each begins to get to know the other. In this area teachers need to develop their listening skills as a most important part of effective counselling.

7. The most far-reaching outcome of a developmental pastoral programme, which gives status and responsibility to form tutors, will be a reduction in the credibility gap between theory and practice referred to earlier. The programme will tackle negative attitudes and self-defeating strategies by making pupils aware of the consequences and encouraging positive modes of behaviour.

Concluding comments

In discussing a whole-school approach to discipline with a focus on three distinctive areas of school organization the significant determinants are good leadership and management at senior and middle levels. From these persons comes guidance but, most especially, the initiation of a consultative process which involves the rest of the staff in policy-making. In the context of disruptive pupils there are a number of responses that need to be considered and within the present climate all three alternatives may be appropriate as schools and local authorities devise a series of strategies. The most violent and aggressive pupils may need to be sent to special units for the benefit of everyone but, as indiscipline is on a continuum of severity, approaches are needed which deal with the less severe cases. Schools have strengths and weaknesses across the staff and it is when all work as a team with effective communications and confident relationships that the general level of discipline will be raised.

References

ADVISORY CENTRE FOR EDUCATION (1980) 'Disruptive units' in *Where*, **158**, pp. 6–7.

ASSISTANT MASTERS AND MISTRESSES ASSOCIATION (AMMA) (1984) 'The reception class today', *Report*, **7** (1), pp. 6–9.

BOXER, R., McCARTHY, M., and COLLEY, B. (1987) 'A school survey of perceived effectiveness of rewards and sanctions', *Pastoral Care in Education*, **5**, 2, pp. 93–102.

BROPHY, J.E. (1981) 'Teacher praise: A functional analysis', *Review of Educational Research*, **51**, pp. 5–32.

BURNS, R.B. (1978) 'The relative effectiveness of various incentives and deterrents as judged by pupils and teachers', *Educational Studies*, **4**, pp. 229–43.

COULBY, D. and HARPER, T. (1985) *Preventing Classroom Disruption*, Beckenham, Croom Helm.

DAWSON, R.L. (1980) *Special Provision for Disturbed Pupils: A Survey*, London, Macmillan.

DEPARTMENT OF EDUCATION AND SCIENCE, (1979) *Aspects of secondary education in England*, London, HMSO.

DUKE, D.L. (1986) 'School discipline plans and the quest for order in American schools', in: TATTUM, D.P. *Management of Disruptive Pupil Behaviour in Schools*, London, Fulton.

FORD, J., MONGON, D. and WHELAN, M. (1982) *Special Education and Social Control: Invisible Disasters*, London, Routledge and Kegan Paul.

FRUDE, N. (1984) 'Frameworks for analysis', in: FRUDE, N. and GAULT, H. *Disruptive Behaviour in Schools*, Chichester, Wiley.

FURLONG, V.J. (1985) *The Deviant Pupil*, Milton Keynes, Open University Press.

GALLOWAY, D.M., BALL, T., BLOMFIELD, D. and SEYD, R. (1982) *Schools and Disruptive Pupils*, London, Longman.

GRIFFITHS, D. (1981) 'A team approach to disruption', *Forward Trends*, 1, pp. 8–15.

HARGREAVES, D.H. (1967) *Social Relations in a Secondary School*, London, Routledge and Kegan Paul.

HARGREAVES, D.H., HESTER, S.K. and MELLOR, F.J. (1975) *Deviance in Classrooms*, London, Routledge and Kegan Paul.

HER MAJESTY'S INSPECTORATE (1978) *Behavioural Units: A Survey of Special Units for Pupils with Behavioural Problems*, London, HMSO.

HER MAJESTY'S INSPECTORATE (1987) *Education Observed 5. Good Behaviour and Discipline in Schools*, London, HMSO.

HER MAJESTY'S INSPECTORATE (1988) *Secondary Schools. An Appraisal by HMI*, London, HMSO.

HIGHFIELD, M. and PINSENT, A. (1952) *A Survey of Rewards and Punishments in Schools*, London, Newnes.

HOLLINGWORTH, E.J., LUFLER, H.S. and CLUNE, W.H. (1984) *School Discipline, Order and Autonomy*, New York, Praeger.

JOHNSON, D., RANSOME, E., PACKWOOD, T., BOWDEN, K. and KOGAN, M. (1980) *Secondary Schools and the Welfare Network*, London, Unwin.

KOUNIN, J. (1970) *Discipline and Group Management in Classrooms*, New York, Holt, Rinehart and Winston.

LACEY, C. (1970) *Hightown Grammar*, Manchester, Manchester University Press.

LAING, A.F. and CHAZAN, M. (1986) 'The management of aggressive behaviour in young children', in: TATTUM, D.P. *Management of Disruptive Pupil Behaviour in Schools*, London, Fulton.

LANE, D.A. (1986) 'Promoting positive behaviour in the classroom', in: TATTUM, D.P. *Management of Disruptive Pupil Behaviour in Schools*, London, Fulton.

LAWRENCE, J., STEED, D. and YOUNG, P. (1984) *Disruptive Children — Disruptive Schools?* Beckenham, Croom Helm.

LAWRENCE, J., STEED, D. and YOUNG, P. (1986) 'The management of disruptive behaviour in Western Europe', in: TATTUM, D.P. *Management of Disruptive Pupil Behaviour in Schools*, London, Fulton.

LING, R. and DAVIES, G. (1984) *A Survey of Off-Site Special Units in England and Wales*, Birmingham, City of Birmingham Polytechnic.

LLOYD-SMITH, M. (1984) *Disrupted Schooling*, London, Murray.

LUFLER, H.S. (1979) 'Debating with assumptions. The need to understand school discipline', *Education and Urban Society*, 11, pp. 450–64.

MAXWELL, W.S. (1987) 'Teachers' attitudes towards disruptive behaviour in secondary schools', *Educational Review*, **39**, 3, pp. 203–16.

MILBURN, C.W. (1980) 'A positive rewards system', in: UPTON, G. and GOBELL, A. *Behaviour Problems in the Comprehensive School*, Cardiff, University College.

MORTIMORE, P. (1980) 'Misbehaviour in schools', in: UPTON, G. and GOBELL, A. (Eds) *Behaviour Problems in the Comprehensive School*, Cardiff, Faculty of Education University College.

MORTIMORE, P., DAVIES, J., VARLAAM, A. and WEST, A. (1983) *Behaviour Problems in Schools*, Beckenham, Croom Helm.

NATIONAL ASSOCIATION OF HEAD TEACHERS (1984) *Council Memorandum on Discipline in Schools*, Haywards Heath, NAHT.

NATIONAL UNION OF TEACHERS (1988) 'Discipline NOP Poll', *Teacher*, June 13, (**9**), pp. 11–14.

PURKEY, C.S. and SMITH, M.S. (1982) 'Too soon to cheer? Synthesis of research of effective schools', *Educational Leadership*, December, pp. 64–9.

RICHARDS, W.H. (1983) 'An investigation of a system of praise, rewards and incentives', *Unpublished M.Ed. Dissertation*, Cardiff, University College.

RUTTER, M., MAUGHAN, B., MORTIMORE, P. and OUSTEN, J. (1979) *Fifteen Thousand Hours*, London, Open Books.

SHARPE, F., WHELDALL, K. and MERRETT, F. (1987) 'The attitudes of British secondary school pupils to praise and reward', *Educational Studies*, **13**, 3, pp. 293–302.

STANFORD, J.P., EMMER, E.T. and CLEMENTS, B.S. (1983) 'Improving classroom management', *Educational Leadership*, April, pp. 56–60.

TATTUM, D.P. (1982) *Disruptive Pupils in Schools and Units*, Chichester, Wiley.

TATTUM, D.P. (1985) 'Disruptive pupil behaviour: A sociological perspective', *Maladjustment and Therapeutic Education*, 3, pp. 12–18.

TATTUM, D.P. (Ed.) (1986) *Management of Disruptive Pupil Behaviour in Schools*, London, Fulton.

TATTUM, D.P. (1989a) 'Violent, aggressive and disruptive behaviour', in: JONES, N. *Special Educational Needs Review*, Vol. 1, Lewes, Falmer Press.

TATTUM, D.P. (1989b) 'Disruptive behaviour — A whole-school approach', in: REID, K. (Ed.) *Helping Troubled Pupils in Secondary Schools, Vol. 2*, Oxford, Blackwell.

TOPPING, K. (1983) *Educational Systems for Disruptive Adolescents*, Beckenham, Croom Helm.

TOPPING, K. (1986) 'Consultative enhancement of school-based action', in: TATTUM, D.P. Management of Disruptive Pupil Behaviour in Schools, London, Fulton.

WATKINS, C. and WAGNER, P. (1987) *School Discipline: A Whole-School Approach*, Oxford, Blackwell.

WEST, A., DAVIES, J. and VARLAAM, A. (1986) 'The management of behaviour problems: A local authority response', in: TATTUM, D.P. *Management of Disruptive Pupil Behaviour in Schools*, London, Fulton.

WITHEY, D.A. (1979) 'Rewards in school: Some sociological perspectives', *Durham and Newcastle Review*, **9**, pp. 22–26.

WRAGG, E.C. (Ed.) (1984) *Classroom Teaching Skills*, Beckenham, Croom Helm.

4
Coping Strategies and Pupil Discipline

Chris Lowe

Introduction

Punishment, inside or outside school, does not exist in a vacuum. It requires a context — and in the late 1980s this has been perceived as one of increasing violence and disruption. But the recent outcry about violence in schools (like its predecessors, since they seem to be cyclic) is alarmist and does a grave disservice to the vast majority of British schools.

The impression has been given by certain journalists, politicians and teacher unions that disruption and oral and physical violence are on the increase. It was in response to this pressure that the Secretary of State for Education and Science, Rt. Hon. Kenneth Baker, MP, set up in 1988 the Enquiry into Discipline in Schools under the Chairmanship of Lord Elton. Curiously this Committee began its work at the same time as a research study *Schools, Disruptive Behaviour and Delinquency* by John Graham was published by the Home Office. This frenetic government activity put alongside the surveys of members conducted by NASUWT and PAT naturally tend to emphasize the gloomier aspects of pupil behaviour. This is further re-inforced in the public's eye by the well-publicized shooting of a deputy head in Northamptonshire by an ex-pupil, and the stabbing of one pupil by another in Manchester.

These also serve as salutory reminders of the extremes which teachers may have to face, and, of course, teachers have legitimate concerns about what support they can expect in such circumstances from heads, governors and local authorities. But there has been no national objective, statistical survey of what the level of serious disruption is in British Schools. The teacher union research may indeed reflect a general, insidious malaise. On the other hand Her Majesty's Inspectors may be right in their 1986 observation that 'the overwhelming majority of schools are orderly communities with good standards of behaviour' (HMI, 1987).

The privilege I have had as Legal Secretary of the Secondary Heads Association of being able to discuss this issue with colleagues, up and down the country, and my own optimistic inclinations, lead me to believe that HMI are right. I feel quite sure that the vast majority of teachers would characterize their schools as well-ordered, caring communities, while acknowledging that there are continual, if irregular, outbreaks of bad behaviour, laziness, insolence, defiance, vandalism and so on — because it is the nature of human beings to be like this at times, and particularly in the nature of adolescents who are in a short span of time discovering themselves and their relationships with society in general. But in the millions of teacher–pupil contacts that take place daily in 30,000 schools these instances form a tiny proportion, while leading to a great deal of time and energy spent in combatting them. Compared with the violence present in some pupils' homes and in the streets our schools are havens of peace, quiet and order.

Why then in the profession do we make such a song and dance about disruption and violence? I suggest that it is not because of any apparent increase, nor because teachers are less able than in the past to deal with each incident as it arises. It is because:

1. teachers now feel freer to talk about disruption in their classrooms; there is less stigma attached;
2. teachers are unsure of what they can do and not do by way of correction;
3. teachers are far too busy with other equally essential tasks and are unable to spend the necessary time on creating good relationships and solving problems;
4. it is one of the symptoms of the low morale in the profession; teachers are expressing a frustration at being undervalued and overworked. They feel that they are isolated and unsupported;
5. teachers feel that they alone are blamed for the moral climate of the country. One chairman of governors at a public meeting in Northamptonshire said that he was disgusted by the thugs being turned out by primary schools! A daft but predictable response from some quarters;
6. teachers believe that too much is expected of them. They have to be in rapid succession — teachers, psychiatrists, counsellors, social workers, detectives. And all with very little preparation and training as far as young teachers are concerned;
7. teachers by and large are unacquainted with modern mediation techniques.

If this diagnosis is correct, it helps us to understand what might be the remedies, and where the concept and practice of punishment fits in.

After all, we *know* why there is disruption and bad behaviour in schools even if we do not know how much. I have over three hundred titles of books and reports on the subject. The research is legion.

We know perfectly well what the symptoms and causes are — psychological problems, family and social background, poor motivation, poor teaching, inappropriate curriculum. They are all singly and collectively causes of tension and frustration likely to result in attention-seeking outbursts.

In schools we are fully aware of these and know that the treatment and remedies are also complex and time-consuming. For a start, dealing with the worst cases is a skilled job — for which social and welfare workers, police and probation officers receive extensive training. Apart from patchy training in *counselling* virtually nothing exists for teachers. Yet teachers are asked to be front-line responders, and initiators of appropriate action. No doubt we shall see a development of such agencies as the Juvenile Liaison Bureau being pioneered in a number of places including Northamptonshire, my own county, where a team of social workers, police, probation officers and teachers have taken cases away from juvenile courts for alternative treatment — with remarkable success. Their technique is to get youngsters to examine and understand their behaviour and to control it themselves, rather than simply to receive punishment for it. The relative amount of time spent on this is enormous, of course, but if we wish to avoid juvenile delinquency turning into adult crime this might have to be afforded. In the meantime we have to recognize that these agencies are not available at the drop of a hat and teachers have to fall back on a first-aid service — which is where punishment came in.

Portia Holman and Nelson Coghill in *Disruptive Behaviour in Schools* write that 'teachers seem to think that disruption should be treated by punishment, if not by barbaric methods, nevertheless by humiliation'. They urge teachers to accept the view that 'the majority of disrupters are suffering, or have suffered, from their family circumstances, and are in need of help'. On the other hand they note that many schools are becoming more child-centred while repeating the canard that many schools possess 'a thoroughly authoritarian structure with a generation gap between heads and the bulk of teachers'. The two researchers report on a meeting of heads considering disruptive behaviour and noted their exasperation with the effects of the disruptive behaviour of disruptive children and their own powerlessness to control it. It seems that this group of heads could only think of bureaucratic procedures and punitive measures to deal with the problem. Holman and Coghill are scathing about the efficacy of punishment as a cure for anything.

I am prepared to believe that it is no cure. I go along too with R.S. Peters in *Ethics and Education* (1966) that 'punishment is one of the most potent devices for bringing about estrangement', and with Jeremy Bentham in *Principles of Morals and Legislation* that 'punishment is in itself evil . . . it ought only to be admitted in as far as it promises to exclude some greater evil'. Bentham's utilitarian view was simply that punishment was of no use if it did not actually do any good. In schools this is frequently the case. We often find ourselves in schools punishing the same Waynes, Duanes and Shanes, Tracys and Sharons over and over again. We give them lines, we keep them in detention, we suspend them — once upon a time we used to cane them — but back they come.

I believe that the general trend away from the punishment of offenders to their treatment, despite occasional hiccoughs, should be, and is, reflected in schools. We know that in schools we should be doing far more with the other agencies — the psychological, social and welfare services, the police and probation services, but we are not trained to do so and we haven't the time. We know that there are behaviour modification techniques — but they require skill and training and again are exceedingly time-consuming and consequently have resource implications.

And so we resort to punishment — we always have — and despite my intellectual acknowledgement that punishment of children might be degrading, might in fact produce the opposite effect to the one I intended to achieve, I feel in my bones — as a parent as well as teacher — that there *is* a proper place for punishment in schools.

One of the reasons has to be that punishment exists in the wider community and in the home. It is a fact of life, and I do not think that will ever change. But I do think our use of it and understanding of its effects will change and have changed.

Plato knew that you have a system of punishment because if you did not, then people would simply take the law into their own hands. We, in turn, know that in schools punishments (sanctions) are only *one* part of the whole apparatus of keeping order and discipline and creating a harmonious climate.

It follows that the purpose of the punishments must be explained, understood and accepted. It is part of the educational process that children should learn that their actions may have consequences, sometimes undesirable ones. The concept of punishment, therefore, must be seen in the context of the total pastoral care offered by the school.

Pastoral Care is itself a huge topic, but for punishment to be effective it must be part of a system of care and concern that has as one of its tenets a belief that on the whole pupils will obey rules and that these rules contain a body of principles that are beneficial to all and are worthy of respect. Pupils will also instinctively expect that punishments for breaking these rules will be applied fairly and consistently, i.e. reasonably, which is a word that crops up frequently in education law.

So much of our teaching in schools concerns notions of equality, fair play, reasonableness, caring and so on, that it seems inconceivable that teachers could resort to the *because I told you so*, or *if you don't do as I say, you will be for it* techniques. But, of course, we do! Not so often nowadays perhaps, but teachers are human, too. Pupils will understand these frustrations if, nevertheless, the ethos of the establishment is *wholesome*, *reasonable* and *caring*. In other words, like the best of homes and families.

What punishment must *not* become is simply the end result of a mass of complicated things that a child is compelled to do or not to do — without explanation or reason — if we intend the growing person to care at all about the school's rules, and later the Law in general. We should never forget in schools that our prime function is educational — the growth of the whole child, and today's children are tomorrow's parents.

Punishment is, therefore, a small important facet of the whole discipline picture, and the approach to punishment in a school must stem from a clearly understood, shared view (staff and pupils, governors and parents) of what kind of behaviour is acceptable and why. The ideas of equity, justice, wisdom, charity that we would wish to be imprinted in adult society must be gleaned from an early age. This will come from the hidden curriculum of the attitudes we take up towards adolescent behaviour and the atmosphere we create in the school.

This is no longer just a professional matter. Local authorities, governors, heads, teachers, parents all have legal responsibilities. Through the 1986 Education Act and new Articles of Government, and conditions of employment, a duty is laid on *heads* to *encourage good behaviour, promote self discipline and a proper regard for authority, secure acceptable standards of behaviour* and *regulate conduct*. That is a tall order when the combined might of the police force and courts cannot achieve it!

Teachers have, according to their Conditions of Employment, to *maintain good order and discipline among the pupils*, while the Governors have a duty to oversee the conduct of the school and have the power to determine what the acceptable standards of behaviour should be. The Secreaty of State in DES Circular 7/87 hoped that governors would consider the influence which the standards and ethos promoted by the school can have on the level of juvenile crime in the area. He suggested that governors might monitor the occurrence of vandalism at the school and in the immediate neighbourhood and report this to parents in the annual report. Governors also have a duty to liaise with the police. The LEA for its part has reserve powers to intervene if there is a breakdown in discipline, and has a duty to provide adequate training and resources. Parents have the right to discuss the discharge of these duties at the Annual Parents Meeting. They also have a general duty to control their offspring, a duty which the Secretary of State has emphasized on a number of occasions.

There is already a duty to set out in the school prospectus what the school's system of punishment is, and this would be a matter that could also be taken up at the new Annual Parents Meetings where the head's, and governors' exercise of their duties can be discussed and questioned. A head, therefore, will need to be able to explain and, if necessary, justify the system of sanctions and punishments.

In addition, the 1986 Act creates new statutory requirements for school exclusions. The government was worried about the inconsistencies involved in suspensions of pupils and the fact that there were many children wandering the streets for whom nothing was being done. The elaborate new rules are expected to prevent this. However, much is still left to the head and governors, and because discretion is intermingled with statutory requirements it might well happen that governors get the technical process wrong. Since parents are much more inclined to know their law and their rights, and frequently bring along solicitors to suspension hearings, there will be difficulties ahead, if heads and governors are not fully conversant with the procedures.

This same 1986 Act abolished corporal punishment — or, at least, partly did so. The abolition applies only to maintained schools, and maintained pupils in independent schools. Fee-paying pupils can still be beaten! However, it is not only formal canings that have gone. Chalk flicking, board duster throwing and shoulder shaking are also outlawed — but those who habitually perpetrated these were not abolished at the same time, and many teachers are already finding it hard to change their ways, which could of course have severe consequences for their careers.

The question of detention — a time-honoured school punishment — is not covered by statute, but since it amounts to false imprisonment if parents do not know about the detention, then it is important that heads and teachers are aware that a parent has the ultimate right to custody of his child — unless a court decides otherwise. Parents can even demand their children back during the school day. If this happened the school could, of course, punish the child by excluding him/her. What it could not do is refuse to hand over the child.

Behind the new statutory provisions, and prior to them, the Common Law offers wise guidance. Close to the beginnings of state education Mr Justice Phillimore laid down the principles of school punishment. In *Mansell v Griffin* (1908) he said that a teacher has the ordinary means of preserving discipline. It is enough for the teacher to be able to say: 'The punishment which I administered was *moderate*, it was *not dictated by any bad motive* and it was *such as is usual* in the school, and such as the *parent might expect* it would receive if it did wrong'. Phillimore did not invent the notion of the teacher being *in loco parentis* but he gave it a nudge in the right direction. If eighty years later we bear those principles in mind we shall not go far wrong. Punishments will not then be dictated by hate, nor even fear perhaps, but by a desire to *encourage good behaviour*.

Where this does not happen we get the worst possible communities. In one school I dealt with as Legal Secretary of SHA, a new head found 1,000 instances of corporal punishment in the Punishment Book. The school was filled with tension and fear; there were reports of riots and constant disruption. The violence was not only in the children, but in the staff, too, and it is difficult to say which prompted or fed from the other. In the middle of the last century the army had to be sent into more than one of the famous public schools to quell pupils rebelling against the harsh regime. But these are worthy of note because they are rare. We can welcome the presence of police in a few of our schools, not because of vicious behaviour from pupils in the school, but because of intruders. It was an intruder who shot the deputy head I mentioned earlier: it had nothing to do with the ethos of the school.

So what should be the response, it would be too daring to say solution, to disruption and violence in school? It seems to me that first and foremost it must be a *local* response — governors, teachers, parents and external agencies working together to serve their schools as well as be served by them.

> All the different agencies — school, social, welfare, police, probation, psychological — must be enabled to get together to understand each others' different perceptions of how to approach and treat delinquency.
>
> The training needs must be addressed and solved.
>
> There must be clear local (LEA and school) policies on discipline matters.
>
> Appropriate staff and the extra resources needed must be on hand.
>
> There must be a local thrust towards crime *prevention* rather than treatment and a consideration of how this can be best done in schools.
>
> The question of appropriate curriculum — and perhaps alternative approaches (as in the 'Low Attaining Pupils Project') needs to be addressed.
>
> The punishment in schools must be positive and consistent and form part of a systematic approach to the creation of an orderly, caring ethos, with values shared by both teachers and pupils.
>
> Parents should be brought into the equation, their responsibilities, and problems, acknowledged and discussed.

It all sounds like a tall order, but in fact most schools are ninety per cent there already. They have positive, workmanlike policies that take into account the local circumstances. Even so problems will still occur in the best regulated schools because the population of pupils, parents and teachers is constantly changing. That is both the frustration and the delight of school teaching.

References

DOCKING, J.W. (1987) *Control and Discipline in School*, London, Harper and Row

GRAHAM, J. (1988) *Schools, Disruptive Behaviour and Delinquency: A Review of Research*, (Home Office Research Study, Number 96), London, HMSO

GRAHAM, J. (1988) *Schools, Disruptive Behaviour and Delinquency*, London, Home Office

HER MAJESTY'S INSPECTORATE (1987) *Good Behaviour and Discipline in Schools*, Education Observed 5, London, HMSO

HOLMAN, P. and COGHILL, P. (1987) *Disruptive Behaviour in Schools*, London, Chartwell and Bratt

PETERS, R.S (1966) *Ethics and Education*, London, Allen and Unwin

Part II
Recommendations to Lord Elton

5
Enquiry into Discipline in Schools:
University of Lancaster

David Galloway
Peter Mortimore
Norman Tutt

How are good behaviour (and their opposites) defined in the school
context

Problems of definition

Good behaviour and bad behaviour are slippery concepts. Whether behaviour is
disruptive depends at least in part on the nature of the task and on the perception of
the teacher. In some lessons pupils talking or moving around the room would be
unacceptable; other lessons require active participation and movement by the
pupils. Further, teachers vary not only in the pupil behaviour they consider acceptable, but also in the behaviour they experience as stressful. This is as true in specialist units for severely disruptive pupils as in the ordinary classroom. For example,
calling out answers without being asked may be highly disruptive to one teacher,
yet appear, at worst a minor irritant to another teacher of the same pupil. It is not
just that one teacher may find this behaviour more troublesome than another. All
classroom behaviour involves interaction between pupils and/or between teachers
and pupils. Most children are quick to identify, and to exploit, any behaviour which
the teacher does not handle with confidence. This is why teachers who find, for
example, continuous calling out particularly troublesome may suffer from more of
this behaviour than their colleagues.

Pupils' behaviour at school does not fall tidily into two distinct groups of
normal and disruptive. Rather it consists of a continuum from highly motivated to
cooperate with the teacher to totally unacceptable. We prefer to define disruptive
broadly as any behaviour which appears problematic, inappropriate and disturbing
to teachers. This emphasis on the teacher's perception implies no lack of concern

about the potentially harmful effects of disruptive behaviour on other pupils and on classroom learning. It does, however, imply that the teacher's needs and the pupils' needs are interlinked, since the teacher needs to establish a high level of motivation in order to meet the pupil's need for achievement in the curriculum.

What behaviour do teachers consider acceptable/unacceptable?

Defining good behaviour is even more difficult. It can be defined in terms of the time pupils spend concentrating on the task the teacher has set, but this tells us little about the quality of learning. The problems again, are that different tasks require different levels of teacher control and pupil involvement, and that teachers vary in the sort of classroom relationships they consider desirable. On the other hand, we do now have considerable information on the classroom behaviour teachers find unacceptable.

Surveys both of secondary teachers (Lawrence *et al.*, 1978) and of primary teachers (Wheldall and Merrett, 1988) report a high frequency of relatively minor behaviour problems. Thus, 51 per cent of primary teachers in Wheldall and Merrett's study thought they were spending too much time on problems of discipline, the most frequent being talking out of turn and hindering other children. Similarly, Lawrence *et al.*, found that only 9 per cent of disruptive incidents reported by staff were described as very serious. The picture, then, is not of any dramatic breakdown in discipline but of frequent relatively minor incidents which, nevertheless, interfere with pupils' educational progress.

Turning to the small minority of pupils whose seriously disruptive behaviour results in long-term exclusion from school, Galloway *et al.*, (1982) found that 'abuse/insolence to teachers' was the most frequent incident precipitating exclusion, followed by unspecified bad behaviour and refusal to accept discipline. The latter usually took the form of refusal to accept corporal punishment which, at that time, was still customary in some schools. Violence towards teachers accounted for only 4.5 per cent of all long term exclusions reported over a four year period from all Sheffield schools. This contrasts with bullying and/or violence to other pupils which was the precipitating incident in nearly 11 per cent of exclusions.

Is there currently a discipline problem in schools: how serious and how widespread is it?

Seriousness of the problem

Minor discipline problems occur in all schools, but some teachers experience many more problems than others. Serious problems occur from time to time in many schools, but again some schools experience many more than others. It is rare for a pupil, including pupils who have been excluded, to be equally troublesome with all teachers.

How widespread is the problem?

Repeated surveys have shown that teachers regard the behaviour of a substantial minority of pupils as a cause for concern. This was as true 60 years ago as it is today (McFie, 1934; Milner, 1938). On the basis of behaviour questionnaires completed by teachers, the National Child Development Study concluded that 14 per cent of seven year olds could be described as maladjusted, (Davie *et al.*, 1972). Using a different teachers' questionnaire, Rutter *et al.* (1975a, 1975b) concluded that 11 per cent of ten year olds on the Isle of Wight and 19 per cent in Inner London exhibited some form of behaviour problem and could be described as deviant, though not necessarily disruptive. By the age of 16, teachers claimed that the statement 'is often disobedient' applied at least to some extent to 18 per cent of the pupils in the National Child Development Survey and the statement 'irritable, quick to fly off the handle' to 20 per cent (Fogelman, 1976).

How widespread, then, is *seriously* disruptive behaviour? While it is clear that violence towards teachers is extremely infrequent (Hansard, 1975; Galloway *et al.*, 1982), there is little information on the prevalence of serious physical attacks on other pupils. The response rate in one well known survey (Lowenstein, 1975) was too low to enable any credence to be placed in its conclusions (5 per cent from primary and 20 per cent from secondary teachers) and even the 'official' survey reported in Hansard (1975) only achieved a 60 per cent response rate from chief education officers.

Another way of looking at the prevalence of the most serious behaviour problems is to examine the number of long-term exclusions for disruptive behaviour. Unfortunately no national statistics are available, and even if they keep systematic records, most LEAs understandably prefer to keep the figures to themselves. The most comprehensive information comes from a four year study in Sheffield from 1975–79. Altogether 277 pupils were excluded indefinitely or for at least three weeks. The number of primary pupils excluded did not exceed 0.01 per cent (1 per 10,000 on roll) in any year. In secondary schools there was a sharp increase, with a peak in the final year of compulsory schooling. Yet even here 0.38 per cent of the total on roll was the highest recorded figure for any one year. Over the four years the absolute number of excluded pupils fluctuated from forty-eight in 1975/76 to ninety-four in 1977/78, representing a theoretical average increase of just over one pupil per secondary school. What it actually indicated was a sharp increase in a small number of schools.

What are the principal causes of disruptive incidents and misbehaviour by pupils? What evidence is there to substantiate any causal connections which may be adduced?

Personal and educational characteristics of disruptive pupils

There is a well established association between reading difficulties and classroom disruptive problems (Rutter *et al.*, 1969; Varlaam, 1974). The causal relationship between reading and behaviour, i.e. whether the reading difficulty causes the behaviour problem or vice versa, has been clarified by recent research. This research — using a longitudinal design — showed that each factor could precede the other (Mortimore *et al.*, 1988). Attention, therefore, to the educational needs of disruptive pupils is essential. This view is supported by research on the most seriously disruptive minority of pupils whose behaviour results in exclusion (York *et al.*, 1972; Galloway, 1982). In his study of all pupils excluded over one year in Sheffield, Galloway found a mean of IQ of 82, with 96 per cent of pupils having an IQ of 100 or below. Altogether 21 per cent had an IQ below 71. Most of these pupils' head teachers recognized their educational backwardness, but attributed it to their general lack of cooperation, not to lack of intellectual ability. The evidence, however, suggested that many of the pupils had special educational needs associated with general low ability. Few of the pupils appeared to be receiving appropriate help; the majority were being taught in ordinary CSE classes whose teachers had little support from a special needs department or learning support team. In these circumstances the behavioural problems they presented could be seen as a response to their daily experience of educational failure.

There is some evidence of atypical autonomic functioning amongst disruptive pupils. Davies and Maliphant (1974), for example, found that disruptive boys in a residential school were significantly slower to learn from punishment than a control group of pupils where teachers had not expressed concern about their behaviour. While the evidence for this particular theory is not strong, it is clear that children with some neurological problems are more likely to be reported as aggressive or disruptive (Graham and Rutter, 1968; Anderson, 1973). Galloway (1987) found a history of serious illnesses or accidents requiring in-patient treatment amongst 69 per cent of excluded pupils, and in 27 per cent there was a possibility of consequent neurological impairment. Overall the evidence suggests that physical factors may contribute to some children's behavioural problems, but cannot be regarded as the sole cause.

Family and neighbourhood characteristics

Whereas studies of persistent absentees from school typically show the overwhelming majority to be living in extremely poor material conditions with a multitude of social, health and economic problems (Galloway, 1985), the picture with seriously disruptive pupils is less clear. They are much less likely than persistent non-attenders to live in materially stressful conditions; in Sheffield 51 per cent lived in the older, less satisfactory forms of council housing, but 30 per cent owned their own homes. In some schools pupils who were excluded tended to live in the most socially disadvantaged parts of the catchment area. In others this was not the case.

It was nevertheless clear that many excluded pupils were living in highly stressful families with frequent tensions in relationships between members. In addition, nearly half of the mothers interviewed were suffering from some form of chronic illness and 44 per cent were either receiving treatment for minor psychiatric symptoms such as depression or described symptoms associated with depression or anxiety. Furthermore, evidence from a study of over 22,000 secondary pupils showed that there was an increased chance of pupil disturbance as other factors of disadvantage increased (Sammons *et al.*, 1983).

The school's contribution

Seriously disruptive pupils, then, appear vulnerable on constitutional, educational, intellectual and social grounds. Does the school also have an influence? Over four years in Sheffield, approximately half of all exclusions were from six of thirty-seven secondary schools from which information was available. An exhaustive study of the catchment areas of all thirty-seven schools showed no consistent relationship between social factors and the number of pupils excluded. Whether a pupil was excluded depended far more on the school he or she happened to attend than on any personal or family characteristic.

Exclusion rates are not always a reliable measure of overall behaviour within a school. Nevertheless, other research on school effectiveness suggests consistently that schools exert a profound influence over the way their pupils behave. For example Rutter *et al.*, (1979) found no consistent relationship between the characteristics of pupils on entering the twelve secondary schools they studied (parental occupation and educational attainment) and their subsequent behaviour within each school. Mortimore *et al.*, (1988) obtained similar results from a larger-scale study of London junior schools. In both studies disruptive behaviour was an infrequent problem in some schools. At other schools it appeared much more frequent and more serious. The differences could not be attributed to differences in the pupils each school admitted. We believe that this evidence should be profoundly encouraging for teachers. It implies that *they* exert an influence over their pupils' behaviour, and that solutions are often to be found within the school. There are seldom grounds for attributing disruptive behaviour mainly to factors in the children or their social backgrounds.

What actions can be taken by relevant organizations and individuals to promote good behaviour in schools, and is there evidence to suggest such action would be effective?

While it is clear that schools as organizations and teachers as individuals do have a very substantial influence on their pupils' behaviour, there is less certainty as to *how* this takes place. The field is rife with speculation and over-optimistic claims for each author's favourite ideas but in many cases the theoretical base is narrow and the empirical evidence weak. In our view the most hopeful leads come from school effectiveness research but we have to point out that no major study of school effectiveness has yet looked specifically at the processes which result in some schools' success in maintaining excellent discipline and interpersonal relations whereas others have substantial problems in these areas. That said, there is sufficient indirect evidence to identify some promising lines of inquiry. We will first discuss action that could be taken by parents, and then turn to teachers, LEAs and the Government.

Parents

An eminent secondary head teacher has argued that schools in Britain compare unfavourably with our competitor countries in the EEC in the quality of relationships established with parents (Marland, 1985). It seems improbable that this relationship will be improved by calls at teacher union conferences for parents to be held responsible for their children's behaviour at times when teachers are legally *in loco parentis*. Moreover, evidence from epidemiological studies shows consistently that although parents are as likely as teachers to express concern about children's behaviour, parents and teachers tend to identify *different* children as problems. Contrary to popular belief, the overlap is relatively small: around 25 per cent of all pupils were identified as difficult either by parents or by teachers (Rutter *et al.*, 1970).

It follows, then, that in demanding greater accountability for children's behaviour at school, some teachers may be asking parents to exercise control *in absentia*, even though they have experienced no unusual discipline problems at home. Unless this is recognized, calls for greater parental accountability are likely to increase tensions between teachers and parents, and may thus increase rather than reduce the likelihood of children behaving disruptively at school.

None of this, however, should be taken to imply that parents have no role in maintaining discipline in school. We believe that they have a vital role. They are less likely to give their support, though, if they feel they are being blamed for their children's difficult behaviour, either when they visit the school or when they hear of teachers making critically dismissive comments about parents at well publicized union conferences. How, then, can parents be enabled to contribute usefully to school discipline?

A characteristic of the most effective junior schools studied by Mortimore *et al.*, (1988) was their success in establishing informal relationships with parents. Formal organizations such as PTAs were not so clearly associated with effective practice. A study in Wales found wide variations between secondary schools in their success in establishing communication with parents (Woods, 1984). The evidence suggests that parents can make an important contribution to discipline, but schools vary very widely in their success in establishing a mutually beneficial partnership. This is an area in which further research is needed. The NFER are currently researching into parent involvement in both primary and secondary schools (Jowett and Baginsky, 1988)

Teachers

It has been known for a long time that teachers who are effective with 'ordinary' children tend also to be effective in teaching disruptive pupils (Kounin *et al.*,

1966). A great deal of enthusiasm has been expressed about the possibility of using behaviour modification techniques to modify disruptive behaviour (O'Leary and O'Leary, 1979; Harrop, 1983; Merrett and Wheldall, 1986). Leading practitioners, however, have been more cautious, arguing that too little is known about failed applications, since only successful studies get published, and that problems of changes continuing over time and transferring to other settings have often been underestimated (Berger, 1983).

Evidence from school effectiveness research suggests that the school's overall climate or ethos is probably the most important single influence on pupils' behaviour. The question is: What factors are critical in determining overall climate. While acknowledging the complexity of this question, we wish to suggest that attention could usefully be directed to eight areas.

1. Our experience suggests that not all schools have a consistent policy on discipline, and that this can be a source of friction for pupils and teachers alike. Schools appear to vary both in the degree of responsibility which class teachers are expected to assume for the pupils' behaviour and in the amount of support which senior teachers offer colleagues in dealing with discipline problems. In some schools confusion still arises because subject teachers are expected to refer behaviour problems to the head of department and 'pastoral' problems to the head of year, yet the decision as to whether a problem is behavioural or pastoral is essentially an arbitrary one, depending in practice on the personal preference of a teacher who may only see the pupil once a week (Galloway, 1983).

2. When pupils feel that their school has dismissed them as examination prospects it is not surprising that they sometimes establish a group identity based on opposition to the school's rules and values (Hargreaves, 1983). In this connection we welcome the proposal in the Education Reform Bill that all pupils should have access to all areas of the National Curriculum. Nevertheless, this will not be achieved without tension in schools which have previously offered alternative curricula to their lower ability pupils. Careful monitoring will be needed.

3. Curriculum process is at least as important as the content. This refers to the manner in which the curriculum is taught, and has not been the subject of detailed study in Britain. Research from New Zealand found substantial differences in behaviour and attainments between pupils in socially disadvantaged primary schools with a multi-ethnic intake. Ramsay *et al.*, (1983) found a consistent tendency in the more effective schools for teachers to introduce the curriculum in ways that built on the pupils' own cultural backgrounds. In contrast, teachers in the less effective schools tended to regard the pupils' cultural backgrounds as having little or no relevance to what they were taught in school.

4. Disruption is unintentionally encouraged in some schools by organizational limitations. Rabinowitz (1981) has drawn attention to the frustration caused when the timetable virtually ensures that pupils arrive late

for some lessons, for example because one lesson starts at the time the previous one stops, so that pupils have to move from one building to another in what amounts to negative time. Similarly Lawrence *et al.*, (1981) noted a peak in disruptive incidents in mid-week and suggested that recreational activities such as a disco might be useful.

5. While all schools claim a commitment to pastoral care, this commitment is not always reflected in the pupils' experience. Schools vary widely in their success in ensuring that each pupil is known by at least one teacher (Galloway, 1983). It has been suggested that the role of the form tutor may have declined with the introduction of comprehensive schools and that this may have led to reduced effectiveness in dealing with problems such as truancy (Reynolds *et al.*, 1987).

6. As we have seen, a high proportion of the most seriously disruptive pupils have marked reading problems and many are educationally backward. In many schools provision for pupils with learning difficulties does not fully address the possible behavioural consequences of failure to meet educational needs. In particular it seems important that pupils should not feel they are being excluded from the mainstream of the school's educational activities, which in secondary schools remains the examination system (for detailed comments on the influence of the examination system, see Mortimore *et al.*, 1986). Galloway (1985) has described provision for special needs at one school that was notably successful in reducing disruption to a minimum. We would like to see 'whole' school-approaches of this sort introduced more widely.

7. The lack of supportive relationships amongst teachers has received considerable attention (Hargreaves, 1978). Too often, teachers find themselves locked into a vicious circle in which they do not seek help in the management of discipline problems because this feels like an admission of incompetence and do not offer help to colleagues because they do not wish to imply that they think their colleague is incompetent. Galloway (1983) argues that support for colleagues in the most effective schools is based on helping them cope with discipline problems themselves rather than on providing a referral channel in which the problem is taken over by senior staff.

8. Schools vary widely in the amount they use the LEA support services and in the way they use them. Gath *et al.*, (1977) found no evidence that these differences were associated with the catchment areas the schools served. Our experience suggests that success is less likely when a disruptive pupil is referred to the support services in the expectation that the pupil should receive some form of treatment or counselling from an expert. Teachers and pupils are much more likely to benefit when teachers and members of the support service work together in a joint endeavour to find effective responses to discipline problems.

Local Education Authorities (LEAs)

We are not convinced that many LEAs have developed a coherent policy on the management of discipline problems in their schools. Such a policy should have regard:

1. To the relatively minor but nevertheless occasionally widespread and persistent problems in some schools;
2. To the problems experienced by some teachers in all schools;
3. To the most seriously troublesome minority who have been excluded or are at risk of exclusion.

Responses to 1. and 2. above will require school-based and school-focused INSET programmes which utilize the expertise of experienced teachers, members of the LEA support services and suitably qualified staff in higher education. Finding solutions to day-to-day discipline problems by motivating pupils to achieve higher educational standards is part of all teachers' professional development. Almost by definition, INSET is also concerned with professional development. Research is urgently needed to identify the ways in which INSET may most effectively help teachers at all levels to respond effectively to discipline problems in their classes in schools.

Responses to the most disturbing minority should be based on the joint needs to ensure:

(a) That normal teaching and learning can continue uninterrupted;
(b) That the probable reasons for the disruption are identified as quickly and accurately as possible.

This requires a full assessment of each pupil's educational needs and a thorough review of factors within the school which may have contributed to the pupils' behavioural problems. If LEAs continue to utilize off-site units for disruptive pupils, admitting pupils from several schools, or on-site units for one school's own pupils, greater attention should be paid to these joint functions. In the past both off-site units (Mortimore *et al.*, 1983) and on-site units (Galloway *et al.*, 1982) have had limited success because their educational rationale has either been unclear or limited. The reintegration of pupils back into mainstream classes is also difficult (Davies and Varlaam, 1985).

Central government

We are not convinced that the distinction implied in the 1981 Education Act between disruptive pupils and pupils with emotional and behavioural problems is helpful. One of us (DG), has carried out a comprehensive assessment of well over 100 pupils following their exclusion from school and / or placement in off-site units for disruptive pupils. Without exception, all these pupils could have been described s having emotional and behavioural problems if a suitable special school had been available. Conversely, a high proportion of pupils placed in special schools could have been described as disruptive if an appropriate off-site unit had been available. The significance of this is that placement of disruptive pupils, unlike that of those with emotional and behavioural difficulties, does not require a statement of their special needs under the 1981 Act. This may be because the government believes that disruptive behaviour requires a rapid response from the LEA. We would not disagree with this view, but would point out that the Act makes provision for emergency placement in special schools or units for the purpose of carrying out a formal assessment leading to a statement of special educational needs.

In the course of their work, HMIs undoubtedly come across primary and secondary schools in which discipline problems are infrequent. While welcoming previous publications (HMI, 1978) we suggest that more could be done to publicize the organizational structure and teaching processes associated with a positive school climate. Similarly, more could be done to publicize innovations in dealing with disciplinary problems.

Finally, we would repeat that although the evidence that schools influence their pupils' behaviour is no longer controversial, relatively little is known about the critical factors within a school's organization, curriculum, classroom teaching process and management style. Nor is there yet an extensive or convincing body of evidence on ways of introducing organizational change to improve discipline and pupil motivation. We hope that the government will consider supporting research that addresses these issues.

References

ANDERSON, E. (1973) *The Disabled Schoolchild: A Study of Integration in Primary Schools*, London, Methuen.

BERGER, M. (1983) 'Behaviour change in the classroom', in: HARRE, R. and LAMB R. (Eds) *The Enclycopaedic Dictionary of Psychology*, Oxford, Blackwell.

DAVIE, E.R., BUTLER, N. and GOLDSTEIN, H. (1972) *From Birth to Seven*, London, Longman.

DAVIES, J.A.V. and MALIPHANT, R. (1974) 'Refractory behaviour in schools and avoidance learning', *Journal of Child Psychology and Psychiatry*, **15**, pp. 23–31.

DAVIES, J. and VARLAAM, A. (1985) 'School support programme: The reintegration of pupils into mainstream schools', London, *ILEA* RS 968/85.

FOGELMAN, K. (1976) *Britain's Sixteen Year Olds*, London, National Children's Bureau.

GALLOWAY, D. (1982) 'A study of pupils suspended from school', *British Journal of Educational Psychology*, **52**, pp. 205–12.

GALLOWAY, D. (1983) 'Disruptive pupils and effective pastoral care', *School Organisation*, **3**, pp. 245–54.

GALLOWAY, D. (1985a) *Schools and Persistent Absentees*, Oxford, Pergamon.

GALLOWAY, D. (1985b) 'Meeting special educational needs in the ordinary school? Or creating them?' *Maladjustment and Therapeutic Education*, **3**, iii, pp. 3–10.

GALLOWAY, D., BALL, T., BLOMFIELD, D. and SEYD, R. (1982) *Schools and Disruptive Pupils*, London, Longman.

GATH, D., COOPER, B., GATTONI, F. and ROCKETT, D. (1977) *Child Guidance and Delinquency in a London Borough*, Oxford, Oxford University Press.

GRAHAM, P. and RUTTER, M. (1968) 'Organic brain dysfunction and child psychiatric disorder', *British Medical Journal*, 3, pp. 695–700.

HANSARD PARLIAMENTARY DEBATES (1975) 863 p. 105, London, HMSO.

HARGREAVES, D.H. (1978) 'What teaching does to teachers', *New Society*, 43, March, pp. 540–2.

HARGREAVES, D.H. (1983) *The Challenge of the Comprehensive School: Culture, Curriculum, Community*, London, Routledge and Kegan Paul.

HARROP, A. (1983) *Behaviour Modification in the Classroom*, London, Hodder and Stoughton.

HER MAJESTY'S INSPECTORATE OF SCHOOLS (1978) *Truancy and Behaviour Problems in Some Urban Schools*, London, HMSO.

JOWETT, S. and BAGINSKY, M. (1988) 'Parents and education: A survey of their involvement and a discussion of some issues', *Educational Research*, 30, pp. 36–45.

KOUNIN, J.S., FRIESEN, W.V. and NORTON, E. (1966) 'Managing emotionally disturbed children in regular classrooms', *Journal of Educational Psychology*, 57, pp. 1–13.

LAWRENCE, J. (1978) 'Monitoring incidents of disruptive behaviour in secondary schools', *Durham and Newcastle Research Review*, 41, pp. 39–43.

LAWRENCE, J., YOUNG, P., STEED, D. and HILTON, G. (1981) *Dialogue on Disruptive Behaviour: A Study of a Secondary School*, South Croydon, PJD Press.

LOWENSTEIN, L.F. (1975) *Violent and Disruptive Behaviour in Schools*, Hemel Hempstead, National Association of Schoolmasters.

McFIE, B.S. (1934) 'Behaviour and personality difficulties in school children', *British Journal of Educational Psychology*, 4, pp. 30–46.

MARLAND, M. (1985) 'Parents, schooling and the welfare of pupils', in: RIBBINS, P. (Ed.) *Schooling and Welfare*, Lewes, Falmer Press.

MERRETT, F.E. and WHELDALL, K. (1986) 'British teachers and the behavioural approach to teaching', in: WHELDALL, K. (Ed.) *The Behaviourist in the Classroom*, 2 edn (revised) London, Allen and Unwin.

MILNER, M. (1938) *The Human Problem in Schools*, London, Methuen.

MORTIMORE, P., DAVIES, J., VARLAAM, A. and WEST, A. (1983) *Behaviour Problems in Schools: An Evaluation of Support Centres*, Beckenham, Croom Helm.

MORTIMORE, J. and MORTIMORE, P. and CHITTY, C. (1986) 'Secondary school examinations', *Bedford Way Paper*, No 18, London University.

MORTIMORE, P., SAMMONS, P., STOLL, L., LEWIS, D. and ECOB, R. (1988) *School Matters: The Junior Years*, Wells, Open Books.

O'LEARY, K.D. and O'LEARY, S.C. (Eds.) (1979) *Classroom Management: The Successful Use of Behaviour Modification*, (2nd edition) New York, Pergamon.

RABINOWITZ, A. (1981) 'The range of solutions: A critical analysis', in: GILLHAM, B. (Ed.) *Problem Behaviour in the Secondary School: A Systems Approach*, Beckenham, Croom Helm.

RAMSAY, P. (1983) 'Fresh perspectives on the school transformation–reproduction debate: A response to Anyon from the Antipodes', *Curriculum Inquiry*, 13, pp. 295–320.

REYNOLDS, D., SULLIVAN, M. and MURGATROYD, S.J. (1987) *The Comprehensive Experiment*, Lewes, Falmer Press.

RUTTER, M., TIZARD, J. and WHITMORE, K. (1970) *Education, Health and Behaviour*, London, Longman.

RUTTER, M., COX, A., TUPLING, C., BERGER, M. and YULE, W. (1975a) 'Attainment and adjustment in two geographical areas: 1. The prevalence of psychiatric disorders', *British Journal of Psychiatry*, **126**, pp. 493–509.

RUTTER, M., YULE, B., QUINTON, D., ROWLANDS, O., YULE, W. and BERGER, M. (1975b) 'Attainment and adjustment in two geographical areas: III. Some factors accounting for area differences', *British Journal of Psychiatry*, **126**, pp. 520–33.

RUTTER, M., MAUGHAN, B., MORTIMORE, P., and OUSTON, J. (1979) *Fifteen Thousand Hours: Secondary Schools and their Effects on Pupils*, London, Open Books.

SAMMONS, P., KYSEL, F. and MORTIMORE, P. (1983) 'Educational priority indices a new perspective', *British Educational Research Journal*, **1**, pp. 27–40.

VARLAAM, A. (1974) 'Educational attainment and behaviour', *GLC Intelligence Quarterly*, **29**, pp. 29–37.

WHELDALL, K. and MERRETT, F. (1988) 'Which classroom behaviours do primary school teachers say they find most troublesome?', *Educational Review*, **40**, pp. 13–27.

WOODS, P. (1984) *Parents and School: A Report for Discussion on Liaison Between Parents and Secondary Schools in Wales*, London, Schools Council.

YORK, R., HERON, J.M. and WOLFF, S. (1972) 'Exclusion from school', *Journal of Child Psychology and Psychiatry*, **13**, pp. 259–66.

6
The Children's Legal Centre: Evidence to the Elton Committee

Martin Rosenbaum

The Children's Legal Centre is concerned with all aspects of law and policy affecting children and young people in England and Wales. The Centre's role is to look at issues from the child's perspective, to ensure that the needs, interests and views of children are properly taken into account in public policy-making. Children too have rights which ought to be respected.

Introduction

The Children's Legal Centre is grateful for the Enquiry's invitation to submit our views. As requested our submission is presented according to the four key questions posed. We are pleased to note from these questions the systematic way in which the Committee is approaching its task and we are particularly pleased by the emphasis which the Committee has placed in its requests for submissions on the use of hard evidence to justify conclusions. Discipline in schools is a controversial area of public debate in which many extremely doubtful claims have achieved a great deal of publicity. Our education system will benefit greatly from a clear, thorough and rigorous analysis of the relevant evidence.

To state briefly the child's perspective on the Enquiry's remit would include making the following points. Schools should be places which children want to attend (some truancy statistics show how far we are from achieving this currently). Children benefit from an atmosphere in schools which promotes learning and enables them to develop their talents and their personality. They are victims if behaviour, which may originate from their peers or from adults, disrupts such an atmosphere. Children want, and are entitled to, interesting and well-prepared lessons which motivate them and their classmates. They want and are entitled to school rules which are well-publicized, fair and reasonable in themselves and are also enforced fairly and reasonably and they should be able to exercise freedom and take decisions for themselves in areas where rules are not necessary. It is wrong to assume that when teachers and pupils are in conflict it is the teacher who is necessarily in the right.

Many organizations are submitting evidence to this Enquiry — some representing teachers, parents, local education authorities, others promoting various educational interests. These organizations will naturally look at the issues from the perspective of those they represent. Pupils, however, at present have no organization of their own to represent their views, and we anticipate that, with some exceptions, most of the bodies making submissions will not be looking at the questions from the point of view of the children — who after all are the people for whose benefit schools exist. Because we anticipate that the approach underlying our evidence will probably not be reflected by many of the other submissions we have therefore felt it necessary to discuss some questions in a fair amount of detail, to ensure that a full range of opinions is available to the Enquiry and that the point of view of the child is fully considered.

Good behaviour and discipline

Good behaviour and discipline in a school involves all members of the school community, pupils, teachers and other staff, showing mutual respect and consideration for each other, creating collectively a pleasant and productive ethos in the school, and working together successfully in the common purpose of teaching and learning. Bad behaviour, which may come from the adults in the school as well as the children, or it may be adults who provoke it, is that which disrupts this state of affairs. It is important to acknowledge that the rules of behaviour in a community place obligations on all its members and in the case of schools not just on the pupils.

Good discipline must be based on self-discipline — which means each individual understanding and accepting rules to govern their own behaviour. This means in turn that in a self-disciplined community any necessary rules must be fair and reasonable for them to be accepted. The rule of fear is no substitute for self-discipline. Apart from anything else, those who are subject to it often seize the opportunity to commit any misdemeanour for which they believe they will not be caught; and this attitude may well remain with them when they leave the more closely regulated school environment. In other words, a school run on fear of sanctions can never inculcate in its pupils the sense of individual responsibility on which the Prime Minister, for example, places so much stress. Schools which concentrate on 'deterrents' will never teach their pupils moral values but only how not to get caught.

The 'discipline' problem

There is clearly some disruptive behaviour in schools. There always has been and doubtless there always will be in any institution which contains some people who are there not because they want to be, but because the law requires it; and who while they are there are required to do things which they do not want to do. There is no magic solution which will entirely eliminate all disciplinary problems from compulsory schooling.

Of course it is much more difficult to answer the question about the seriousness and extent of any discipline problem in schools. Conditions vary widely in the United Kingdom's 30,000 plus schools and the fact that incidents of a certain kind happen in some particular schools is by no means a necessary guide to the national picture. However, the public have undoubtedly been given the impression through recent well-publicized claims that there is an extremely serious and widespread and quite unprecedented problem of disruption. We believe that it is important to spell out three reasons why these claims should be treated with a great deal of scepticism. This is necessary to prevent claims which may well be myths becoming accepted without good reason and then taken for granted. There is also the risk that public concern which may not be justified by the facts could lead to the adoption of more authoritarian measures in schools which would be counter-productive as well as unfair and damaging to pupils.

The reasons for scepticism are firstly that there are many important voices denying the existence of such a serious and widespread problem but they get very little publicity; secondly that there have always been people concerned about widespread and serious disruption in schools; and thirdly that the surveys of increasing disruption which have created so much fuss have invariably turned out to be methodologically flawed and therefore quite unreliable.

The first important reason for scepticism about the discipline problem is that there are many who argue that the problem has been much exaggerated. It is necessary to draw particular attention to their views because, and this does not only apply to education, those who say things are dreadful and/or getting worse invariably get much more public attention than those who say things are all right and/or much the same as they always have been.

The Enquiry will of course be aware that last year's HM Inspectors' report *Good Behaviour and Discipline in Schools* stated: 'The overwhelming majority of schools are orderly communities in which there are good standards of behaviour and discipline; poor behaviour is unusual, and serious indiscipline a rare occurrence.' The Inspectorate is undoubtedly in a better position than any other body to form an overall objective view of the disciplinary situation in schools.

There are many other examples one could give but it is worth quoting another teaching union view from the speech given in February 1988 to the Institute for the Study and Treatment of Delinquency by Chris Lowe, Legal Secretary of the Secondary Heads Association (and Headteacher of Prince William Comprehensive, Peterborough):

> The recent outcry about violence in schools is alarmist and does a great disservice to the vast majority of British schools . . . Whether deliberately or not, the general public has been given the impression that our schools are violent places — and that is a travesty of the truth . . . It is time we said firmly and unequivocally that, compared with the violence present in many of our pupils' homes or in the streets, our maintained schools are

> havens of peace, quiet and order... In the millions of teacher–pupil
> contacts that take place daily in 30,000 schools, these instances [of bad
> behaviour] form a tiny proportion.

Mr Lowe added: 'Why then in the profession do we make such a song and dance about disruption and violence? I suggest that it is not because of any apparent increase, nor because teachers are any more or less able to deal with each incident as it arises.' The reasons Mr Lowe cites instead are: teachers feeling freer to talk about disruption; teachers being unsure what they can do by way of correction; teachers being too busy on other tasks to spend the necessary time; low morale in the profession; a feeling amongst teachers that they alone are blamed for the moral climate of the country; and a belief by teachers that too much is expected of them.

It is also clear that many members of other unions which have been publicizing instances of disruption are dissatisfied with the stance their leadership has taken, for example the NAHT members at their conference earlier in 1988 who said the problem was being exaggerated. To give one further but different kind of example the Independent reported (8 January 1988) that 'Researchers at Birmingham University found that, even in secondary schools, physical aggression was cited by fewer than 1 per cent of West Midlands teachers as a problem'.

To take the second point, it is important to set this issue in its historical context. Many who claim that discipline is sharply deteriorating forget — or perhaps choose to ignore — the extent to which there has always been concern about standards of behaviour in schools, including violence. Disruption, violence, vandalism and so on are unfortunately traditional aspects of the British education system.

In any case it is often not clear which period is in mind when it is alleged behaviour was significantly better. Five years ago? The 1970s? Before the permissive society? Perhaps even before the war? The historical record sadly does not lend credence to the idea that there was ever a golden age of school discipline. Clearly in this submission it is impossible to give a detailed historical account of British school discipline but we can say enough to cast doubt on the claims under consideration.

In 1983 for example the Assistant Masters' and Mistresses' Association issued a pamphlet 'Assaults on Teachers' which stated 'Teachers are often the victims of vicious attacks ... It is not unknown for parents to enter schools and attack the first teacher in sight'. In the 1970s there was certainly no shortage of news stories about school disruption: many of them around the start of the decade were inspired by the National Association of Schoolmasters which had been fighting a rearguard action against the raising of the school leaving age. A report on discipline produced in 1970 by the London 'Joint Four' (the then Association of Assistant Mistresses, Association of Head Mistresses, Assistant Masters' Association and Head Masters' Association) stated: 'There should be a national policy for the protection of teachers against abuse and assault ... The growing frequency of cases of assault on teachers by pupils must be stemmed'. Similarly a 1972 pamphlet 'Violence in Schools' issued by the NAS contained a survey reporting 178 cases of violence against secondary school teachers including assaults with knives and bottles, 176 cases of 'verbal violence' (obscene language and abuse), and forty-nine pupil attacks on primary school teachers.

A decade previously, the teacher unions had not asserted themselves in the same way but there are other sources. A 1962 article in the *British Journal of Sociology* ('The Sociology of a School' by John Webb) presents an account of 'what goes on in a large number of secondary modern schools for boys'. It says: 'Hostility between teachers and boys is the key factor . . . It is present whenever a teacher deals with boys but varies in intensity . . . The most common hostility lies between the mild and the ferocious and is, on the boys' side, almost a guerilla war against the teacher's standards'. The author gives one example of a boy with a flick-knife fighting a teacher and then describes as typical an incident in which a teacher grapples with one boy while another boy tries to spill ink on the teacher's suit.

This extract from a speech given to the Conservative Party Conference in 1959 is also remarkably similar to the kind of statements one hears today. Mr K.L. Lockstone said:

> To my mind, over the last twenty-five years we in this country, through misguided sentiment, have cast aside the word discipline, and now we are suffering for it . . . Ask the teaching profession what they think, and you will be told that they are not allowed to enforce discipline — or at least if they do, they stand every chance of a complaint from the parents and being brought before the management committee.

The National Foundation for Educational Research's 'Survey of Rewards and Punishments in Schools' in 1952 also provides striking echoes of other frequent contemporary claims — e.g. that children are disruptive at a younger age. It reported that: 'Chief Education Officers have noted an increase in the number of children, some of them less than seven years old, who are referred to Child Guidance Clinics as being out of control'. The report also refers to lax moral standards and parents who are 'actively antagonistic to the teachers and to the standards represented by the schools'. According to the report teachers want 'stricter home discipline and parental control', another familiar theme today.

If we want to continue our historical journey back before the war, then this NFER report also gives a schools inspector's description of an elementary school where 'during the 1930s parents of the pupils regularly visited the school to "have a go" at the head. Some of them had to be ejected forcibly from the school premises'. Or take Stephen Humphries' account of pre-war schooling (in 'Hooligans or Rebels — an Oral History of Working-Class Childhood and Youth 1889–1939') in which he writes: 'Among boys disobedience usually took the form of spontaneous and volatile outbursts of physical aggression, and they would disrupt lessons or seek immediate revenge on authoritarian teachers by throwing inkpots or by kicking or punching them.' Indeed this book gives several graphic first-person accounts of pupils kicking teachers and smashing up school desks, even whole classes cheering while an irate mother drags a teacher out of the classroom into the playground by her hair, and so on.

We can finish in Victorian times with a quote from Sir Rhodes Boyson who, writing in *The Spectator* (28 February 1970) described how 'my first deputy head told me that when he started teaching in 1890 in a small Lancashire textile town, he, along with other young teachers, dared not go to the station at the end of the school day without the presence of the headmaster or he would be attacked in the street by groups of boys throwing stones and sods of earth'. If one wished to go back further to the early nineteenth and late eighteenth centuries it is a well-known fact that full-scale riots — some put down by the army — were common at Harrow, Winchester and other major public schools, and that George III's standard question to boys at Eton was 'Have you had a rebellion lately?'

Of course all this information, although only a small selection of examples, is anecdotal and is not conclusive evidence on the growing or decreasing extent of school disruption. But it should at least make us think twice. The point is that there is no hard evidence from the past — even the recent past — about the extent of a discipline problem. The only possible verdict on whether it has significantly increased or decreased is 'not proven'.

The third point is that the well-publicized surveys which have undoubtedly fostered a public impression that there is widespread indiscipline in schools do not stand up well to critical examination. It is also the case that some of the publicity they have generated has presented a much worse picture of school life than even the proclaimed results of the surveys indicate. One particularly defective survey was that published by the Professional Association of Teachers last November. It has been claimed that this showed that 32 per cent of teachers had suffered physical violence at the hands of pupils. In fact this applied to 32 per cent of the 1500 PAT members who replied to the survey, 4 per cent of the total membership. Clearly those who had been attacked were much more likely to reply, so the sample is obviously completely unrepresentative. Those who responded and said they had been assaulted in fact amount to roughly 1 per cent of the union's membership. The most striking aspect of the survey is that 96 per cent of the members of the union which has recently made the most public fuss about this issue do not think violence and disruption is a sufficiently severe problem for them to take the effort to fill out a brief union questionnaire about it.

Other similar surveys have also been unreliable for various reasons. For example according to press reports the recent National Association of Head Teachers survey was only returned by 45 per cent of the heads it was sent to, and is therefore contaminated by self-selecting bias. Again it would be the heads who wanted to report increased problems who would have been much more likely to respond. Such surveys cannot be treated as representative and reliable unless they get much higher response rates. Similarly the Enquiry itself is doubtless aware that teachers, parents and others who believe that there is a serious and widespread discipline problem are much more likely to submit evidence to it than those who do not, and that those who submit evidence will therefore not constitute a representative sample.

The National Union of Teachers/NOP opinion poll published recently avoids this trap but falls into others. Respondents were apparently asked whether indiscipline was a regular or frequent occurrence in their school, but these terms are too vague and subjective to place much weight on the answers.

Other problems crop up with surveys which, again like the NUT poll, ask teachers to compare the situation today with their impressions of a previous time. This is an unreliable technique which probably reveals as much about the respondents' preconceptions as about anything else. Memories are often faulty. There is a tendency to see the past through the proverbial rose-tinted spectacles, well-documented with regard to youth violence and crime in Geoffrey Pearson's classic work *Hooligan*. There is also a tendency to see past incidents less seriously, sometimes as pranks say, rather than serious disruption. Futhermore it is possible that teachers may have become more sensitized to violence. This factor is acknowledged by AMMA, for example, in its 1983 pamphlet on assaults on teachers referred to above. Indeed, it is possible that increased concern about disruption could mainly reflect demands for better standards of behaviour. Finally, it would be naive to entirely ignore the possibility that some teachers may think that if they say disruption is increasing the ensuing publicity will help to ensure that they get paid more. In short there is no guarantee that the answers to such questions can be relied on. Some academic research claiming to measure increased disruption is also based on unreliable impressions of the past, as well as being very small-scale.

It is also interesting to note that the details of the press reports of the NUT and NAHT surveys suggest a much less disturbing picture than the impression given by the headlines. Since we have not seen the actual surveys we only have the press reports to go on but for example buried deep in *The Guardian*'s report (17 June 1988) of the NAHT survey was the statement: 'The vast majority of heads however said there had been either no increase or only a marginal increase in disruptive behaviour since 1985'.

What conclusions should be drawn from our explanations of the reasons for scepticism about claims regarding the discipline problem? First, let us say that there is no excuse for complacency. Some very unpleasant and vicious incidents have occurred in schools and it is important to try to prevent them. Later we explain what action we think should be taken to improve school discipline. Nevertheless the fact is that at far as we are aware there is no hard evidence for the claim that there is a serious and widespread and deteriorating discipline problem in our schools. This view is shared by HM Senior Chief Inspector Eric Bolton who told *The Sunday Times* (17 January 1988): 'Most teachers are not in a blackboard jungle situation. It is very difficult to discover the extent of school violence. Nobody keeps trustworthy or regular data. So it is impossible to say if the problem has got better or worse'. Similarly the recent research review from the Home Office Research and Planning Unit ('Schools, Disruptive Behaviour and Delinquency' by John Graham, published in May) concludes from its survey of the research that 'there is no clear evidence' for 'an increase in the prevalence of disruption in schools'.

It is essential that any research in this field is thoroughly and critically examined before any weight is placed on its results, and we are sure that the Enquiry will do this. Several leaky buckets placed one on top of another do not hold water; not do several surveys with similar apparent results, but holes in their arguments, lead one to a justified conclusion.

The causes of disruptive behaviour

Disruptive behaviour has many causes and not all of them are subject to the influence of schools or education policy-making. But it is clear that there are factors under the control of the school which can reduce — or increase — disruptive behaviour. In this submission we make no attempt to give a comprehensive account of the causes of disruption. Instead we concentrate on some factors which we believe play an important if partial role. We focus on these firstly because they are particularly significant when one looks at schools from the point of view of the pupils, which as explained peviously is our perspective, and secondly because they can be influenced by education policy-making.

There is a substantial amount of research on the causes of disruption and some consistent messages emerge from it. The research identifies a number of disparate causes. We will not present all the messages from this research which the Enquiry will presumably be examining, but just those relating to the factors we are concerned about. Some of the most important work comes from those researchers who have in the 1970s and 1980s focused on school effectiveness and compared schools in order to isolate the factors which make some schools more successful than others, after accounting for the nature of their intakes.

David Reynolds and others made a thorough study of several comprehensives in South Wales in the 1970s which had similar social and intellectual intakes. They found that schools which were more successful (i.e. had better classroom behaviour, less vandalism, less truancy, less juvenile delinquency, and better exam results) were characterized amongst other factors by a certain set of attitudes towards the pupils. These schools had more tolerant attitudes to the enforcing of certain rules regarding 'dress, manners and morals', low levels of institutional control, low rates of physical punishment (at that time in this area no school had abandoned it entirely) and a high proportion of pupils in authority positions.

David Reynolds draws the distinction between schools whose basic strategy is 'incorporation' and those whose is 'coercion'. The former involves concentration on developing good teacher–pupil relationships, giving pupils an active role in lessons, 'minimal use of overt institutional control (so that pupil behaviour was relatively unconstrained), low rates of physical punishment, a tolerance of a limited amount of 'acting out' (smoking, gum chewing), a pragmatic hesitancy to enforce rules which might have provoked rebellion, and an attempt to reward good behaviour rather than punish bad behaviour'.

On the other hand coercive schools were marked by 'high levels of institutional control, strict rule enforcement, high rates of physical punishment and very little tolerance of any acting out'. Reynolds concludes that there is a causal relationship and that coercive schools promote disruption and incorporative schools reduce it. (The quotes are from 'The effects of school — a radical faith re-stated' by David Reynolds and Michael Sullivan in *Problem Behaviour in the Secondary School* edited by Bill Gillham (Croom Helm, 1981), one of the many articles by Reynolds and others about this work. Incidentally the radical faith which is re-stated is that some schools are better than others and these differences between schools do make for important differences in the achievements and behaviour of their pupils).

A similar message is conveyed by the major study of twelve Inner London secondary schools by Michael Rutter, Barbara Maughan, Peter Mortimore and Janet Ouston, *Fifteen Thousand Hours: Secondary Schools and their Effects on Children*. Like the work of Reynolds and his colleagues, the investigation by Rutter and his team found firstly that 'secondary schools varied markedly with respect to their pupils' behaviour, attendance, exam success and delinquency'... 'even after taking into account differences in their intake' and secondly that these differences between school outcomes were systematically related to their characteristics as social institutions. Again they draw a causal relationship.

The conclusions of Rutter *et al.* included the following:

- That 'frequency disciplinary interventions' in the classroom are likely to be counter-productive;
- That 'the tensions and resentment which stem from the negative atmosphere created by constant nagging and reprimands may actually provoke and perpetuate disruptive behaviour';
- That 'an excessive use of punishments is likely to be discouraging and lead to low morale. Praise, rewards and encouragements need to outweigh negative sanctions';
- That 'children's behaviour was better in schools where teachers were readily available to be consulted by the children about their problems';
- That behaviour was better in schools 'in which a high proportion of children held some kind of position of responsibility in the school system';
- That 'unofficial' physical punishment is linked to worse behaviour. 'If teachers react with violence to provocation and disruptiveness this may well encourage pupils to do the same';
- That good schools provided 'pleasant working conditions' for their pupils including 'features such as access to a telephone, availability of refreshments and being allowed in the buildings during breaks'.

It is useful to cite above some of the most important research to provide support for our arguments in the next section, but of course we do not have the space to quote all the relevant studies with similar outcomes and in any case it is all directly accessible to the Enquiry. It is simpler to refer to the similar conclusions reached by the research review 'Schools, Disruptive Behaviour and Delinquency' published very recently in May 1988 by the Home Office Research and Planning Unit (Home Office Research Study 96, by John Graham). This report summarizes much of the relevant research which the Enquiry should consider and identifies from the research 'three main features of schooling as the most important influences' on disruptive behaviour and truancy — 'teaching skills and teacher/pupil relations; rewards, sanctions and rule enforcement; pastoral care and pupil welfare'. The report goes on to say:

Where rules are too frequent, too petty and insensitively enforced, incidents of disruptive behaviour are likely to flourish... Teachers need... to allow for the developing adult status of older pupils... Those teachers who... estabish stable, firm and friendly relationships with pupils based on mutal respect and trust are likely to be the most effective.

This Home Office research review also quotes other studies which show for example that confrontations between teachers and pupils are precipitated when teachers 'enforce rules perceived by pupils as illegitimate' and that teacher–pupil relationships are damaged by the enforcement of 'petty' rules. The latter study (Hargreaves *et al.*, *Deviance in Classrooms*) based on an analysis of two secondary schools in northern England details some characteristics of teachers who provoke deviance. They tend to regard pupils as confrontational and treat them with suspicion, and pick on certain pupils, humiliating them in front of the class and issuing them with ultimatums. Their more successful colleagues regard pupils as co-operative and avoid confrontation, treating pupils with respect and showing concern for their welfare.

The research review also draws points from a review of the literature on disaffection from school (A. Skinner, *Disaffection from School*) produced by the National Youth Bureau. This refers to 'research which illustrates the provocative effects of teachers who exercise excessively strict authority and the resentment experienced by pupils who are picked on unfairly, called names, physically manhandled, treated disrespectfully, persistently supervised and denied the opportunity to use their initiative'. There is also for example the work of Delwyn Tattum on the reasons disruptive pupils themselves give for their behaviour, among which 'not being treated with respect' and 'rules being applied unfairly and inconsistently' figure prominently. One should also note the North American research such as that by J.L. Epstein and J.M. McPartland which demonstrates a link between pupil participation in school decision-making and better relations between pupils and staff.

Outside the field of academic research a similar message in terms of the kind of role pupils should play in schools is advocated in the 'Burnage Inquiry' report: the report of the enquiry chaired by Ian MacDonald QC into the circumstances surrounding the death of Ahmed Ullah at Burnage High School, Manchester. The full report has not yet been published, but the recommendations in the extracts leaked to the *Manchester Evening News* (25 April 1988) included the following:

> We propose a democratically elected school students' union, to be resourced and provided with accommodation from the school establishment, and from whatever fund-raising they might do themselves. The students' union would be part of the 'umbrella working group' or 'school development council' and would have a share in the responsibility for the well-being of the school and would be involved in the shaping and reviewing of school policy on such issues as violence or racism. If a disciplined, well-organised, democratic and vibrant student union had been operating at Burnage High School, the school might have been able to avoid the great disruption of the events of March 1987. We believe that the rather belated attempt by that school to set up fifth-form student councils was a limited recognition of this need.

A final point which must be made is that children learn very powerfully by example: there is of course a vast amount of psychological evidence to confirm this. Teachers must, therefore, maintain high standards of behaviour themselves. In this context it is worth mentioning the research which has been done into children and smoking, since this is one of the aspects of schoolchildren's behaviour which has been examined in most detail. Studies on what schools can do to discourage, or encourage smoking, such as those carried out for the Health Education Council, have consistently found that a major influence on pupil smoking rates is whether or not teachers smoke at the school. In other words pupils are more likely to smoke if teachers do, and as the work of Rutter *et al.* confirmed, they are more likely to be late in a school where teachers are frequently late, and are more likely to be violent if teachers are violent. This reinforces the point made earlier that a school must be seen as a community of all its members, all of whom are bound by rules. Teachers who have double standards and whose implicit motto is 'do as I say, not as I do' undermine good school discipline.

Action which should be taken

As we have already said, there are many causes of disruptive behaviour and therefore there are many tactics one could use to reduce it. Our submission is not intended to provide a comprehensive strategy but rather it concentrates on some important factors which can be influenced by schools and education policy-making. It is clear from the evidence above that behaviour is better when schools:

- Treat pupils fairly and with respect;
- Strive to build co-operative rather then antagonistic teacher–pupil relationships;
- Do not impose petty and unnecessary rules;
- Have a tolerant and positive rather than punitive and authoritarian atmosphere;
- Are quick to reward and slow to punish;
- Give pupils responsibility and rights to active participation;
- Exhibit concern for pupils' welfare and responsiveness to their needs;
- Ensure that teachers themselves provide good models of behaviour.

It is not always easy to meet all of these criteria but we set out below some measures which we believe would help schools satisfy these aims and achieve better behaviour. We must emphasize that we support these measures not only because they would make schools more harmonious and productive places but also because they will provide rights which we believe pupils in principle are entitled to.

School rules

Schools should avoid petty and unnecessary rules. Where they exist these vary from school to school but the most common example which should be eliminated is compulsory school uniform. Punishment for not wearing school uniform is one of the most frequent causes of quite unnecessary hostility between teachers and pupils. In some schools it is enforced at a tremendous cost in terms of damage to teacher–pupil relationships and wasted time and effort. Schools who wish could have voluntary dress codes, but to punish pupils for not complying is making a mountain out of a molehill.

School rules which are necessary should be clearly and unambiguously stated and well-publicized so that pupils are fully aware of them. Another frequent cause of resentment among pupils is being punished for breaking a school rule they did not know existed. The Government should ensure that heads fulfil their obligations under Section 22 of the Education (No 2) Act 1986 to make school rules and disciplinary measures generally known within the school.

Disciplinary procedures

Any disciplinary procedures must be operated fairly. Schools must ensure that pupils are not punished for offences they did not commit and that any punishment is proportional to the offence involved. Pupils should be protected from degrading punishments and should have adequate appeal rights if their education is interrupted through being excluded from school.

This means, for example, that there should be an end to the practice of mass detentions, say of whole classes, where the particular culprit cannot be identified. There is no circumstance outside school where it would be considered acceptable to punish a whole group because of the actions of one or some of its members who cannot be identified. It is just as morally unjustifiable within school and quite rightly creates outrage amongst innocent pupils who are punished in this way. In a case two years ago (*Terrington v Lancashire Education Authority*, Blackpool County Court, 26 June 1986) the judge went much of the way in this direction when he said: 'Punishment must not be indiscriminate. A blanket detention such as the punishment of a whole class must only be used as a last resort, otherwise people who are quite innocent may be detained incorrectly and unlawfully'. However, the logic of the argument is that blanket punishments, when individual culprits cannot be identified, should be prohibited altogether. This is the only stance which is fair to the innocent.

Exclusion procedures are particularly important since they involve interrupting a pupil's education and some pupils are out of school for months as a result. The rights of pupils to natural justice in such circumstances were upheld in the recent case of a boy expelled from London Oratory School in Inner London. Mr Justice McCullough said there was no reason why

> the rules of natural justice, the rules of ordinary fair play, should not apply to the procedure for expelling a school-boy as to the procedure for sending down a university student . . . It must be right that a boy about to be expelled should know the nature of the accusation, have the opportunity to state his case and be judged by a tribunal which acted in good faith (*The Times*, 17 February 1988).

While of course pupils are sometimes suspended for extremely serious offences, sometimes they are suspended for very trivial ones. Examples which have come to the Centre's notice include the following:

- Frequent cases of pupils suspended for not wearing school uniform including for example a boy who was suspended for wearing the wrong colour raincoat on the way to and from school;
- Several instances of boys suspended because their hair had been cut too short and not being allowed back to school until it had grown to a length the headteacher considered sufficient;
- A boy suspended for buying an ice cream on his way home from a van outside the school gates in breach of the school's 'healthy eating' policy;
- A boy suspended (at a different school) for bringing bars of chocolate in with his sandwiches in his lunchbox;
- A boy suspended for what was described as 'a serious act of theft from a member of staff' and turned out to mean that he had eaten a teacher's apple.

Pupils and parents are entitled to adequate safeguards against unjustified suspensions and expulsions. The current rights should be extended by:

Providing a right of appeal to an independent body against short-term and indefinite exclusions as well as permanent ones (as already exists in Scotland);
Providing pupils under 18 with the right to initiate appeals against exclusion on their own behalf;
Providing pupils under 18 with the right to be present and be heard when their appeals are considered.

Attempts to weaken their existing rights should be resisted.

It is essential that schools and LEAs distinguish clearly between procedures for exclusion on disciplinary grounds and special needs provision. Removing pupils perceived as disruptive to segregated special schools or units is no panacea. The educational and equal opportunities arguments against segregrated schooling mean that the days of separate special schools are numbered. The tendency to exclude such pupils rather than try to meet their needs in the mainstream setting is an indication of failure. It may also reflect the failure of LEAs to use the 1981 Act framework for multi-disciplinary assessment to determine the additional support schools require to cater for the needs of such pupils. Concentrating pupils categorized as disruptive or having emotional and behavioural difficulties in separate schools or units implies accepting that their difficulties are not produced by inadequate or inappropriate educational provision.

'Informal' referrals to units, whether within school premises or grounds or separately housed, are not acceptable. Pupils in units generally have access to a very limited curriculum and correspondingly limited exam opportunities. Any such referral should be subject to 1981 Act assessment and placement procedures.

It is essential to resist any calls for the reintroduction of corporal punishment.

Research such as that by Davis Reynolds referred to earlier has consistently demonstrated that it is a counter-productive as well as a damaging and degrading form of punishment. It creates hostility and resentment and makes the use of violence seem acceptable. It was unfortunately predictable that some teachers who did not want it abolished would now be making claims about resulting difficulties. But the experience of those LEAs (over 30) who had already banned it successfully as well as that of every country in Europe demonstrates that it is entirely unnecessary. A glance at any punishment book would always show the same names again and again, sometimes for the same offences, demonstrating its ineffectiveness as a 'deterent'. In any case reintroduction is clearly impractical since the ruling of the European Court of Human Rights means it could only be brought back for some pupils — those whose parents were willing for them to be beaten.

Responsibility and participation

Pupils should have rights to involvement in school decision-making and mechanisms should be established to ensure this. The Government should lift the ban on under 18 school governors imposed by Section 15 of the Education (No 2) Act 1986 and legislate to include pupil governors on the governing bodies of secondary schools. Secondary schools should have school councils elected by pupils which would have a real say over important procedures. Pupils are more likely to accept such rules and procedures when they have been able to play a part in drawing them up.

Each LEA should establish a Pupils' Parliament, as for example the Inner London Education Authority did, which would be elected by secondary school pupils, possibly via their school councils, and consider motions relating to the LEA's policies. Motions passed should be considered by the education committee and the Parliament or a committee elected by it should be consulted on all educational decisions by the education committee.

The school system must also recognize the rights of pupils to have adequate choice over their courses to study. The Government's proposed National Curriculum is so prescriptive it will probably be disastrous from the point of view of preventing disruption in schools. As the School Curriculum Development Committee said in their response to the consultative paper on the National Curriculum last year, 'Pupil disaffection is likely to increase by their being required to continue the study of subjects in which they have demonstrated neither interest nor aptitude and which they feel is irrelevant to their plans for the future'. Forcing pupils to do the full range of subjects laid down in the National Curriculum all the way up to the age of 16 is bound to promote disruption especially among fourth and fifth year pupils who feel entitled to greater flexibility. We must just hope that the subject working groups will at least mitigate the situation by introducing as much flexibility as possible.

Complaints procedures

Pupils need a route by which grievances and complaints which cannot be resolved at school level can be aired and investigated. An education ombudsman service should be established to which pupils could complain about any aspect of school life. It is essential that the pupils themselves have direct access and the right to complain is not limited to their parents. This service could be an extension of the role of the local government ombudsmen or could be a separate body. Until one is established nationally, LEAs should set up their own. Such a service would help to prevent the build up of resentment and bitterness and would also ensure that where pupils had valid complaints the situation was put right.

School ethos

Schools should strive to create a positive and tolerant atmosphere as opposed to an authoritarian one, in terms of teacher–pupil relationships, procedures in the class-room and the role pupils have in lessons, and all other aspects of school life.

A charter of rights and responsibilities

One way to promote the measures we have listed would be for schools to draw up a *Pupils' Charter* — a charter which would specify rights and responsibilities for pupils. This would include for example, the right to ensure that any necessary school rules are reasonable, clearly stated and well-publicized; the right to ensure that any disciplinary procedures are operated fairly; the right to participate in school decision-making and to express opinions freely; the right to have access to a grievance procedure; etc. It would also include responsibilities for example to show concern for the welfare of others, to have respect for the property of others, and to co-operate in the educational process. Ideally the Charter would be extended so that it also laid down rights and responsibilities for school staff, to emphasize the extent to which the school should be one community.

Summary

The Children's Legal Centre's submission is based on the child's point of view. Children, too, have rights which ought to be respected.

Schools will only give pupils a sense of moral values and individual responsibility by developing self-discipline. Those which concentrate on 'deterrents' only teach how not to get caught. Creating self-discipline requires that school rules must be fair and reasonable and enforced fairly and reasonably.

There is no hard evidence that there is an unprecedented serious and widespread problem of disruption in schools. The well-publicized surveys which have claimed there is have been flawed, for reasons which include unrepresentative samples and vague and unreliable questions. The public have been misled by the publicity these surveys have created. Historically there has always been a problem to some extent and some important sources argue that today's problems have been much exaggerated.

Research into the causes of disruptive behaviour provides consistent messages. These include that behaviour is better when schools:

- Treat pupils fairly and with respect;
- Strive to build co-operative rather than antagonistic teacher–pupil relationships;
- Do not impose petty and unnecessary rules;
- Have a tolerant and positive rather than punitive and authoritarian atmosphere;
- Are quick to reward and slow to punish;
- Give pupils responsibility and rights to active participation;
- Exhibit concern for pupils' welfare and responsiveness to their needs;
- Ensure that teachers themselves provide good models of behaviour.

Disruption is caused by alienation and resentment. Schools which treat pupils with respect achieve better behaviour and create a better environment for learning. For discipline to work it must be fair and pupils must see it to be fair.

Measures to provide pupils with the rights they are entitled to also help to promote a harmonious and productive atmosphere in schools. Our recommendations include:

the elimination of petty and unnecessary rules including compulsory school uniform;

eliminating mass punishments;

extending the safeguards of pupils and parents against unfair suspensions;

pupil governors, school councils with significant powers, and LEA-organized Pupils' Parliaments;

introducing more flexibility into the National Curriculum;

setting up an 'education ombudsman' service for pupils' complaints;

drawing up charters of rights and responsibilities for pupils and school staff.

References

ASSISTANT MASTERS AND MISTRESSES ASSOCIATION (1983) *Assaults on Teachers*, London, AMMA.

BOLTON, E. (1988) 'School violence inquiry', *The Sunday Times*, 17 January.

BOYSON, R. (1970) 'Law and order in school', *The Spectator*, 28 February.

HUMPHRIES, S. (1970) *Hooligans or Rebels — An Oral History of Working-Class Childhood and Youth, 1889–1939*, Oxford, Basil Blackwell.

GRAHAM, J. (1988) *Schools, Disruptive Behaviour and Delinquency*, London, Home Office Research and Policy Unit, May.

LIELL, P. and SAUNDERS, J.B. (1986) 'Terrington v. Lancashire County Council, in *The Law of Education*, London, Butterworths.

LONDON 'JOINT FOUR' (1970) *Discipline*, London, 'Joint Four'.

LOWENSTEIN, L.F. (1972) *Violence in Schools*, Birmingham, National Association of Schoolmasters.

NATIONAL FOUNDATION FOR EDUCATIONAL RESEARCH (1952) *A Survey of Rewards and Punishments in Schools*, London, Newnes Educational Publishing.

PEARSON, G. (1983) *Hooligan*, London, Macmillan.

REYNOLDS, D. (1976) 'The delinquent school', in HAMMERSLEY, M. and WOODS, P. (Eds) *The Process of Schooling*, London, Routledge and Kegan Paul.

REYNOLDS, D. and SULLIVAN, M. (1981) 'The effects of school — A radical faith re-stated', in GILLHAM, B. (Ed.) *Problem Behaviour in the Secondary School*, Beckenham, Croom Helm.

RUTTER, M., MAUGHAN, B., MORTIMORE, P. and OUSTON, J. (1979) *Fifteen Thousand Hours*, London, Open Books.

SKINNER, A. (1983) *Dissaffection from School*, Leicester, National Youth Bureau.

WEBB, J. (1962) 'The sociology of school', *British Journal of Sociology*, 13, pp. 264–72.

7

The National Children's Bureau: Evidence to the Elton Committee

Ronald Davie

The National Children's Bureau is one of the country's leading independent agencies concerned with the education, care and health of children. Its corporate membership of 500 includes most of the statutory authorities, voluntary and professional bodies involved in children's services in the U.K. Its primary activities are research; development work; information dissemination; and policy analysis and review.

Introduction

The response of the Bureau to the four questions posed by the Committee is as follows:

Definition of good behaviour and discipline (and their opposites) in the school context

Definitions of such terms can be very simplistic and the value laden implications of 'good' and 'bad' in this context might not be helpful. In particular, there is a danger of seeing good behaviour by pupils as that which is merely compliant and conforming, which is comfortable for and acceptable to teachers; and of viewing discipline as a system of control which brings about such compliance.

It has also to be said that what is acceptable and appropriate behaviour for one teacher or school may not be for another. Furthermore, the particular teaching situation as well, of course, as the age of the child are relevant factors. The behaviour of children in school therefore has always to be viewed in context and related to educational aims and objectives.

With this in mind, we would favour a definition of desirable behaviour by pupils which refers to the degree and extent to which the behaviour (individual and corporate) enables and promotes appropriate, constructive and healthy learning.

Such behaviour will be embedded in corresponding underlying attitudes, which can only grow out of a relationship of mutual respect and regard between teacher and pupil.

As we have indicated above, there is a temptation to define 'discipline' narrowly in terms of sanctions and control, of school rules and regulations. Whilst these concepts and the realities which lie behind them are an important part of the framework which a school sets for its pupils in an attempt to ensure that effective learning and teaching takes place, the picture is more complex than this (Docking, 1980).

In particular, it ignores the fact that self-discipline for its pupils must be the ultimate goal for which schools are striving. It also tends to emphasize punishment and sanctions at the expense of reward, recognition and encouragement. However, it should not be overlooked that the latter can be instruments of control — often more effective ones, too.

Discipline in schools is therefore quite a complex concept and issue. It cannot be separated meaningfully from other aspects of school life, nor can strategies for responding to the issue be viewed or developed in isolation. We are inclined to define effective and productive discipline in schools as the various means by which desirable pupil behaviour — as defined earlier — is facilitated and encouraged.

Is there in your view currently a discipline problem in schools and, if so, how serious and widespread is it?

It is not possible to give a rigorous or unequivocal answer to this question. Such evidence as there is from those who can view the situation with some objectivity, e.g. HMI (DES, 1987), suggests that 'the overwhelming majority of schools are orderly communities'. A recent enquiry in Northern Ireland tended to confirm that conclusion in the province, although 'conclusive evidence is not easy to obtain' (DENI, 1987).

Two enquiries carried out recently by the Professional Association of Teachers and the NAS/UWT are unfortunately methodologically unsound, since they rely upon returns from teachers who chose to respond to a general request for completion of a questionnaire. In addition, some of the questions put to the teachers lacked the rigour needed for an objective enquiry. The most recent enquiry, undertaken by NOP on behalf of the NUT, is clearly a more structured piece of work. However, the questions used in this survey also appear highly subjective. Nevertheless, it strengthens the case for a properly constituted and independent research study. We return to this point shortly.

One member of the National Children's Bureau Board of Management, an experienced teacher–trainer with special knowledge of this topic, reports that his in-service training students feel that the problem of misbehaviour and disruption is on the increase, although he emphasizes that their perception and the reality may not necessarily be the same. The other teacher–trainer on the Board, specializing in primary work, reports:

> Excluding some specific inner city areas, my visits around the country to primary schools do not immediately cause me to think that a 'discipline problem' exists.

In summary, then, there is no clear evidence for any serious or widespread prevalence of serious disruption or violence in schools, nor for any significant increase in such behaviour. There may well be cause for genuine concern but this is most likely to be restricted to particular areas and particular schools. The claims by some that there is a national crisis and that chaos reigns are alarmist and without foundation.

However, this should not be cause for complacency, for a number of reasons. First, our ignorance on such an important issue is inexcusable. The DES should as a matter of urgency commission a research study to investigate this question. Furthermore, the methodology for such a study should be designed to permit replication at intervals in order to keep the situation under review. In this context, the Department's recent reversal of a prior decision to fund some research on pupils with emotional and behavioural difficulties has baffled the research community and seems highly regrettable.

Secondly, in this area, a relatively few pupils can have a damaging effect out of all proportion to their numbers, so the fact that the overwhelming majority of pupils present few problems may be less relevant that at first it seems. Thirdly, there can be little doubt that substantial numbers of teachers take the view that there *is* a significant and growing problem; therefore, that percpetion — valid or not — must be confronted in its own right.

> *What are in your view the principal causes of disruptive incidents and misbehaviour by pupils? What evidence is there to substantiate any causal connections that you may be suggesting?*

The extensive literature on children's emotional and behaviour problems is no doubt readily available to the Committee and does not need summarizing here. However, this tends to focus on children with special educational needs, many of whom will still be in special schools or units, although trends to integrate such pupils into mainstream schools without adequate staffing and support services are likely to cause difficulties. The remit of the Committee on the other hand is centred on more normal problems of misbehaviour and disruption in mainstream schools.

Secondly, this literature largely concentrates upon the social, socio-economic and familial factors which may lead to behaviour problems. Whilst such factors are of undoubted importance, schools have little or no control over them and therefore must primarily be concerned with what can be achieved within their own walls to provide the best preventive, supportive and responsive strategies.

The literature in this latter area is less extensive and more recent. Again, no doubt the Committee will have its own resources to synthesize this, but the principal conclusion to emerge from these studies (Rutter *et al.*, 1979; Davie *et al.*, 1984 and 1985; Reynolds, 1985 and 1988) is that *what* schools offer, and *how* they offer it, has a significant impact not only upon pupils' learning but on their behaviour also. These and other references confirm what every practitioner and every parent knows, namely, that the leadership and example set by the head-teacher and senior colleagues, the effectiveness of the various systems in the school, the consistency with which the whole staff apply and interpret procedures and rules, the ways in which the school makes clear that it cares about its pupils and their work, are profoundly important in determining the standards of academic performance and of behaviour and relationships throughout the school.

Finally, to answer this question more directly, the principal causes of disruptive incidents and misbehaviour by pupils will vary from child to child, from situation to situation and from school to school, both as regards extra-school factors, intra-school factors and the interaction between the two. However, the kinds of school factors identified above are in our view ones for which a causal connection is strongly indicated. No doubt there will be some evidence submitted to the Committee which will point out that these kinds of connections established by research thus far are correlational and not necessarily causal. Whilst this is true, the fact that the research findings tend to confirm practical experience should permit positive planning and action on the basis of the findings — at the same time, building in the essential monitoring and evaluation.

> *What action could be taken by relevant organizations and individuals (e.g. teachers, parents, local education authorities, the Government, etc.) to promote an orderly atmosphere in schools? What evidence is there to suggest such action would be effective?*

Many specific suggestions and courses of action have been advanced by members of the National Children's Bureau, which range from involving school and community health staff more to encouraging schools to use rewards much more extensively, since as one such member reminded us about a recent piece of research:

> In schools where the headteachers emphasised punishments more than rewards, pupils' progress tended to be inhibited; the greater the number of punishments listed, the more negative were the effects (Mortimore *et al.*, 1988).

However, in the time available — and perhaps in any event — we felt it best to summarize our response to this question in nine major points:

1. General exhortations by the Committee — or by Ministers — to parents or to teachers about the necessity to 'improve standards of behaviour' etc. are unlikely to be effective or of value.
2. The clear message needs to be conveyed to schools, by the Committee in the first instance, that although a number of the familial and other factors which may predispose some pupils to disruption and misbehaviour in school are largely outside the school's control, there is now a great deal of

evidence to indicate that the way a school is led and organized and the quality of the relationships which are developed between staff and pupils are of very considerable importance in determining the behaviour of pupils. Further, this behaviour cannot meaningfully be viewed — nor steps be taken to improve it — in isolation. It is in particular related to the relevance of the curriculum and also to the general ethos of the school. It therefore needs to be tackled in the context of what has come to be termed *whole-school policy.*

3. Local education authorities have an important role to play here in helping their schools to make a rigorous assessment of their problems, procedures and policies; assisting them, where necessary, in the formulation of strategies to tackle any problems; and further assisting and supporting them, as necessary, in implementing and in monitoring such strategies. The LEA's role in this should be supportive and sympathetic. At the same time it should be more proactive and firmer than has often been the tendency in the past. This is, of course, a sensitive issue because, given our system, the effectiveness of headteachers will be under scrutiny and they in particular will need to be consulted and may need professional support in such an exercise. In addition, the teaching unions will need to be consulted. The understanding, co-operation and active involvement of school governors will also be necessary.

4. Two areas of teacher training need to be given higher priority. First is classroom management and control. At the initial training level, for example, recent central directives have once more fuelled a tendency regrettably present in many training institutions to give more time, resources and status to subject studies at the expense of classroom management skills and practical experience. At the in-service level, too, both within schools in their procedures for guiding probationary and younger teachers, and at the local authority level in their INSET priorities, classroom management and skills seem not to be taken very seriously. The other neglected training area, albeit gaining some ground of late, is that of management and organizational development as related to schools as institutions.

5. One specific course of action which we would urge is the encouragement of schools to find ways of listening to and heeding the views of pupils in relation to school procedures, policies and curriculua. School councils are not the only, nor necessarily the best, way of achieving this. Tutorial lessons and House meetings, for example, can also be used for this purpose and questionnaires, especially if they are constructed in consultation with pupils, can be particularly valuable. The experience of schools which have used these and other methods to tap the views of pupils is that the responses are on the whole frank, honest, perceptive and useful. A working group of the NCB's Children's Policy Review Group is currently gathering evidence on this issue.

6. We have thus far said little about the contribution of parents but we regard it as axiomatic that the more schools can succeed in actively involving

parents in formulating and reviewing their policies and procedures, the more understandable, acceptable, and successful they are likely to be. Again, however, we would caution against the presentation of this issue to parents as merely one of the rules, regulations and sanctions. Furthermore, if the involvement of parents is seen merely, for example, in terms of a circular letter from the school setting out its rules and procedures and inviting parents' co-operation, it is unlikely to be seen as partnership.

7. It seems to us that sufficient is now known about the nature of the problems in schools and the practical possibilities for promoting institutional change in schools, including the ideas expressed in paras. 2–6, so that a small national development team might usefully be established to help bring about such change. The National Children's Bureau would be happy to discuss this idea further with the Committee, if the Committee wished, and in any event to be associated with any such initiative.

8. One longer term strategy which should be given higher priority by schools is the teaching of personal and social education and preparation for parenthood. This is desirable for a number of reasons and in our view it should be included as a subject area in the core curriculum (NCB, 1987). However, it has particular value in this context because parenting skills in the next generation of parents can help facilitate healthy learning and adjustment in children and can prevent many of the problems which otherwise schools have to deal with.

9. The Government also has an important role to play in this area. We have made it clear that desirable behaviour and appropriate discipline in schools is inextricably bound up with the other important aspects of school life: academic curricula and pastoral care; organizational systems and personal relationships; the perception of the pupils and the morale of the teachers. In our judgment, morale and job satisfaction are rather low in the teaching force at present. The nature and extent of new legislation, with the Education Reform Act still to come, plus the not too distant industrial action, all set against the changing role and status of teachers in society over the past twenty to thirty years have resulted in an unsettledness which has undermined confidence. The Government has an important part to play in restoring this confidence and improving job satisfaction. The Government's declared intention of raising the quality of education will not be achieved unless this can be done. And the quality of education is not to be measured simply in terms of pupils' attainment, however well assessed, but also in the quality of respect and regard implicit in the person-to-person behaviour seen in schools.

The final question has to do with evidence. The kernel of the problem, leaving aside the macro issues referred to in the previous paragraph, is how to facilitate constructive change in schools. A recent Home Office review (Graham, 1988) comments that 'initiating change in schools is complex and fraught with difficulties, particularly with respect to behavioural problems'. There is very little hard evidence on this question, although as indicated earlier (para. 7), in our view enough is known of the practical possibilities to justify the establishment of a national development team to help facilitate the process and to provide a national database for local initiatives and results. In addition, more research in this area would undoubtedly be of value.

Ouston *et al.*, (1985) did some useful work based upon some of the secondary schools in the earlier study by Rutter *et al.*, (1979). However, perhaps the best documented attempt to promote institutional change in schools with particular reference to behaviour problems was undertaken by Davie and his colleagues in Cardiff. The evaluation of that attempt (Davie *et al.*, 1984 and 1985) documented an encouraging degree of success, most of which was shown to have been sustained some six years later (manuscript in preparation).

References

DAVIE, R., CALLELY, E.M. and PHILLIPS, D.D. (1984) *Evaluation of INSET Course on Behaviour Problems*, (A Report Submitted to the Welsh Office.) Cardiff, Department of Education, University College.

DAVIE, R., PHILLIPS, D. and CALLELY, E. (1985) *Change in Secondary Schools*, Cardiff, Department of Education, University College. (Shortened version of above).

DEPARTMENT OF EDUCATION AND SCIENCE (1987) *Good Behaviour and Discipline in Schools*, A report by H.M. Inspectors, London, HMSO.

DEPARTMENT OF EDUCATION FOR NORTHERN IRELAND (1987) *Report of the Working Party on Discipline in Schools in Northen Ireland*, Belfast, HMSO.

DOCKING, J. (1980) *Control and Discipline in Schools*, London, Harper and Row.

GRAHAM, J. (1988) *Schools, Disruptive Behaviour and Delinquency: A Review of Research*, Home Office Research and Planning Unit, London, HMSO.

MORTIMORE, P., SAMMONS, P., STOLL, L., LEWIS, D. and ECOB, R. (1988) *School Matters: The Junior Years*, Wells, Open Books.

N.C.B. (1987) *The National Curriculum 5–16: Response to the Department of Education and Science and Welsh Office Consultation Document*, London, National Children's Bureau.

OUSTON, J., MAUGHAN, B. and RUTTER, M. (1985) *Innovation and Change in Six Secondary Schools*, Report to the Department of Education and Science, London, HMSO.

REYNOLDS, D. (ed.) (1985) *Studying School Effectiveness*, Lewes, Falmer Press.

REYNOLDS, D. (1988) 'Changing comprehensive schools', *Children and Society*, **2**, pp. 68–77.

RUTTER, M., MAUGHAN, B., MORTIMORE, P. and OUSTON, J. (1979) *Fifteen Thousand Hours: Secondary Schools and their Effects on Children*, London, Open Books.

8
National Association for Pastoral Care in Education: Evidence to the Elton Committee

Chris Watkins

The National Association for Pastoral Care in Education was established in 1982, and commands a membership of over 2,500, the majority of whom work in secondary schools. It is an organization that is managed nationally, regionally, and through local groups. The Association was established to support the pastoral aspects of the teacher's role, and in particular, those aspects recently stated in the new conditions of service as the professional duties of teachers.

The Association is uniquely well placed to submit evidence to the Elton Committee on discipline because many of its members are in positions of responsibility in the pastoral care system of secondary schools. In their roles as tutors, heads of year or house, as deputy heads, they are able to observe and enagage in responding to many of the disruptive incidents in our schools. In fact, it is not uncommon to see the role of tutors described in terms of a responsibility for welfare and discipline of pupils. Pastoral care systems in school are seen by the Association to have the goals of encouraging everyone in a school or college to foster a caring and orderly environment within which all students can exercise initiative and responsibility, and grow socially, emotionally, intellectually and morally. These aims are set out in the Association's 1986 publication called *Preparing for Pastoral Care: In-Service Training for the Pastoral Aspect of the Teachers' Role*.

Introduction

It is the view of the National Association of Pastoral Care in Education that a positive contribution to understanding, and the debate about school discipline, can come out if the Elton Committee utilizes this opportunity to disseminate some of the known effective practices which some schools have developed in recent years. NAPCE welcomes the Committee's emphasis on collecting evidence, and on asking contributors to specify the evidence which leads to their views. School discipline is, however, a topic that engages the emotions, and as a result, there is the danger that evidence collected will in itself be selected, and a further risk that proposals will be based on what is a limited view of the problem. As in other areas of disturbing behaviour, it is all too easy to give excessive weight to those that shout the loudest, calling for something to be done, and who thereby promote the existence of a problem without clear evidence of its scale or seriousness. NAPCE also welcomes the inclusion in the Committee's terms of reference of a wide range of stake holders in the education system: central government, local authorities, voluntary bodies, governors, headteachers, teachers and parents. The Association takes the view that when these different groups act in effective partnership then schools are characterized by having fewer discipline problems, while conversely, when there is conflict between these parties then pupil behaviour may well mirror it.

Responses to the committee's four main questions

The first question concerns the definition of good behaviour and discipline, and their opposites in the context of a school. In the opinion of the Association, it is not meaningful to give a list of good behaviours. The meaning of behaviour varies according to many features, including the context, and we can look at this in terms of pupils singing in a maths lesson, a music lesson or in the headteacher's room, and the difference in meaning that this particular behaviour has in each of these contexts. It is meaningful to say that undisciplined behaviour is generally that which disrupts the teacher's goals and the teaching process. This definition can incorporate the fact that behaviour which is seen as indisciplined can vary across time, place, person, and victim. Evidence from the Brunel University Education Studies Unit (Bird, *et al.*, 1980), suggested that there was a trend in the general sorts of behaviours which teachers were likely to define as disruptive. These included refusal to be taught, or to obey, to work, or as a response to authority. Also included in the definition is talking and rowdy behaviour and this, together with the different kinds of refusal, were found by the Brunel researchers to cover half of the reported disruptive incidents. Disruptive behaviour also refers to pupils using bad language, being insolent, slow in settling down to work, lateness for lessons, and the throwing of objects in classrooms. Behaviours which are defined as indisciplines, therefore, occur in a context both of the school and individual classrooms, and any attempt to understanding them should start with an understanding of these respective contexts.

The Elton Committee is enquiring as to whether currently there is a discipline problem in schools and whether it is serious and widespread. The Association knows no systematic convincing evidence that could lead to the conclusion that there is more indisciplined behaviour in schools currently than there has been at any other time. Although there are occasional attempts to put forward this argument, members of the Association do not believe that the systematic data which would be needed to support this view is available, in relation to both the present and past. Where there have been surveys of discipline problems in recent years these have typically suffered from a loaded approach aand loaded questions.

The evidence from the National Association of Pastoral Care in Education

Membership is not direct but from the Association's conferences on this particular theme. It was found that such a theme did not regularly attract greater numbers to these conferences than other areas of school management, such as personal social education, and school guidance. This has happened despite the fact that the membership of the Association is closely associated with the phenomena of discipline and behaviour in schools on a daily basis. The impression is that this concern about behaviour and discipline stands evenly alongside a number of other concerns. This view of the Association is consistent with that put forward by HMI in their Report (DES, 1984) when they published a review of published reports by Her Majesty's Inspectors. The Association is also aware of historical evidence that showed that phenomena of hooliganism were a feature of the Victorian era (Pearson, 1983).

The NAPCE considers that the multiple causes of disruption in schools can be encompassed under three headings: social issues, school issues and personal issues. The Association considers it wrong to ignore the social contexts of the school, and in the possible contribution to school and discipline, features such as youth employment and the more widespread polarization in society have their effect. The Association draws attention to the evidence which appears in documents viewing causes of disruptive behaviour in terms of *within* the pupil in the home background. But as teachers, members of the Association are also aware that there is evidence that does not support this tendency in our thinking (Dierenfield, 1982). Pupils who are associated with behaviour problems in primary schools are not the pupils who are associated with problems in secondary schools (Mortimore, 1980). When disruptive incidents do occur they do engage over time more than a tiny minority of pupils (Lawrence *et al.*, 1981). Teachers and parents describe different behaviours in young people as problematic (Graham and Rutter, 1970). Pupils from the full range of social backgrounds express similar disaffection with the later years of schooling (ILEA, 1984).

With this evidence in mind the Association considered a range of aspects. Schools in the same area with comparable intakes are associated with different delinquency rates (Power, 1976). Schools in similar areas show large and consistent differences in the number of pupils excluded or suspended on disciplinary grounds (Galloway, *et al.*, 1982). A number of aspects of pupils behaviour vary across schools and may be related to school climate or school ethos (Rutter, *et al.*, 1979). These are all aspects of schools.

If we consider organization and curriculum within schools then we find that schools which group pupils according to ability are associated with higher disruption in the lower bands (Lawrence, *et al.*, 1981). Most schools find more disruptive incidents in the final years of compulsory schooling, where attention can be drawn to the curriculum. If we look at aspects of classroom interaction and teaching methods then the evidence of studies of classroom behaviour (Kounin, 1976) leads to the conclusion that the action teachers take in response to a discipline problem has no consistent relationship with their managerial success. However, what teachers do before misbehaviour occurs is crucial in achieving success. Some research data suggests that whole class teaching methods are associated with greater incidents of disruption than group work methods. There is also evidence (Clarke, 1981) which suggests that hard strategies on the part of teachers are less likely to lead to the diminution of disruptive incidents than soft or discursive strategies.

In relation to action that is required to promote an orderly atmosphere in schools there needs to be action that is long-term and developmental rather than short-term and reactive in responses on the part of central government, LEAs, schools and teachers. In relation to central government action it is important that the status and standing of our education system is maintained to a high level in the eyes of all who have a stake in it. Continued challenges to the professional standing of teachers will not help (DES, 1988) nor does the continued lack of opportunity for young school leavers (Coffield, *et al.*, 1986). Schools are presently being subjected to a large number of changes initiated from outside and this can lead to extra stress for teachers (Health Education Authority, 1988). If the stress is not alleviated by support then there is a risk of increased under-achievement and polarization within and across schools. Poorer standards of behaviour could result. In relation to the curriculum of schools, a curriculum which meets the needs of young people, is flexible and engaging, and which is associated with the appropriate teaching methods and valuing of achievements, will reduce disaffected behaviour by pupils. The government needs to be alert to the danger that an excessive emphasis on a fixed curriculum, with imposed achievement targets, will increase disaffected behaviour in pupils. The government now has considerable control over the content of in-service training for teachers and it should set a continuing national priority to address the aspects of school behaviour and its multiple causes. If the government is concerned to promote an informed view of school discipline it will fund appropriate research.

Action that can be taken by Local Education Authorities is covered by support to schools, the question of suspensions and exclusions, and staffing. LEAs should insist that in-service and staff development is available to promote positive discipline. This should be reflected in local authorities for GRIST and should include training in the relation between pastoral care and discipline. Local LEAs should promote a process of positive self-review in schools on areas associated with discipline. LEAs should maintain the spirit of the Warnock Report, and the 1981 Education Act, and support provision in the ordinary schools as a general priority. In relation to suspensions and exclusions, LEAs should investigate and experiment with new practices regarding exclusion, so that this really is a last resort, and ensure that some schools do not over use it. Local research is urgently needed on school differences. In relation to staffing, LEAs should make sure that their staffing priorities for schools include consideration of the team and its leaders which are involved in promoting positive discipline. With regard to action that can be taken by schools and teachers, then schools should review and up-date their long-term staff support provision and take seriously the pastoral care of staff. They should continue the process of curriculum review with an emphasis on the affiliation of pupils. There is a need to prioritize some time for staff to review and develop teaching methods through staff workshops, for example; also to develop effective mechanisms for gathering and discussing clear information (Watkins and Wagner, 1987) on patterns of discipline. Schools should clarify the positive long-term role of pastoral care (Galloway, 1983) in relation to patterns of discipline pertaining to achievement, and discourage over-emphasis on short-term crisis management. It is necessary to clarify the role and importance of the form tutor as a first point of regular contact and information regarding individual pupils and discourage extensive referral of pupils. Schools should review formal rules and prune counterproductive examples. They should also promote structured tutorials for pupils to reflect on, and give their perspectives on patterns of behaviour and discipline in school. With all this, parents' advice and co-operation should be enlisted and valued through frequent informal contact. In a concluding section in the Association's evidence to the Elton Committee the following observations were made:

1. LEA statistics on suspensions and exclusions are not a good indicator of pupil behaviour and tend to reflect the operation of divergent local and school policies and practices. Like all official statistics on deviance, they reflect variation over time which are not linked to variations in pupil behaviour, for example, trends in teachers' tolerance across terms or a school having a drive on disruptive behaviour. Statistics on the exclusion of black pupils demonstrate that teachers' and schools' perceptions are at work in such figures (Commission for Racial Equality, 1986)

2. LEA and school policies on discipline can have some positive effects through the process by which they are drawn up. If this process is consultative and discursive it can aid the school's coherence in general terms. It is disturbing to note that the Elton Committee focuses on policies for excluding pupils and not on policies for achieving positive discipline.

3. The Elton Committee enquiry concerning in-service training, which is specifically rated to classroom control, could be counterproductive if such training were narrowly conceived. Much in-service training on management, curriculum and teaching methods, pastoral care, and on individual pupils has clear pay off for positive discipline in schools.

4. The Elton Committee enquiry concerning alternative provision for pupils is founded on the view that particular pupils are responsible for indiscipline, that they can be identified, and that they should not be taught in the ordinary school. This is a partial and questionable view. There is growing evidence to show that alternative provision in ineffective in the long term, since it tends to fill up in the short term and stimulates further demand for such provision. Other evidence (Daines, 1981) suggests that alternative provision is ineffective in the short-term, since problem behaviour reappears in connection with over 60 per cent of pupils who return from such provision.

References

BIRD, C., CHESSUM, R., FURLONG, J. and JOHNSON, D. (1980) *Disaffected Pupils*, Brunel University, Education Studies Unit.

CLARKE, D.D. (1981) 'Disruptive incidents in secondary school classrooms: a sequence analysis approach', *Oxford Review of Education*, 7, pp. 111–17.

COFFIELD, F., BORRILL, C. and MARSHALL, S. (1986) *Growing Up at the Margins*, Milton Keynes, Open University Press.

COMMISSION FOR RACIAL EQUALITY (1986) *Suspensions and Exclusions in Birmingham LEA*, London, CRE.

DAINES, R. (1981) 'Withdrawal units and the psychology of problem behaviour', in GILLHAM, B. (Ed.) *Problem Behaviour in Secondary Schools*, Beckenham, Croom Helm.

DEPARTMENT OF EDUCATION AND SCIENCE (1984) *Education Observed No. 2*, Review of published reports by HMI, London, HMSO.

DEPARTMENT OF EDUCATION AND SCIENCE (1988) *Qualified Teacher Status: A Consultative Document*, London, HMSO.

DIERENFIELD, R.B. (1982) *Classroom Disruption in English Comprehensive Schools*, St. Paul Minnesota, Macalasater College Education Department.

GALLOWAY, D., BALL, T., BLOMFIELD, D. and SEYD, R. (1982) *Schools and Disruptive Pupils*, London, Longman.

GALLOWAY, D. (1983) 'Disruptive pupils and effective pastoral care', *School Organisation*, 3, pp. 245–54.

GILLHAM, B. (1984) 'School organisation and the control of disruptive incidents', in FRUDE, N. and GAULT, H. (Eds) *Disruptive Behaviour in Schools*, Colchester, Wiley.

GRAHAM, P. and RUTTER, M. (1970) 'Selection of children with psychiatric disorders', in RUTTER, M., TIZARD, J. and WHITMORE, K. (Eds) *Education, Health and Behaviour*, London, Longman.

HEALTH EDUCATION AUTHORITY (1988) *Stress at Work*, London, HEA.

INNER LONDON EDUCATION AUTHORITY (1984) *Improving Secondary Schools*, Research Studies, London, ILEA.

KOUNIN, J.S. (1976) *Discipline and Group Management in Classrooms*, New York, Holt, Rinehart and Winston.

LAWRENCE, J., STEED, D. and YOUNG, P. (1977) *Disruptive Behaviour in a Secondary School*, Educational Studies Monograph No. 1, University of London, Goldsmiths College.

LAWRENCE, J., STEED, D. and YOUNG, P. (1981) *Disruptive Children — Disruptive Schools?* Beckenham, Croom Helm.

MORTIMORE, P. (1980) 'Misbehaviour in schools', in UPTON, G. and GOBELL, A. (Eds) *Behaviour Problems in the Comprehensive School*, Cardiff, Faculty of Education, University College.

PEARSON, G. (1983) *Hooligan: A History of Respectable Fears*, London, Macmillan.

POWER, M.J., ALDERSON, M.R., PHILLIPSON, C.M., SCHOENBERG, E. and MORRIS, J. (1967) 'Delinquent Schools', *New Society*, 19th October.

RABINOWITZ, A. (1981) 'The range of solutions: a critical analysis', in: GILLHAM, B. (Ed.) *Problem Behaviour in Secondary Schools*, Beckenham, Croom Helm.

RUTTER, M., MAUGHAN, B., MORTIMORE, P. and OUSTON, J. (1979) *Fifteen Thousand Hours*, London, Open Books.

WATKINS, C. and WAGNER, P. (1987) *School Discipline: A Whole-school Approach*, Oxford, Blackwell.

9
Oxfordshire LEA:
A Response to the Elton Committee Enquiry

Tim Brighouse and Neville Jones

Following discussions with colleagues in the Oxfordshire Education Service the following responses are made in relation to the specific issues raised.

Good behaviour and discipline in schools are encapsulated in that which:

1. enables, enhances and secures positive participatory learning between individuals and within groups;
2. values the views of others and makes use of interaction;
3. results in the pupil's self esteem, and his/her esteem for others;
4. enables an effective learning partnership to exist between teacher and pupil;
5. allows pupils to be interactive in all aspects of their learning so that behaviour standards are self set and not determined largely by external deterrents, for example, sanctions and punishments.

The discipline problem is comparatively modest in the county based on teacher reports and the number of pupil suspensions. It is estimated that it is no greater than was experienced in the grammar schools and secondary schools in the 1950s.

The breakdown of discipline, where it occurs, is usually symptomatic of the breakdown of relationship between pupil/school as represented by the teacher. The solution is to be found in this area.

Major causes of disruptive incidents and behaviour spring from:

1. Pupils' expectations, learning needs and interests not being satisfied by the existing curriculum;
   Little negotiation between teacher and pupil due to subject based learning bias of curriculum;
2. Dominance of examination relevance to those pupils intending to pursue further education;
3. Learning difficulties which may arise from cognitive deficiency, cultural deprivation or affective factors tend to lead to emotional blocks, avoidance behaviour and disaffection unless sensitive, skilled mediation is available;

4. Non-existent or low priority pastoral care in schools, not only as part of the inherent organization but by individual teachers;
5. Media coverage of negative incidents in school life with little effort being made to *spread good news*;
6. Little emphasis being placed on qualities of leadership, character and education philosophy in the selection of school heads and senior staff.

Suggested action to help promote orderly atmosphere in schools could include:

1. Teaching staff: greater self esteem and professional conduct, supported by government;
   Absorption into the staff of schools of the peripatetic services of remedial teams, even one day perhaps, educational psychologists and education social workers. This could also be achieved by enhancing staffing for all comprehensive schools;
2. Curriculum initiatives: inclusion of pastoral and social education as part of the core curriculum and the provision in the timetable for pastoral care to be carried out;
   Diversity of curriculum to cater for students marginalized by the current system;
   Greater emphasis on student orientated learning. LEA utilization of national and local projects, such as TVEI and LAPP;
3. Students: to be encouraged to carry out self assessments in work and behaviour. The management of behaviour could be negotiable with pupils being offered opportunities to renegotiate their place in the school community.
   Students to be actively encouraged to develop self esteem and a sense of belonging and identify within their schools.
4. Prevention strategy: to replace crisis management. This should be implemented through school and classroom rules, effective teaching techniques and developing positive pupil self concepts.

The climate set by a school, an LEA, and by government will affect behaviour. The LEA tries to encourage schools to find good practice and publish it: it has established a framework for recording achievement (OCEA) which influences all that goes on. It encourages the belief that there is a touch of genius in every child and that it is the main task of teachers and schools to find each child's talent and develop it with high expectation. In consequence the LEA believes that it has harder working teachers, a closer partnership with parents and less of a problem that might be the case elsewhere.

Suspensions have, overall, remained static from 1985–1987 at 287/285 although three areas have dropped quite dramatically, including Oxford City from 138 in 1985/86 to 64 in 1986/87.

The statistics are too flimsy to draw too definite a set of conclusions. We believe the figures are very low and reflect the success of curriculum initiatives over the last decade. Quite specifically, it is interesting to note that those schools which had already abandoned the cane before formal abolition have also reduced their suspensions whereas those few which had been forced to abandon it by committee decision have increased suspensions.

Quite often school brochures of information contain subliminal messages of discipline policies varying from the punitive-heavy at one end of the spectrum to praise-orientated at the other. Schools do have policies which they review through the Evaluation Process. A fairer snapshot of school policies should be obtained from HMI.

In addition to the usual courses which include elements of classroom management, there have been special initiatives since April, 1987 (introduction to GRIST), which have identified the areas of concern in the management of classroom problems. These are:

— understanding individual differences and the implication for classroom management.
— the meaning of disruption and deviancy to the classroom teacher.
— teacher authority in the classroom.
— stress in teaching directly relating to this area.
— the implication of disruptive behaviour in the classroom.
— management of behaviour problems with whole class groups.
— recording difficult behaviour.
— teacher response to difficult situations.
— the use of sanctions.
— seeking and gaining support within and without the school.
— working effectively with parents of disaffected pupils.
— fostering positive relationships with pupils.

The above subjects have been arrived at as a result of requests from schools. Thirty-three schools have been involved in in-service training on the above, ranging from one day to ten two hour sessions within a term. Small primary schools have grouped together in clusters to take part and in secondary schools twenty-two to sixty members of staff per school have been involved. Three of the Authority's teachers on secondment made an excellent commercially produced video at Oxford Polytechnic 'In the Heat of the Moment' with backing notes. The University Department also has an excellent classroom craft booklet in its PGCE course.

Oxfordshire LEA makes alternative provision for disturbed/disturbing pupils in five special units, each offering help with differing behavioural problems.

We are also well into a three year project (1986–1989) to examine maladjustment and disaffection within schools. The project began with a period of academic research, some in conjunction with Oxford University Department of Education, and has now progressed into practical modelling involving thirty-five local schools. A grant of £135,000 p.a. for three years was made by the Education Committee for this work.

We feel it important not to have an identification system of disruptive pupils as this would seem to institutionalize the problem and nurture its emergence. It is preferable that teachers, as part of their individual pastoral care, are watchful for students displaying behavioural problems and/or becoming socially isolated from their peers, and share their expertise in the handling of these pupils. Strategies need to be devised and developed for individual schools to reflect their staff's chosen path of management of these problems, and for staff to retain their control.

As a result of research and work in Oxfordshire schools, we are acquiring an understanding into the causes of bad behaviour in our schools which forms the basis of an approach from a whole school perspective.

We feel it is important to produce a curriculum which could be interest-led to inspire pupils who are not GCSE motivated and delivered on a part-time basis with children attending both mainstream schools and units.

10
Discipline in Schools: the SHA Submission to the Elton Committee

Chris Lowe

Introduction

The Secondary Headteachers Association is aware that the Elton Committee owes its existence to the government's concern to investigate the incidence of violence and disruption in schools. Although SHA believes that it is minor indiscipline that causes more daily disruption to children's learning and frustration to teachers, we wish to concentrate on disruptive behaviour of a more extreme nature which usually has a disproportionate effect on a school's atmosphere and which has to be tackled by the senior management in a school. This behaviour is often categorized confusingly as violence, disruption, vandalism and delinquency. We wish to make positive suggestions for tackling this problem.

In this submission it is accepted that there is no agreed definition of *violence* or *disruption*, but it is understood that for the purpose of the survey the two terms mean behaviour of an extreme nature that causes personal injury or hurt.

SHA sees two strands to the issue. Firstly, the schools' reaction to violent/disruptive incidents as they occur, and secondly, the schools' pro-active schemes to promote law and order within the school and community. These two approaches are not necessarily separate. However, the first section of this submission touches on responses to disruption within schools. The second section, the curriculum and Annexe A, deals with strategies for improving young people's understanding of law and order issues.

The Association is aware that members are perforce treating the symptoms rather than the causes of delinquency, but do not feel it is appropriate in this submission to enter into the legal, psychological, medical and social factors that relate to juvenile delinquency.

Responses to disruption

At national level there has been a great deal of rhetoric about violence in schools but no attempt at serious statistical research. The well publicized teacher union findings from their surveys were taken from small, subjective samples and naturally highlighted those members who had been involved in violent incidents. SHA believes that these surveys bear out what SHA members have also reported — that there has been an increase in violent behaviour in schools (both verbal and physical) over the past ten years. *But* SHA also maintains that the incidence of violence, when considered in the context of pupil hours in schools, is nevertheless small and instances of extreme violence which attract publicity are very rare. SHA agrees with HMI that 'the overwhelming majority of schools are orderly communities with good standards of behaviour' (Education Observed: Good Behaviour and Discipline in Schools, 1986).

However, members of SHA would acknowledge that their own estimates of the general situation are subjective, based on their own particular experiences and *feel* for the school climate.

> SHA suggests that there is a need to carry out an objective study of the precise nature and seriousness of the problem.

> SHA further suggests that the 1977 study carried out by the U.S. Department of Health, Education, and Welfare and the National Institute of Education into Violent Schools in the USA might be a useful model (see Annexe B).

It would not be helpful to quote in detail from the findings of this American survey as the schools and the times are different. However, the Report, emanating from carefully regulated research, did throw up data about the extent of, the quality of, the time and place of, the victims and perpetrators of, the institutions reaction to, the communities reaction to, violent incidents. Although there have been many researches into and studies of aspects of discipline and behaviour in schools in Britain, there has not been an objective, statistical survey, as far as SHA knows.

The USA Report concluded that strong and effective school management, particularly by the principal, could help greatly in reducing crime and misbehaviour. The principal's leadership and initiation of a structure of order seemed to differentiate *safe schools* from those having trouble. SHA would wish to underline its belief that a fair, firm and consistent system of student management is just as important in Britain, but clearly the support and co-operation of the governors and teachers will be of paramount importancee.

Heads, senior management teams and the assistant teachers, therefore, should collaborate in the establishing of consistent and well understood structures that create climates where disruptive behaviour is minimized and produce prompt responses when violence threatens. Most heads and deputies and their senior colleagues have achieved this by instinct and experience.

> SHA feels that it is possible and desirable for better training in appropriate techniques to be made available for teachers in senior positions.

Attention should be drawn to the 1980 White Paper *Young Offenders* (Cmnd 8045) in which the government emphasized the importance of local co-operation, and pledged to encourage inter-agency co-operation at local level. SHA believes that much has been achieved since then (See Annexe A for example) but much remains.

The Association wishes to record appreciation of all the external agencies who co-operate with schools in their efforts to combat social problems. However, it is clear that most teachers do not understand the different ways that officials of other services (social services, psychological service, remedial health service, police) are trained to approach problems and why they develop these methods. Similarly, it is also apparent that these officials do not always understand the teachers' approach. There is evidence that much misunderstanding (and in some cases bitterness) has been caused by this.

> SHA suggests, therefore, that more attention should be paid to this aspect in the development of staff in schools and also in the other services.
> In the first instance a study of this particular problem would pay dividends. SHA further suggests that inter-agency Standing Committees should be the norm in each LEA.

SHA accepts that, despite the relatively minor nature of the problem of violence in schools nationwide, each violent incident is nevertheless serious for the particular victim, the perpetrator, and the school and must be met by *appropriate action*. SHA believes that the legal framework and the administrative machinery for that action is already in place, but that there is generally inadequate training in the recognition and implementation of *appropriate action*.

Teachers have in general not been trained in the skills required to cope with extreme conflict or to recognize signs of potential violence. Teachers need the confidence to maintain appropriate standards of behaviour secure in the knowledge that they will be properly supported by the senior management, governing bodies and LEA.

> The classroom teacher needs to be made aware during initial teacher training of modern mediation skills and problem-solving skills, and ought also to receive regular up-dating during his/her teaching career. It would seem to be a fundamental right of every teacher to have command of necessary front-line skills.

> Other employees in the school (e.g., ancillaries and mid-day supervisors) should also be entitled to adequate training since they are equally at risk and have a part to play in combatting disruption.

It is the job of *senior managers* in the school to have a clear policy on tackling any violent behaviour. The policy should include the training of staff, the reporting procedures, the immediate action procedures, the sanction system, the exclusion procedures, the role of particular members of staff. This follows from the clearly laid down duty of head and teachers in the Conditions of Employment and the 1986 (No. 2) Act SS22–27.

The *governing body* has a part to play both through its statutory responsibilities and its general watchdog function, acting as the agent of the local community. Governing bodies can also help to create links between the school, the parents and the local community. They can also act as a sounding board for ideas, and offer lay advice general to the needs of the school once they have come to know the school — which in itself is a difficult enough problem.

> Governing bodies need the training to understand their responsibilities
> and the means of meeting them.

The local authority and the government have the responsibility to ensure that schools have the staff and resources to enable them to create orderly communities. SHA has already emphasized in its publication *The Staffing Implications of Better Schools* the heavy demands on staff time to minimize disruption in schools. SHA regrets the wide disparity in quantity and quality of the support services which LEAs ought to have to meet the problems caused by disruptive pupils. LEAs also have reserve powers to take action when pupils' education is threatened by bad behaviour in the school (S28 Education [No. 2] Act 1986).

SHA agrees with HMI's view in *Secondary Schools: An Appraisal by HMI*, 1988, that the very small numbers of pupils who are a persistent cause of worry consume a great deal of teacher time, especially for those with pastoral responsibility. Schools have to resort to short or longer-term exclusion of such pupils in order to cope. Most schools do this with reluctance as exclusion generally solves nothing. LEAs should be very wary of reinstating, against the wishes of the school, pupils who have been excluded. Instead they should ensure that they have agencies and machinery for meeting these problems without causing more problems to the school.

Parents too, have a large part to play. SHA is convinced that a positive parental attitude is the best guarantee of good pupil behaviour. It is generally true, however, that the parents of violent or extremely disruptive pupils have the least control over their offspring. Simply exhorting them to do better will be useless. They will more than likely need help from one or other of the social service agencies that exist to varying degrees in each local authority.

> Where parents of a violent pupil are inadequate they should be entitled
> to speedy and appropriate advice and guidance.

Strategies for improving an understanding of law and order issues

The curriculum

SHA acknowledges that schools in Britain have traditionally been at the centre of moral education of young people. However, the time and effort put into the personal and social education curriculum has, ironically not been rewarded by a place for personal and social education in the National Curriculum. Protestations by government ministers that such education can still be included in other areas or outside the National Curriculum illustrate a lack of understanding of the nature and development of a structured, pro-active pastoral curriculum in many schools.

SHA suggests that the National Curriculum Council should give a lead in ensuring that programme of personal/social/moral education are given a prominent place in the National Curriculum.

SHA endorses the conclusion reached by John Graham in his *Schools, Disruptive Behaviour and Delinquency: A Review of Research* published by the Home Office in May 1988, that the character and organization of a school influences the behaviour, attendance and academic performance of pupils and also that pupils in trouble at school are more likely to get into trouble with the law outside school. SHA also agrees with Home Office Minister of State, Mr. John Patten MP, who said when presenting Mr. Graham's study, that 'Schools along with parents, the family and the media, have an important role to play in diverting children from the criminal justice system'. The Association contends that many schools up and down the country are actively involved in working with other agencies in positive schemes to heighten youngsters' awareness of the importance of acting within the law and making positive contributions to society. Attached in Annexe A are descriptions of schemes designed to combat delinquency and vandalism that have come to our attention. There are no doubt many more. They deserved to be given publicity and encouragement.

Their effectiveness both in the short and long term should be studied and evaluated in collaboration with the Institute for the Study and Treatment of Delinquency. SHA would wish to offer their services in helping evaluate and monitor these developments which it considers to signify a welcome trend in school — community co-operation.

Finally, SHA hope that the Elton Committee will recommend a positive programme of research and action accompanied by appropriate and specific funding so that the thrust of the work of the Committee is not lost.

References

GRAHAM, J. (1988) Schools, Disruptive Behaviour and Delinquency, HER MAJESTY'S INSPECTORATE (1986) *Education Observed: Good Behaviour and Discipline in Schools*, London, HMSO.

Annexe A

Initiatives (involving schools) to tackle crime/vandalism

LEA	SCHOOL(S):	SHORT DESCRIPTION OF INITIATIVE	NOTES:
(1) Hampshire	Southampton	Mutli-agency Summer Camps at Police Training School, Netley. 100 Secondary School pupils will participate in 1988. This follows a successful pilot camp in the New Forest involving Mount Pleasant Middle School.	The Hampshire thrust is via police/school liaison and co-operation.
(2)	Deanery School, Southampton	Two police officers regularly involved in PAVE Curriculum	HMI have been commissioned by the DES to evaluate schemes country-wide and Hampshire is one of the LEAs to be visited and evaluated.
(3)	Bridgemary School Porchester S Oak Farm S Farnborough S Crestwood S Eastleigh	The PSE Advisory Team of the Education Dept has organized training courses for police schools' liaison officers at these schools. Some 30 officers being trained.	

Annexe A (Cont'd.)

LEA	SCHOOL(S):	SHORT DESCRIPTION OF INITIATIVE	NOTES:
(4)	Four Schools in Winchester plus a Children's Home	Seven Police Officers involved for one full day per month in their respective Schools. Areas of the curriculum where police involvement would be of help are negotiated with Staff (so far, English, PSE, Humanities, Science, Special needs and tutor periods). Several Staff have accompanied police on patrol. Offices are involved in pastoral and Heads of Year meetings.	
(5)	Cowplain/Cobham	Similar scheme to the above.	
(6)	Basingstoke	A teacher has been seconded full-time for one term to develop police/school liaison. One policeman has also been seconded full time to develop school liaison in Secondary Schools. He has developed many work modules. Teachers have useful police establishments.	
(7)	Isle of Wight	Similar scheme to the above.	
(8) Cornwall	East Cornwall Schools	An Early Warning Scheme initiated by a police Chief Superintendent. Schools are grouped in clusters of 6 or 7 to alert each other (and police) of any incidents — particularly occasions where pupils might be approached by strangers.	

Annexe A (Cont'd.)

LEA	SCHOOL(S):	SHORT DESCRIPTION OF INITIATIVE	NOTES:
	Liskeard/Looe Schools	The Schools are working with the Communities Project Foundation on developing community education, targetting the 16–24 age-group in terms of their particular needs in this area.	
(9) Gloucestershire	Winchcombe School	School co-operating with local police and residents arranged for 4th/5th Formers to fit safety chains to senior citizens' houses.	
(10) South Glamorgan	Llanilltud Fawr School Bryn Hafren Girls School	Junior Crime Prevention panel. Groups working with Community policeman, marked personal property for people in Shopping Centre.	
(11) Stockport	All	School Watch Scheme. The aim is to raise parent's awareness of vandalism on School property. Letter from the Director of Education has gone to all parents requesting their co-operation in reporting suspicious incidents seen in school grounds from their home or as they pass.	
(12) Wolverhampton	Various	Junior crime prevention panels — 'Junior Crimebusters'. ('Young People Against Crime') being set up in many Schools, initiated by West Midlands police. A leaflet 'Help Smash Crime' has been distributed.	

Annexe A (Cont'd.)

LEA	SCHOOL(S):	SHORT DESCRIPTION OF INITIATIVE	NOTES:
(13) Northumberland	King Edward VI School, Morpeth	An anti-alcohol abuse project is run jointly with the 'Stay Dry' Campaign. Involves all 4th Years through the PSE course. Youth Leaders run non-alcoholic cocktail bars at School Discos.	
(14) Cheshire	Various in Runcorn	*Kops and Kids Scheme* — a five week Summer activities scheme run in conjunction with YTS support for supervision, aim being to offer alternative to being on the streets. *Clean up Campaign* — once per month on Saturday mornings the police organize local clean-up service. (Litter and Graffiti). They pay youngsters for their time. Any institution wanting graffiti removed would provide the material.	
(15) Croydon	Various	Befrienders' Scheme — a 'behaviour modification' Scheme for youngsters who have come to the notice of the police. Scheme run jointly by Education, Social Services and the Police. Funded by LEA.	

Annexe A (Cont'd.)

LEA	SCHOOL(S):	SHORT DESCRIPTION OF INITIATIVE	NOTES:
(16) Cambridgeshire	St Neots' Secondary Schools	Co-operating with Town Council and Local Police in Scheme to provide greater leisure/recreation facilities for teenagers. 5th and 6th Formers have been co-opted to a joint committee to develop the project. So far a 'club night' has been arranged on a weekly basis and a regular disco organized by the town council.	
(17) Kirklees	Honley H.S.	School's Junior Crime Prevention panel has transformed the local graffiti-scarred railway station into pleasant place for travellers, helped by BR and police.	
(18) St Helens		Plans are afoot to establish Youth Crime Prevention Panels in every Secondary School.	
(19) Derbyshire	Sinfin Community School, Derby	School Youth Clubs and Derby Community Arts have joint project on a district centre mural where graffiti was a major problem.	It is reported that the mural is still in good condition.
	Six Secondary Schools	Secondary Schools Development project is now addressing whole-school issues identified by the Schools with intention of reducing disruption.	

Annexe A (Cont'd.)

LEA	SCHOOL(S):	SHORT DESCRIPTION OF INITIATIVE	NOTES:
(20) Doncaster	Mexborough School	(a) Local police involved in PSE curriculum. Work and role of the police are covered. Pupils' awareness of what is legal and illegal is raised.	
		(b) Co-operating with Psychological Service on behaviour modification programme for group of pupils with behavioural problems.	
(21) Staffordshire	Stafford Area Schools	A detailed GRIST submission focussing on the prevention of disruptive behaviour, recommending a two-year pilot project in the Stafford Area has gone to the Staffordshire Education Committee from Heads and AEOs in the Stafford Area. One of the thrusts would be to improve staff expertise in identifying problems and minimizing disruptive behaviour.	
	Stoke Area	Junior Crime Prevention Panels being set up. Youth activities run jointly by police and schools.	

Annexe A (Cont'd.)

LEA	SCHOOL(S):	SHORT DESCRIPTION OF INITIATIVE	NOTES:
(22) Northamptonshire	Various	(a) Juvenile Liaison Bureaux. The pilot ones were successful enough to encourage expansion in 1988–9. (b) Many Schools involved in Schools/police liaison. (c) Inter-agency 'Case Conferences' — intended to catch potential problems early. (d) Pupils take part in Crime Prevention Panel work.	The number of adolescents appearing before magistrates has been dramatically reduced.
(23) Durham	Chester-le-Street	Junior Crime Prevention Panel — issue ultra violet pens for pupils to mark equipment; puts up posters. Initiated a School Watch System.	
	Other Schools	Some Schools involved in Neighbourhood Watch Schemes.	
(24) Kingston	Two Schools	A joint proposal by Kingston Friends Workshop Group, Kingston Learning Difficulties Project and the Institute for the Study and Treatment of Delinquency, for research into personal and group problem solving in the classroom.	Funds for this project are being sought.

Annexe A (Cont'd.)

LEA	SCHOOL(S):	SHORT DESCRIPTION OF INITIATIVE	NOTES:
(25) Sefton	Various	School/Police liaison. Police organize a 5 a-side football and arrange an annual 'Schools' Day'. Initiating a PALS (Police and Leisure Pursuits) Scheme. Crime Prevention Poster Competition.	
(25) N. Yorkshire	Five Harrogate Schools	Schools and Crime Prevention Panel and Harrogate Anti-Theft Group are investigating consequences of shop theft for thief, family and community. Hoping to set up Junior Panels.	
(26) Avon & Somerset	Various	*SPLASH* (School and Police Liaison Activities for Summer Holidays) Summer holiday activity scheme co-ordinated by police. Glossy brochure produced by police with many advertisements. Enormous number of activities and centres.	
(27) Lincolnshire		A multi disciplinary Vandalism Working Party. Concerns itself mainly with the symptoms of vandalism rather than the causes, but has recently been considering 'causes' following a paper by an AEO on the subject.	

Annexe A (Cont'd.)

LEA	SCHOOL(S):	SHORT DESCRIPTION OF INITIATIVE	NOTES:
(28) West Sussex	Various	(a) Juvenile Liaison Bureaux	
	Chichester HS for Girls	(b) Alcohol Abuse amongst Young People Project in conjunction with police, highlighting the relationship of drugs, alcohol with crime.	
		(c) Behaviour Modification Project — organized by police with input from teachers and School Liaison Officer.	
	Various	(d) Police Volunteer Cadet Corps — recruits in local schools. Also input into Police Service element of Duke of Edinburgh Award Scheme.	
	Chichester	(e) Police and Schools have introduced an 'Adopt A School' scheme to improve liaison between police/parents/teachers/pupils.	
	Chichester Schools	(f) A Schools Early Warning System — Schools liaise over 'incidents' particularly those of a sexual nature.	
	Chichester	(g) 350 Neighbourhood Watch Schemes in being. Schools are situated within them.	
		(h) Teachers and Police have talks (including Women at Risk Video) and also practical self-defence instruction by PE Staff.	

Annexe A (Cont'd.)

LEA	SCHOOL(S):	SHORT DESCRIPTION OF INITIATIVE	NOTES:
	Chichester HS for Girls	(i) First four years have Law, crime and Police lessons organized by School/Police Liaison Officer.	
(29) Oxfordshire	Witney	(a) Town Forum under auspices of County Council Chairman met to discuss a worrying trend of alcohol related petty crime.	Have since then made greater efforts to curtail under-age drinking by introducing ID cards for those likely to be suspected of being under-age.
		(b) Young People and Alcohol Conference, May 1988, produced list of recommendations which townfolk hope will be implemented.	
		(c) Close liaison with schools sought by local police over crime prevention.	
(30) Kent		CSV Kent in partnership with Kent Social Services and Education Departments set up a pilot scheme of intermediate treatment to help avoid Custodial Sentences for young people. Funding came from the Government under DHSS (Circular LAC 83/3).	A final report on the Kent schemes was published in Sept. 87.

Annexe B

Methodology by NIE in USA

The National Institute of Education (NIE) conducted its study of school crime in three phases. In Phase I, a mail survey asked more than 4,000 elementary and secondary school principals to report in detail on the incidence of illegal or disruptive activities in their schools. Nine one-month reporting periods were assigned to participating schools on a random basis.

In Phase II, field representatives conducted on-site surveys of nationally representative cluster samples. Principals kept a record of incidents during the reporting month, and supplied additional information about their schools. Students and teachers were surveyed and asked to report any experiences they might have had as victims of violence or theft in the reporting month. In addition, they provided information about themselves, their schools, and their communities, which was later used in statistical analyses to sort out some of the factors that seemed to affect school crime rates.

Phase III involved a more intensive qualitative study of ten schools. Most of the Phase III schools had had a history of problems with crime and violence, but had improved dramatically in a short time.

Part III
Curriculum Approaches to Prevention

11
Curriculum: The Changing Framework

Richard Pring

The educational context for the work with young people with special educational needs, and for the inter-agency co-operation required to meet those needs, is changing at a bewildering rate — and not all the changes are easy to reconcile with one another. The aim in this chapter is to give the background to these changes, and to tease out some of the ideas that underpin them.

Changing context

The inadequacies of the educational system have been emphasized in recent years in several quarters. Often the criticism is based on ignorance or prejudice and it is easy to blame schools for the ills that beset society on a wider plain. Nonetheless, there are social and economic changes, and no educational system can remain static in the wake of these. It must be responsive. As in the case of all institutions such responses may be slower than people wish. They will not leave old ideas and philosophies intact. They require a constant rethinking of the aims and purposes of education and of the ways in which these might be fulfilled.

Economic context

This is particularly true if we try to see the connection between the educational service and employment. Schools and colleges have been criticized for not preparing young people properly for the future, in particular for the world of work. This criticism has come from employers, but it has been taken up by politicians and by officials. It was a major theme of Mr Callaghan's (then Prime Minister) Ruskin College Speech in 1977 'Preparing future generations for life', and he suggested four areas where this preparation of young people was lacking.

1. Basic skills that industry needed;
2. Positive attitudes towards industry and towards the economic needs of society;

3. Technological knowledge and know-how for living effectively in a technological society;
4. Personal qualities for coping with a changing and difficult world.

Subsequent government White Papers, MSC papers, and ministerial speeches developed these themes, pointing to the need for:

— More integration of education with training
— A greater degree of vocational relevance
— More explicit statements of standards to be achieved
— More emphasis on basic skills
— More focus upon personal development and effectiveness.

Employers are not the best, when tackled on this theme, to say precisely what is required of school-leavers. But there is now some consensus, in what little research there is, that above all they require basic skills in language and in mathematics, increasingly a 'literacy' in information technology, and above all the personal qualities required to sustain responsible, flexible and creative approaches to working and to maintaining good working relationships. An excellent craftsman who can't work in a team may well be a disaster for a struggling employer.

Furthermore, part of the personal development required lies in the attitude to industry as the basic of our social and personal welfare. There has been some scholarly and trenchant criticism of the deeply rooted cultural bias against the wealth-creating part of our society, especially that of making and of manufacturing.

The economic context, and the relation of this to education, need to be spelt out in more detail. Employment patterns are changing, from manufacturing to service industries, from unskilled to skilled (although there is a lot of unemployment, there are many vacancies at the technician level), and from region to region.

Hence, a new challenge has been given to education. Can it so educate the next generation of young people that they are better prepared in attitudes, in personal qualities, in basic skills to move into a swiftly changing and more technically oriented world of work?

Social context

Swift economic change brings with it social disruption, and this is reflected in the growing concern over violence, hooliganism, and young people with special needs. Again schools have often been criticized for wider social ills, and yet that is most unfair. It is too often that ill-resourced schools, and the youth service, remain the few areas where young people can find helpful and constructive responses to their difficulties. Nonetheless, there are social problems and a public concern, and schools, colleges, the youth service, and other support agencies, are asked to respond. A survey published in 1988 on drug taking in London schools reveals that one in twelve are 'into' drugs (including glue sniffing). The response? Better and more forceful *educational* programmes. Once again schools are in the front line.

It is difficult, in general terms, to argue against this. Schools are there to educate the next generation: those who shortly will shape society in a particular way. If you believe, as I do, that schools *do* make a difference then you have to admit to a rather awesome responsibility that cannot disappear simply because it is not acknowledged. Schools do acknowledge it and are doing something about it but it is sad that so few of those that criticize schools recognise this.

Personal context

Unemployment patterns vary from region to region, but in some areas unemployment among young people remains very high. Even where there is employment, the future is much less predictable than it was a generation ago. This must affect what the educational system is about. How can we prepare young people not simply economically (basic skills, attitudes, technological know-how), but psychologically for a future that is so unpredictable? Certainly industry requires its new recruits to have certain personal qualities, often referred to as *personal effectiveness*, but these may not be the same personal qualities as those required to sustain young people with hope, with inner security, when objectively there seems little ground for hope. Personal development easily trips off the end of the tongue, but it must be central to the plans of a responsive school, given the changing context.

Changing standards

'Falling standards' is, as it always has been, a banner behind which the critics of education march. It is one that the unprincipled politician will always follow: it is easy to find faults with schools, struggling with inadequate resources to teach reluctant learners, and to receive instant, though superficial public support by doing so. But there is little evidence to suggest that standards have fallen, and if anything, they have risen, judged by increased examination activity and by the results of the national surveys of the Assessment of Performance Unit.

But as the economic, social, and personal contexts of education seep through into the reappraisal of its aims and values, so the definitions of standards begin to alter too, thereby affecting what is taught and how it is taught, affecting also the role of other agencies in the overall process, as we shall see.

Changing courses and organisation

One outstanding feature of the last ten years has been the rapidity with which schools and colleges have adapted to the changing context, often in the most difficult of conditions. I shall outline certain key features of this.

Prevocational

In the mid-1970's, many young people remained in full-time education beyond the age of 16, though not prepared for the 'A' level route and undecided over any specific vocational direction. What should be done with these young people? They were there; they had to be taught; but most post-16 provisions were either the traditionally academic 'A' level courses or the vocational skills courses.

A first task of the Further Education Unit (FEU), recently established at the DES, was to advise FE establishments on how to respond to a problem that had arisen mainly from the impact of unemployment. After all, most of the young people wanted to be at work.

The solution, published in 1979 in a Report called *A Basis for Choice* (ABC), was that general education should continue, but that there should be an orientation towards different kinds of employment and that there should be work experience. The Report's conception of general education was a radical departure from how it is normally conceived. 'General Education' is usually understood to signify an aggregate of disconnected subjects which, between them, provide a broad initiation into different kinds of knowledge. It tends also to be rather academic in so far as it promotes a rather theoretical, non-practical approach to learning, reinforced by a predominantly literary form of assessment. The Report started from different premisses. It began with questions about the aims of education, and then about the programmes of study and the activities which would help realise these aims, keeping an open mind on whether subjects were the necessary or best vehicle for doing so.

In establishing the aims of the curriculum, the Report looked in two directions — compatible directions if rightly handled. First, how might the curriculum develop the personal qualities (knowledge, attitudes, abilities, understandings) that would be good for the individual? Secondly, how might it develop those qualities that society needed if it was to remain socially and economically buoyant? The Report spelt out aims which included such goals as the ability to work effectively with other people, to establish co-operative and creative relationships, to develop a set of defensible moral values, to communicate effectively, to have the social and political awareness to operate constructively within democratic arrangements, to have the knowledge and know-how to live within a technologically sophisticated environment. Sometimes these aims tallied closely with the aims of traditional subjects; sometimes they did not. Indeed, to meet the aims, it was often not necessary to think in terms of subjects or specific contents at all but rather in terms of effective relationships and of processes of learning.

The principles of the ABC Report were soon translated into courses by the City and Guilds of London Institute (CGLI) and by the Royal Society of the Arts (RSA). The CGLI 365 Course proved immensely popular, not only with post-16 students, but also as a solution to the problems that many schools saw in motivating students from 14. Roughly speaking, one had here a *prevocational* curriculum that provided a more practical, more relevant, more activity based curriculum with different working relationships with teachers and with an orientation towards the world of work which, for many young people, is what they require. Furthermore, it had built into it an approach to assessment through profiling which gave a much more generous picture of what the young people had done and could do than did the traditional forms of examination.

The ABC Report was followed by the CGLI 365 Course, and in a roundabout way, this begat the Certificate in Prevocational Education. This Certificate provides the general principles of general education, as outlined in the ABC Report, through modules which, at different levels (introductory, exploratory, and preparation) introduce students to different areas of work. We should note the concept of general education which was to be provided through vocational preparation, for part of general education lies in non-specific attitudes towards enquiring co-operatively, tackling problems systematically, communicating effectively to different audiences, applying technological processes to different contexts.

The principles behind CPVE attracted sufficient interest from schools to encourage the Business and Technical Education Council (BTEC) to initiate pre-vocational Foundation Programmes, designed to make learning more *relevant* for those aged between 14 and 16, to be sufficiently flexible to incorporate GCSE (after all, subjects *taught in a particular way* and with the addition of profiling and work experience could meet the criteria of the prevocational curriculum), and to provide that continuity from 14 to 17.

Finally, from a quite different quarter, the Technical and Vocational Education Initiative (TVEI) was announced in 1982 and commenced in 1983. This was financed by the Manpower Services Commission (MSC), now the Training Agency, on a massive scale in order to encourage schools and colleges to work in consortium in order to orient the curriculum much more effectively to the world of work. It established broad criteria for the different schemes:

— Provide equal opportunities;
— Provide a four-year curriculum designed as a preparation for adult life in a society liable to rapid change;
— Encourage initiative, problem-solving, and other aspects of personal development;
— Contain a vocational element throughout;
— Relate vocational and technical elements to potential employment opportunities;
— Plan work experience within the programme;
— Establish links with subsequent training and educational opportunities;
— Include regular careers and educational assessment;
— Prepare students for one or more nationally recognised qualifications;
— Design courses so that they might be usefully replicated.

TVEI brought a different source and a different mode (namely the MSC) of funding to education. This is most important. One way of ensuring that the educational service responds to the contextual changes outlined above is to provide financial leverage — previously not within the government's power. The shift towards specific grants to local education authorities (LEAs) from general grants is one of the most significant developments in the control of education, for it enables the government, in making resources conditional upon agreed programmes, to shape the curriculum in the way that it requires. In this case, TVEI has affected work in schools and colleges profoundly, seeking a closer orientation of education to subsequent training possibility and at the same time, by being seen as more relevant, meeting the personal needs of otherwise disillusioned young people.

Vocational training

The 'preparation for the future' envisaged within the prevocational curriculum points to general qualities rather than specific skills, although it does aim at a transformation of attitude towards the world of work.

However, specific vocational training has to begin some time, and there has been much criticism, especially from the MSC, that there is not enough of it at the appopriate levels and in the right places. In this, so we are told, we lag behind our major industrial competitors.

Two aspects of this I want to emphasize. The first concerns vocational schemes and the second concerns qualification.

The most significant programme has been the Youth Training Scheme (YTS). This (funded by MSC) provides a two-year programme for 16 year olds which includes at least 20 weeks 'off the job' training, planned work experience, occupational training, and personal guidance and assessment.

The schemes are located, by and large, in industry which receives a grant for each trainee. To take on trainees, and to be in receipt of the grant, employers need to be awarded Approved Training Organisation (ATO) status. As such the employer is responsible for planning and implementing the whole training programme under the conditions set out in the last paragraph.

The Youth Training Scheme is now the major route for young people into employment. It is, therefore, an important element in the government's aim to provide a better trained workforce — although it has often been seen (wrongly) by its critics as a way of mopping up the unemployed. The scheme aims to broaden the training horizons, making individual programmes more educational in the sense that there is greater focus on personal development. To that end, progress on the scheme can and should be recognized in different levels of qualifications, mainly by CGLI and BTEC. This links the Youth Training Scheme to what has occurred previously at school and, through well marked out progression routes, to further training and educational possibilities.

There inevitably are various problems. Many major firms are now wanting to opt out of the programme, preferring instead to develop their own. There often can be difficulty in finding enough suitable managing agents to ensure that there is good quality training. The successful managing agents can be selective in whom they take on. Employers after all want to make a profit, and there are limits to their altruism where connection with profit is not self-evident, and those with special needs (physical, mental, emotional) might once again be the ones most vulnerable in the vocational preparation for the future.

Secondly, however, there has been a reform of vocational qualifications. It was felt by government (in this case, the Department of Employment and its MSC) that the jungle of qualifications at different levels needed to be brought up to date and into some more comprehensible and coherent system. Time-serving should give way to competency-based assessment.

There is no doubt that the present arrangement for vocational qualifications are confusing — with so many different and competing validation bodies (BTEC, CGLI, RSA, Pitman's for example). To help bring order to a confused situation, the National Council for Vocational Qualification (NCVQ) was established in 1986 to design and implement a national framework for vocational qualifications (NVQ) at four different levels — from operative and craft up to technician level. Qualifications would require proof of occupational competence in the skills that it has been decided persons so qualified should have mastered. Eventually, no doubt, the model will extend to higher and professional levels, thus giving clear routes of progression.

Already, therefore, the framework is changing with fairly dynamic and comprehensive policies towards prevocational and vocational education and training that are aimed to meet the criticism of the disconnections between economic and social needs on the one hand and, on the other, the educational provision. One can envisage the possible routes through the system if there is the political will and coherence to establish them from Prevocational Foundation at 14 either to CPVE or to NVQ, with the possibility of later transfer from CPVE to NVQ at higher levels. This could one day be a route through to the professional levels which will no doubt come.

There is, however, one major problem, namely, the reconciliation between these developments and the reassertion of the traditional academic route, such that, instead of the integration of education and training, there is likely to be a reinforcement of the division.

Academic courses

One criticism that has constantly emerged from teachers, but also from many employers, is the way in which we examine students and record achievement. This clearly affects the flexibility of the system, the possibility of integration between education and training, and progression from one part to another.

The secondary curriculum has traditionally been seen in terms of an aggregate of subjects. These are reflected in a subject based examination system, pass or failure, which in part has been determined by the 'normal curve of distribution'. The system has encouraged a certain style of learning, neither practical nor experiential, but celebrating memorized and prepared answers. Moreover, at the end of it all, employers are not much the wiser about what the students know or can do.

The reform of the 16+ examination, by replacing GCE 'O' level by GCSE, aims to meet some of these criticisms. The examination encourages more practical work and it spells out more clearly the criteria against which the student is to be assessed. The aim is to shift the emphasis from pass or fail to levels of performance which are described by the different sets of criteria. There is, therefore, a link between the GCSE philosophy and that of the NCVQ.

Nonetheless, the GCSE reinforces the subject based approach to the curriculum. But so does the National Curriculum which specifies foundation subjects, and only belatedly has shown interest in the cross-curriculum themes, the links with industry, and the processes of learning which are the hallmark of the pre-vocational courses.

There is therefore a problem in the contemporary framework that is emerging. There is clearly more progression than before, but flexibility between the pre-vocational developments and the subject-based courses seems to have escaped these reforms, although brave attempts are being made to remedy this. The fact that different government departments are funding different initiatives clearly makes the coherence of the system more difficult to establish.

Outside links

One element in these developments that requires special reference is the link being established between the educational service and industry. Clearly this is important if schools are to be seen as a preparation for the world of work: important because the schools need to be aware of the qualities, attitudes, and skills that industry does highlight as important, but also because employers themselves need to be educated about the problems faced and efforts made by schools in providing a broader educational base for preparing young people for an unpredictable future.

There are many schemes and initiatives, but there are signs now of much firmer policy and resources to support these as a result of the Department of Trade and Industry's White Paper in January of 1988 according to which (i) 10 per cent of all teachers should have a spell in industry in any one year; (ii) all students should have a couple of weeks' of work experience before leaving school; and (iii) initial teacher training must prepare students for this closer schools/industry co-operation.

There is at the same time closer involvement of employers within governing bodies of schools and of colleges.

The curriculum

The National Curriculum reinforces traditional approaches to the curriculum, and ignores the educational advances made through the prevocational routes that are relevant to students across the ability range and that attempt to meet the problems of the changing context.

The key features of the new curriculum thinking (quoted from R. Pring, R. White, and D. Brockington *14-18 Education and Training: making sense of the national curriculum and the new vocationalism*, Centre for Secondary and Tertiary Inservice Training, 1988, p. 10) are the following:

Encouraging a shift of responsibility for learning from teacher to student (thereby challenging traditional teaching styles and requiring the learner to develop skills of independent enquiry);

Making learning more project and activity based;

Relating what is learnt to future needs of the students and of society (whether or not these are employment needs);

Linking educational programmes more closely to community resources (including employers, parents, other institutions of learning);

Focusing upon personal development and effectiveness (thus stressing the importance of guidance and counselling);

Seeing the central value of the creative arts and humanities in meeting those personal needs;

Introducing the student to the principles and practices of technology;

Developing social, economic, and political awareness;

Recognising the overriding importance of communications skills;

Promoting equal opportunities for people of different race, sex and class.

There is a much greater stress upon the process of learning: approaching new problems with confidence, developing the study skills that create greater autonomy, sensitizing the enquirer to wider social and moral implications, encouraging through practice the capacity to communicate with different audiences, and seeing the significance of what one is doing for further training and education.

There is, of course, a danger that such stress upon process content devalues. That would be foolish. Intellectual development requires the mastery of concepts, of principles, and indeed of facts which are frequently to be located and organized within subjects. There must be a place for subjects in any general education. But the subjects themselves need to be re-thought so that they do incorporate the processes stressed by prevocational curriculum, and they must, too, reflect in their style and content the cross-curriculum themes (economic awareness, for example) that so easily are omitted in the aggregate of discrete and disconnected subjects. The process of learning within subjects should be transformed by the possibilities opened up by technology, rather than technology being added to an unreformed set of subjects.

One significant development in the prevocational curriculum is the focus upon personal development in a world, including an educational world, which so often seems indifferent to the impact of the courses upon the individual — upon attitudes, interests, feelings, and appreciation. The more person–focused curriculum establishes criteria of relevance and of educational value against which the subjects or indeed the vocational orientation might be judged.

Therefore, two key elements in the curriculum must be the system of assessment and the provision for guidance and counselling. On the one hand there is

developing a way of recording achievement that ensures a closer tutorial arrangement between teacher and learner, a more generous recording of what students can
do and have experience of, and thus a basis for a negotiation of relevant learning
objectives. Such a system, although characteristic chiefly of prevocational courses,
will be extended to all pre-16 courses in the early 1990s, thus facilitating much
greater continuity from school to college and from prevocational and general
education into vocational courses and employment.

In addition, the counselling and guidance skills that are required in such profiling of students will establish a different *educational* relationship between student
and teacher. At the very practical level, more help is needed to enable the student to
see constructively a route through from school to further training and employment.

Philosophical issues

Beneath these curriculum changes are more fundamental ideas of a philosophical kind that ultimately affect the way in which the curriculum will be
reshaped and the link established between the educational and training systems
and the changing context of employment and the wider society.

Liberal education and vocational training

There is a long tradition of tying the concept of education to that of academic
subjects — academic in the sense of valuing exclusively the more theoretical
pursuits, approached in a relatively non-practical and non-experiential manner,
and assessed in a predominantly literary or numerical mode. Education, in this
view, is an initiation into different forms of knowledge which are pursued for their
own intrinsic interest, not for their usefulness. Hence, education for its own sake
(organized through discrete subjects) is contrasted with 'training', which is not
pursued for its own sake and which is geared to the skills required for quite specific
(often vocational) ends.

What the prevocational curriculum has done it to challenge this dichotomy. It
has promoted a broader vision of education which sees this to be a development of
people as reflective and sensitive, concerned with practical and personal issues as
much as with theoretical and impersonal ones. One can be educated (empowered to
think, to imagine and to reflect more effectively) through vocational interests, and
training on specific tasks is part (though not the whole) of that. It has thus linked
education also to the deep-seated concerns that young people have about their
future because *to them*, if not to those who philosophize about education, what
they will do after school, and what they need to do to qualify for that, is of supreme
importance.

Practical and theoretical knowledge

The prevocational courses in particular have challenged that disdain that many share for the practical or the experiential. So much learning has been 'book-learning', the absorption of facts or theories in abstraction from the concrete, practical world to which they relate. The experience that the young people themselves bring to school or engage in outside the formal curriculum would have no place in the reflective learning that takes place in schools.

There are, however, practical problems in motivating young people, and these possibly reflect deeper philosophical problems about the way in which 'school knowledge' is understood and organized. 'Knowing-how' (the practical ability to engage intelligently in an activity — driving a car, being a politician or a teacher, participating in a discussion) is as much a kind of knowledge, making demands upon the intellect and thoughtfulness, as is the 'knowing-that', the grasp and reproduction of propositions about facts or theories. Indeed, the 'knowing-that' is so often the articultation of the 'truths' embodied in the intelligent 'knowing-how'. I may know *how* to teach, but not be very good at articulating that knowledge. On the other hand, I may know a lot about the theory of teaching, but be useless in practice. What kind of knowledge is of most worth?

The prevocational curriculum has re-assessed the importance and the merit of *practical* knowledge, and has thought through ways in which this might be assessed. To some extent, the GCSE has followed suit, but only 'to some extent', and therefore there remains the difficulty of reconciling, too, different traditions that reflect different values attached to different modes of knowing.

School and society

There are those who argue that schools should be rather like monasteries, cut off from the distractions of the world so that the students might concentrate on their studies — which themselves have no immediate and obvious relevance to that world. Indeed, many private schools are placed in very rural places, not the most obvious places for forming minds of future captains of industry.

Such a view, however, is challenged by many recent developments — closer links between school and community and between school and industry, the involvement of employers and parents in the school, practical work experience, project work within the community, and links between schools and various community agencies. TVEI and CPVE have attached much educational significance to these links, and they have been appreciated by the students.

But there *are* these quite different perceptions of schooling, and in the case of school/society continuity much needs to be done to work out in practice and educationally what the connections should be. It is strange that the national curriculum, and the wider issues of educational control contained within the 1988 Education Act, should have learnt so little from the community school movement.

The way forward

The changing framework can still change in quite different directions, depending on who is allowed to control education and training.

There are, as we have seen, different traditions competing for allegiance. It is possible to find ways of merging these traditions — of seeing how training can be conducted in an educational way, how vocational interests can be liberally interpreted, how theoretical studies can be based on practical know-how and experience, and how what happens in school can reflect and be critical of wider social experience.

But these different traditions are deeply entrenched within our culture and received values, and it may not be easy to merge them — as the prevocational courses have attempted to do.

For that to happen there is need for:

1. Greater overall cohesion in educational planning — *but* there are three government departments involved in these initiatives and the Education Act, by diminishing the responsibilities of LEAs, would lessen the likelihood of such planning;
2. An integrated system of assessment and recording of achievement — *but* different examination systems prevail, embodying different views about assessment, and all alongside a developing system of profiling;
3. Flexible routes through the academic, prevocational and vocational course‹ — *but* that very flexibility is elusive in the maintenance of three traditions, embodying different educational values and controlled by different bodies.

The issues therefore that confront us are these:

The content of the curriculum

To what extent should the curriculum of schools be subject-based, thereby ignoring many of the lessons to be learned from TVEI, CGLI/BTEC, CPVE and excluding a more experience-based and practical approach to the development of understanding? If it is to be subject-based, how is it to cope with those other areas of knowledge which are not prescribed but which educationally are seen by many to be important: economic awareness, health education, personal and social development?

The control of the curriculum

If there is to be a nationally prescribed curriculum, what safeguards do there need to be against the detailed control from whoever happens to be in political power?

Where will there be scope for the innovation and curriculum development, characteristic of the TVEI and other prevocational initiatives, which would not have been possible under the subject-based highly prescriptive national curriculum?

Or, at the most local level, what role should parents or employer have in determining the details of the curriculum, especially in the new governing bodies which, from September 1988, are being asked to reflect business interests?

How to assess students

Will the national assessment at ages 7, 11, 14 and 16 produce a narrowing of the criteria whereby standards are judged, excluding the innovative forms of assessment (of co-operative learning, of the process of learning, of designing and problem-solving, for example) that pre-vocational education has encouraged? Will these now overshadow the development of profiling which, unlike national standardized testing, is aimed at giving a positive picture of what young people can do and not of what they have failed to do?

Personal and Social Development (PSD)

How far should PSD be a central focus of the curriculum, thereby relegating the acquisition of knowledge and understanding to a less important place in the overall concerns of the schools? Are there specific values that schools ought to be promoting (self-confidence and self-reliance; equality of respect between gender, races, abilities; entrepreneurial attitudes; civic virtues; political and social criticism)?

Linking schools with the community

What sort of partnership should be established between schools and industry with regard to: work experience for pupils, industrial experience for teachers, school experience for industrialists, curriculum materials about industry, for example? Is not the lack of clarity here one concrete manifestation of the deeper philosophical debate about the relevance of education?

Maintaining the system of education

Should we pursue the path, which seems implicit in the 1988 Education Act, whereby, in pursuit of greater freedom of choice, we undermine the *system* of education whereby our educational objectives might be achieved? Thus we are quickly reaching the following hierarchy of schools which will no doubt reflect differences vis-à-vis the academic, pre-vocational, and vocational distinctions:

Independent independent
Dependent independent (depending on assisted places)
City Technology Colleges (dependent on business)
Grant Maintained Schools (independent of LEAs)
Popular Maintained Schools (benefiting from the Open Admissions Policy)
Unpopular Maintained Schools (suffering from the Open Admissions Policy)

Conclusion

We are now witnessing the most radical changes in Secondary Education since the 1944 Education Act. In brief, these changes involve:

1. A greater degree of central political control;
2. A tightening up of an essentially subject-based curriculum;
3. The contemporaneous development of pre-vocational education characterized in a very different way;
4. The greater stress upon vocational relevance;
5. The transformation of the system of examination and assessment that seem to move in quite opposite directions;
6. The attempt to link schools with the community, particular employers.

Underpinning these changes are differences in what different protagonists see to be the value and purpose of education, how knowledge should be defined and organized, and how the educational service should serve the wider community.

References

Further Education Unit (1979) *A Basis for Choice*, London, HMSO.
Pring, R., White, R. and Brockington, D. (1988) *14–18 Education and Training: Making Sense of the National Curriculum and the New Vocationalism*, Bristol, Youth Education Service.

12
TVEI: All Change or Small Change?

Lawrie Walker

Introduction

When I first put together the two phrases *classroom discipline* and *Technical and Vocational Education* I was conscious of a strangeness, as if a dog were to marry a horse, or a horse was tied to a cloud. Nobody who writes about TVEI ever mentions discipline: the whole manner of discourse looks in another direction. The teachers of course, who actually have to carry out in practice the theories behind TVEI, think about discipline all the time. They have to, they are teachers. This year's government scheme might be next year's old hat but students will always be there on Monday mornings.

I am going to argue in the following pages that TVEI can in some senses stand for many other acronyms that have been travelling around the educational system, more or less purposefully, for the last two decades. The reader can check out his or her perceptions against my own as we proceed because there can't be many people working in education who haven't been touched (or, in some cases, manhandled) by educational *innovation*.

I shall suggest in what follows that TVEI can be seen as a paradigm for the dynamics of change taking place in British education during this particular slice of history, and that *discipline* is a very useful key to understanding the value of systems of learning in our society. For it is quite clear that our concept of *learning* is evolving, under pressure of reality rather than through educational philosophy, and the role of *teacher* is moving with it, sometimes painfully.

In exploring the nature of TVEI and of discipline we may discover ways in which certain tensions within our educational system are being resolved through a process of adaptation . . . and we may find contradictions that we will have to live through and which are a direct consequence of a society struggling to control massive, uncertain change.

Schools are currently operating in what might be called a *project economy*, a state of affairs which has enormous impact on their ability to deal effectively with change. Funding for curriculum developments now comes from many sources, and is targetted at different subjects, groups of students and sectors of schooling.

Facilitating agencies abound — to co-ordinate work-experience, build industry links and to act as management consultants, for example. No one has a clear picture of how it all fits together, because it doesn't. Not yet. There is an enormous amount of energy around and a deal too much entropy.

What we are experiencing in education is an aspect of a larger confusion, in which the number of acronyms abounding is directly related to the level of response generated by a society trying to cope. It is, I think, a creative confusion, a necessarily piecemeal attempt to deal with crises as they arise and not, as we might be forgiven for believing, a game of musical chairs. It can even be seen as a time of great excitement for those who are active; the strong thrive, success can be tasted. Change can be shaped.

Except, of course, by those who cannot be active — the weak, the dispossessed, the vulnerable, the powerless. In education, they are the students. Sometimes they are the teachers, struggling to walk a tightrope in a storm. At the heart of teaching is a relationship between teacher and learner. In difficult times, relationships intensify, roles blur, responsibilities collide with rights. Discipline is a short-hand term for the social contract operating within a teacher–learner relationship. In times of alteration, discipline is redefined.

Technical Vocational Educational Initiative

The TVEI is one of many current interventions into our educational system. The initials stand for the Technical and Vocational Educational Initiative, an unpleasing phrase which attempts to express the lines of development the scheme was expected to take. I have never read a philosophical justification for TVEI, though many teachers ask for it. This is because TVEI did not spring from educational theory; it came fully armed from the head of the Manpower Services Commission (currently called the Training Agency) as a response to what was described as a failure of education to prepare young people for the world of work.

In its very crude form, TVEI would improve skills training, particularly in areas of new technology, which would in turn lead to the creation of new jobs, make British industry more competitive and create wealth. Its inspiration was political, economic, pragmatic.

Now there is undoubtedly a degree of truth in the charge that the curriculum of schools, and to a lesser extent of Colleges of Further Education, is out of phase with the realities of late twentieth century life. Our curriculum has grown by accretion; it is overcrowded and out of shape. It is a kitbag full of many useful things, and some useless things, but it is not fully guaranteed to see its owner safely through the next ten years. Yet I believe TVEI, in its initial conception, was founded on a half-truth. The relation between skills and wealth creation is not causal. Wealth creation is more complex. Moreover, many teachers question the utilitarian impulses behind TVEI. They are right to do so.

What has happened since TVEI began, about five years ago, is fascinating. A philosophy has been created. TVEI has evolved into something more subtle and, I believe, more useful. This has happened through an inevitable process of colonization by educators. The Training Agency, too, has been quick to learn and respond. Teachers have accepted the need for new methodologies and new skills areas but have relocated them in the context of a liberal education, arguing that a *whole* man or woman, equipped with the knowledge, skills, experiences and confidence to make decisions and act effectively is more than ever necessary to a society driven forward by a continuing technological revolution.

What exactly *is* the TVEI? I have given up trying to explain it at dinner parties, because it is not a subject, or a qualification, or a place or a thing. It is, essentially, a sum of money and a set of ground rules (criteria). The strength of TVEI lies, paradoxically, in its lack of specificity. Teachers can respond to it in their own terms, using it as a springboard for the high dives they always wanted to try. I know of no teacher who has taken exception to the criteria, which we can summarize as follows.

The TVEI seeks to develop programmes of learning which are fully certificated, relevant to career opportunities, offering students a range of experiences (including a practical understanding of industry) and skills training (particularly those of handling new technology) through participative, problem-solving activities. Sensitive counselling through the progressive choices made between the ages of fourteen and nineteen should be tied into a system of recording positive achievement. There is an especial emphasis on the promotion of equal opportunities.

If you ask me 'what exactly happens in TVEI classes that's any different?' I would have to be honest and reply 'Nothing'. I've not seen anything or read about anything that doesn't take place in other projects and in good teaching generally. TVEI varies from place to place, depending on the local plans, but you can expect to see such things as an emphasis on group work and student projects, mini-enterprise, problem-solving activities, close collaboration with local industry, adults other than teachers in classrooms, students working in the community, an emphasis on the applications of technology, including information technology, an attempt to involve students more thoroughly in decision-making, careful counselling and tutorial work linked to a formative recording of achievement — a roll call of new approaches to teaching and learning, yes, but in some ways it's old wine in new bottles.

The difference lies not in what's being done but in the scale and scope of what's being attempted. The amount of corporate energy operating in the TVEI schemes I know about is enormous. It is not the individual examples of good practice which are so striking; it is the inter-relation of good practices.

This scale of change is being actively encouraged by the Training Agency. In the 'Extension' of the TVEI currently on offer to all local authorities in England and Wales, schools and colleges are urged to plan *whole-curriculum* developments for all students. Time will tell. Whole-curriculum approaches are notoriously slippery and sly: they tend to spread themselves thin and disappear or find a safe place and huddle there. Any school attempting TVEI Extension is taking on a course of action for which there are no experts. Sensible schools will, I believe, recognise that *whole curriculum* is better expressed as *student-centred*, where the emphasis is on an *entitlement* to agreed areas of study, forms of support and guidance, and worthwhile certification. If we start from the individual student and his or her needs and rights (for example, the right to accurate, full information about courses of study available within and outside the institution) we are much more likely to find the keys and levers to whole curriculum change.

The TVEI, then, has the avowed purpose of affecting a school at every level of operation — option systems, assessment and recording procedures, careers guidance, methodology of teaching, timetabling structures, staff responsibilities, student rights to an entitlement curriculum. This is a radical manifesto, and it is dangerous. If it is badly managed it will be at best inefficient and wasteful, at worst destructive, splitting staffrooms and destroying a school's commonly held agreements about its purpose and methods of working.

Some readers will find that too dramatic; others may recognize it. What you see depends on where you stand. I will come back to the TVEI and the notion of institutional change, but first it may be helpful to identify some of the concepts that operate within the term *discipline*.

Discipline

When I started teaching, discipline meant survival. All teachers know that a large group of young people, particularly adolescents, needs to be controlled if the teacher is to get safely from one end of the lesson to the other. One can talk of time-management, task management and group management, but the essence is control. Such is the realpolitik of education, operating as the baseline for professional survival, however experienced the teacher. It can be the stuff of nightmares. From this baseline one can interpret other notions of discipline, either positively or negatively.

Negatively, all forms of teacher behaviour can be seen as strategies for survival. Team-teaching, project work, out of school activities, can all be interpreted as ways of avoiding the conflicts generated by closing twenty young people in one room with one adult until a bell rings to release prisoners. Positively, one can claim that there can be no creativity without grounds of order. Only chaos can come from chaos. Teacher control is a pre-requisite for learning to take place. Team-teaching, project work and out of school activities, if properly organized, are ways of making education more interesting and useful for both students and teachers, of controlling through involvement.

I am quite sure that during any teaching day both positive and negative aspects of discipline can be found operating, often at the same time: different explanations are not necessarily exclusive. Yet to restrict discipline to control is to seriously undervalue the nature of the learning relationship and the integrity of teachers.

Most teachers would perhaps agree that there is a continuum of discipline ranging from strictly rule-governed behaviour enforced within a relationship of power and obedience, to self-regulation based upon self-knowledge and respect for the rights of other people, with many intermediate stages; and that any one student within a group will relate to a teacher with an individual understanding of the rules.

One can go further and say that the relationship will change over (often short) periods of time, for innumerable reasons. We might also say that it has been traditionally easier for the teacher to work within a ritual, authoritarian mode, where individual responses are quite deliberately subordinated. A teacher who encourages more open relationships, where negotiation plays a formal part in behaviour, is taking risks; but I believe those risks are now essential, for the following reasons.

First, our culture has changed. Young people in Britain, at the back end of the twentieth century, operate within a highly organized consumer-society, which offers personal fulfilment in the form of physical goods. One has only to study a television advert for a pair of jeans or a soft drink to recognize both the potency and the absurdity of the promise. Our children, and of course ourselves, are courted with images of empowerment such as social success and sexual satisfaction. Our society deliberately and systematically offers a false interpretation of life to unformed young minds, and packages the promise in short, dramatic sounds and images. A pop song is three minutes long.

When our children are continually wooed by excitement it is very difficult to sit twenty or more of them in a room for one or more hours and ask them to obey rules, listen and write. The passivity and sense of personal importance nurtured by a media-driven culture has destroyed the possibility of education based upon passive learning within a rule-governed environment which denigrates personal importance. If I labour an obvious point it is because there is still a very powerful nostalgia among parents, and government ministers, for a form of discipline in schools which runs contrary to the prevailing culture. We cannot have it both ways. Nor do I believe we should; for a second, more positive reason.

Passive learning, where teachers are experts who tell children what they should know and children learn it, operates successfully in a relatively stable culture. Teachers are traditionally conservative, their job has usually been to pass on received wisdom and ensure intellectual and moral continuity of the culture. While there is still a strong element of this mediation in teachers' jobs today, there is an equally strong element of ambivalence. We do not live in a stable society with a single culture; we do not agree on moral values; yesterday's solutions are suspect; today's problems are continually redefining themselves. Teachers find themselves in the unenviable position of being expected to ensure cultural continuity and stability in a society which does not possess those attributes.

Moreover, the last thing we want today is a society made up of convergent young people unable to interact with knowledge and values in a critical way. You do not need a high degree of self-motivation, self-knowledge and critical aptitude in a stable culture, though individuals who have that will do well; you do in a culture like ours, if you and the culture are to survive. In a world where rules are evolving, intelligent responses are essential.

For reasons of expediency and necessity, therefore, teachers are obliged to move away from rigid rule-governed, autocratic forms of discipline; a role-shift which is undeniably fraught.

This is not to claim, of course, that rules cannot operate within classrooms, or that teachers cannot expect children to listen: just as there are occasions when the most efficient form of learning is by a lecture or by memorizing, so there are occasions when silent obedience is the most useful context for learning. The fact is that today's teacher is expected to have both a larger repertoire of teaching methods and a more complex set of rules to adapt to circumstances. The rules of discipline governing a free discussion are different from those operating in a chemistry experiment. This in turn means that both teacher and student have to be aware of the changing behaviour expected in changing contexts — the rules have to be continually negotiated.

We will consider later on the implications for a community where codes of behaviour alter with circumstances, and of the difficulties attendant on role-shift for teachers and students alike. For the moment I will point out the obvious; that people aren't always very good at knowing how to move from one relationship to another, and they don't always agree with other people's interpretation of how to behave.

Teaching and learning

There are also epistemological reasons for shifting from traditional models of teaching and learning. Secondary teachers who have been trained as specialists in one or two subject areas are increasingly being asked, and particularly in TVEI, to broaden their teaching role within and beyond their specialisms. There are at least three reasons for this: development of the ways in which knowledge is made available; extended definitions of what can be legitimately included within particular disciplines; and new or reformulated categories of knowledge within the curriculum.

Knowledge now comes to us through many channels — television, radio, book, newspaper, videoscreen, microcomputer. The communications network which makes information and opinion available worldwide has made personal expertise a very shaky possession, if by expertise we mean being one of a few sources of knowledge. A teacher is now only one of many who offer instruction. His or her authority cannot any longer stand upon more possession of information, nor can the subject matter of education be dominated by the recall of learned information.

It is one of today's truisms that 'I don't know but I know where to find out' has replaced 'I remember'. There has been, accordingly, a desire to teach methods of information retrieval to students. Fine, as far as it goes. Yet it is also true that knowing where to look is only useful if we know exactly what we are looking for. Today's teacher needs, paradoxically, to be a greater expert in, say, History or Chemistry, if he or she is to help students formulate the right kind of questions and select from all the available answers.

I believe there is now an acknowledgement that young people do not need to know a vast amount of readily recallable information — such information is readily to hand — but more than ever need to know the basic principles of a particular discipline, its structure, concepts, limits, the kind of questions it can ask and the ways it can answer. They do not necessarily need to know about the Hapsburgs, but they do need to know the nature of historical evidence, to understand the concepts of kingship and democracy, to recognize ways in which societies organize power.

A teacher, then, has to be very expert indeed, not only as a source of factual information, but as an organizer of learning and a manager of resources. Lessons must still have content. You cannot teach History or Chemistry without it. But the factors governing the choice of content are now more subtle, related to usefulness for action, or relevance as we call it now, and for elucidating principles and key concepts.

Furthermore, teachers do not know everything. As our curriculum continues to adjust to action in the world outside school, teachers seek help from others — from business managers, office secretaries, local politicians, doctors, geologists, practicing chemists — people whose living depends upon the usefulness of knowledge.

Developments in communications have, therefore, obliged teachers to develop strategies for organizing and applying information, and skills in working with other people. If students are to gain power in handling information critically and usefully they must be given opportunity to exercise control over it. They have to ask questions, define tasks, propose methods, analyze solutions, talk it over with each other, present findings accurately . . . which can only happen if the teacher is very skilful at setting tasks and sensitive in shaping the student's progress.

If one accepts that school subjects are not simply concerned with information, but with application, the subject teacher has to reconsider what can legitimately be included in his or her work. Technology in general, and information technology in particular, can operate in many subject areas. Enterprise activities, where students work together to design and deliver a service or product for other people, now occur in subjects other than Business Studies. Business Studies itself has matured considerably from typing for lower-ability girls. CDT can include the business application of project work, incorporating computer-aided design; students in English classes use word processors to write plays for the local community; local people work with students in Home Economics. All these and more can be found in TVEI schemes. Such a liberation of activity has its real source in a growing recognition that the peculiar British distinction between *academic* and *applied* knowledge has stifled students and teachers and, as a consequence, has hindered social and scientific development.

Furthermore, new areas of study are arriving in schools, imported from higher up the system as recently formulated disciplines such as Computer Studies or Biochemistry, or as responses to broad vocational areas, often modelled on further education courses.

An example of the latter, from the Oxfordshire TVEI scheme, is the GCSE course 'Services to People'. This is a modular programme which considers the varied ways in which a community supports its members by offering services. The subject matter includes Travel and Tourism, Catering, Childcare, Accommodation Services, and Care of the Handicapped. Its purpose is not to train people for jobs — that is not a school's function — but to look critically at the notion of service, the way services are organised for particular client groups, how new technologies have altered the possibilities for service industries, and to alert students to a range of possible future career options. Such a course cannot be run on traditional lines. Apart from the fact that there are no secondary teachers trained to teach *Services*, the course demands a large input from people actively engaged in the service industry and a significant degree of out-of-school experience, which in itself requires changes to a school's organisation of time.

The *Services to People* course meets the TVEI criteria: it is active, useful, related to career opportunities, offers positive experiences for boys and girls of all ability and has worthwhile certification. It cannot be delivered other than through active, participatory styles of teaching and learning. However, it will not survive a National Curriculum unless it becomes cross-curricular.

Cross-curricular or integrated courses derive from the belief that the world cannot be understood or controlled solely in terms of separate disciplines of knowledge, and that students should experience the integration of knowledge through case studies (genetic engineering demonstrates the inter-relation of science and technology, throws up moral dilemmas, expands the medical profession, alters family planning and social evolution, and redefines the concept *human*) or through projects which incorporate a wide range of skills traditionally associated with distinct subjects (mounting an opera involves music, drama, technology, group skills, graphic design and communication, business advertising, and applied mathematics, for example).

Such programmes are notoriously hard to design and sustain, because the *state of the art* is in infancy and because organizing a cross-curricular team of teachers is logistically and socially difficult. Nevertheless, the impulse to provide for the practical integration of knowledge is one that education is trying to grasp because that's the way we interpret the world and how we get things done. Students on such programmes can expect highly participative sessions.

To summarize

I hope I have made my point by now. Schemes such as the TVEI force teachers to behave more flexibly. Discipline has to operate with a more open relationship based upon the responsibility of the learner and the managerial expertise of the teacher. This more open form of learning does not guarantee success but it does permit teachers to explore a wider range of responses and understand their students more fully. Individual acts of indiscipline still occur, and need to be understood in all their complexity, but I am here describing a general style of behaviour which allows players to interact in more adult ways.

I have spoken of discipline as behaviour within a relationship centred on learning. Relationships between teachers and students when engaged in learning have certain characteristics: they involve a number of bodies in a relatively small shared space and within a formally allocated time, beyond which the relationship is temporarily abandoned; they are based upon shared tasks, but the authority and accountability differ between the teacher and the students. The temporary relationship itself operates within a larger set of relationships which is the school community, and it may or may not be in accord with that larger set of values. Formal rules of behaviour are continually modified under pressure of the personalities and the changing dynamics of a lesson as it proceeds. The relationship is not one event but a continually adapting process as the teacher's attention shifts and students change tasks and interact with each other. Practical agreements about behaviour are enacted through a series of negotiations which are both conscious and unconscious, explicit and tacit, controlled and uncontrolled.

Studies of classroom behaviour have shown in an imperfect way what a subtle, strange thing a lesson is. Yet teachers and students do it all day and every day. Each lesson offers potential conflicts which are diverted, suppressed, driven underground, result in displacement activity, or surface into verbal or physical confrontations. It is a testimony to the skill and sensitivity of students and teachers alike that open conflict is, relatively, rare.

Given the difficulties of maintaining a healthy, fluid relationship in which agreements about behaviour outnumber disagreements, one has to ask whether the kinds of teaching necessitated by schemes such as TVEI help or hinder agreements. Because if it becomes significantly more difficult for a teacher to control a class involved in *active learning*, the teacher will revert to more closed, authoritarian methods and TVEI will become redundant.

It would be easy to just say 'Yes, it works', because that is what educational theorists want to believe. Many teachers want to believe it too and express their beliefs in the following pragmatic terms, which I personally find convincing.

People, they say, relate well and work more efficiently when they are respected by the ones they work with, are doing things they find useful and interesting, within their capabilities but challenging, are given support when necessary but feel they have control over their work, share ideas and activities with other people, and are rewarded for doing it. People do not relate well or work efficiently when they are not respected, are doing things they find useless or uninteresting — students are people.

If such a simple statement of faith seems as valid to you as it does to me, and if you are in general agreement with the argument so far, then we have reached a position which looks too good to be true. I have argued that for reasons of desirability and neccessity certain 'new' methods of teaching are redefining the more traditional notions of discipline. I have then said — O lucky chance! — that this new relationship of learning is more effective and agreeable to everyone. Before I close down the word processor and send to the printer this happy conclusion, however, I must listen to the sceptic in the corner of the staffroom who asks me where the evidence is, and what are the hidden costs, because you never get something for nothing. Good questions. Difficult answers.

Let me try some answers

There *is* a price to be paid for *active learning* and more open relationships between students and teachers; at its most simple, everybody has to work harder. In the TVEI, these relationships are being developed within a context of wider change, in school management structures, time-organization, curriculum content, and links with the local community. Desired changes in personal relationships between teachers and students are accompanied by, and to a degree are dependent upon, institutional change. Beneath the excitement of innovation is a continual sense of strain.

The strain arises for a number of reasons. All active change means more work, if only in terms of hours spent thinking, talking and preparing. New courses need new materials, learning and assessment objectives have to be co-ordinated, assessment methods have to be trialled and moderated. Also, we all use too much energy when we try to do something we've never done before. All teachers remember their first years of professional life, before they learned the tricks, the short cuts, effective gestures, tones of voice, classroom rituals — coming home exhausted and sinking in front of the television watching cartoons, appalling soap operas, anything at all until you could relax enough to mark and prepare for tomorrow morning. For teachers well into their careers a demand that they dismantle years of successful tactics for relatively untried ways of working can with some justification be seen as a bad gamble.

Students too feel the strain. They tend to be more conservative than teachers. It is hard to be deprived of the support that has been traditionally offered — carefully set tasks of a standard kind, with the teacher offering supporting information, telling them how to do it and when it has to be done. Group projects don't always feel like *real work*; discussions don't seem to be as important as written exercises. And because students aren't fully adult there is always a strong chance that it will go wrong. When a teacher lightens his or her control over a group, the danger of timewasting is always present.

Now there is a sense in which these kinds of strain are temporary. Courses are put in place. Teachers in time familiarize themselves with novel arrangements. Students learn to accept the new responsibilities that come with decision-making. But the effort and uncertainty demanded by more complex work patterns will always be greater than that of more closed teaching methods.

I would go further, though you may not follow me. I believe that current active approaches to learning are widening the gap between effective and ineffective teachers, because of the personal confidence and group management skills required. TVEI is seized on by some staff as a liberation; for others it is the last straw. When innovations such as the TVEI move beyond the small teams of committed *project teachers*, as is intended by the TVEI Extension, a significant number of teachers will feel they are unable to deliver and will in consequence attempt to neutralize innovation. More of that later.

Furthermore, there is methodological anxiety as well as that generated by the extra work and the sometimes uncertain outcomes of new teaching styles. It is much harder to control learning once we move away from instruction, set tasks and familiar processes, and it is correspondingly easier to misunderstand or misread the nature of the learning that is or is not taking place. New approaches to learning have to develop more sophisticated methods of appraisal, involving students' own recorded evaluations and clearly stated objectives. Such checking systems are necessary to overcome the very human temptation to believe useful learning is going on just because students are busy and content.

Let me continue with the qualifications. There is no hard evidence, that I know of, that the TVEI methodology produces superior outcomes for students. Many local evaluation reports from around the country comment favourably on improved relationships and attitudes between students and teachers. One would expect this, because the work is usually more interesting and seen to be useful, and the experience of working outside classrooms and being taken more seriously as participants in learning is inherently satisfying. In this sense discipline is better, and we can answer those who believe that football hooligans and muggers will disappear if we all get our canes out of the cupboard.

Where is the evidence, however, that the TVEI produces more effective learning? How do we begin to chart the relationships between teaching styles, discipline, and outcomes? It is too early to measure improvements by GCSE results, even if one were sure of the value of such an instrument and could disentangle student populations, the contribution of new and therefore strange work programmes, and the usual *halo* effect. Undoubtedly examination results will be used as a *measure*: we will have to wait and see and judge carefully. The evidence we do have tends to be personal, based on teacher and student perceptions, generally favourable to date, or relatively objective in estimating how far the *performance indicators* TVEI schemes set for themselves are being met. Such indicators are, however, in their infancy. We can measure attendance — TVEI students would seem to attend more regularly than others, though not in all schemes — and entry to options (more girls are taking technological subjects, but not, it seems, in the critical mass hoped for) but when we try to measure the quality of learning that has taken place we find it much more difficult.

One way through the difficulty is to set very clear targets for youngsters in the form of *competency statements*, a practice encouraged by GCSE grade criteria. The TVEI teachers are developing useful skills in describing such behaviours and this form of assessment is both more precise and more diagnostically useful than traditional norm-referenced tests. I am aware that the relation between norm-referenced and criterion-referenced testing is more interdependent than proponents of each usually admit, but the shift towards the individual measured against a specified objective rather than as a relative value within a peer group is to be welcomed. Supporting this system of regular target-setting and immediate feedback is the increasing opportunity for students to comment on their own performance through formative *recording*. Such developments hold out high hopes for improving our agreement about what is being achieved by our children and are, I think, useful in motivating students and teachers alike.

Performance indicators, as we currently call our attempts to specify measures by which we can detect desirable forms of behaviour, may provide evidence of the success or otherwise of students involved in more open learning environments and thus, in a general way, of the correlation between styles of discipline and outcomes of learning, but there are limits. We have to assume the indicators represent real targets, identify the most important behaviours, and are capable of relating to whole populations of students. We cannot, of course, with any degree of certainty, compare the results with those of students who are *not* working towards competencies within a supporting system.

When the sceptical teacher or politician, asks how successful these new methods of learning are, therefore, we can point to improved social behaviour and the more positive perceptions held by students, and we can indicate how many students are meeting the targets set; but I doubt whether anyone with a naive concept of educational standards will be satisfied. It is, perhaps, more important at this stage of the development of our educational system that the actors themselves are convinced. It is after all one of the necessary ironies of any curriculum development that the worst of the new is measured against the best of the old: for change which is unresisted is unlikely to be ultimately profitable.

I offer the above comments to counterbalance the optimism of my earlier statement of faith in more open, adult relationships. I do not believe they invalidate the notion that such relationships are necessary to our society, but they do suggest a more realistic context for the actual processes of change colleagues are undertaking.

Whole-school implications

This essay, so far, proposes that discipline is as an expression of a complex relationship between teachers and students; that contemporary interventions into the way we teach and learn, as in TVEI, attempt to involve students as much as possible in the processes of their own learning; that such an attempt is essential for our society; and that the implementation of new methodology involves a significant and strenuous role shift for both teachers and students.

I would like now to move on to the whole-school implications of developing these more open relationships, because my comments so far have been restricted to those teachers who are formally committed to curriculum change.

Staff involved in successful projects have many advantages. They tend to work as a close-knit team with a clear sense of purpose and, usually, a considerable degree of support from the LEA in the form of in-service and material resources. Perhaps most significantly, they feel important and experience a sense of control. Sometimes they have smaller groups of students to deal with; in the nature of projects they are doing things which break the daily routine of school life. This sense of power and worth helps to compensate for the uncertainty and the strain of working in open territory. Students too, begin to identify with a successful project: teachers are after all spending much more time and effort on them, which helps to ease the tension of trying out new relationships.

The other staff in the school, however, may be doubly disadvantaged. Not only do they perceive the lack of support and attention they, by comparison, receive; their own working patterns suffer disruption. The negative side of curriculum innovation includes students missing lessons to go out of school or to work on day-long projects, timetable dislocations, staff absent for yet more meetings; and, it may be felt, a general imbalance in the school's priorities. The tail, it is inevitably said, wags the dog. Staff who complain about the effects on the school's daily life often do so legitimately; sometimes the unhappiness derives from envy ('TVEI gets everything. If we had their resources . . .'); sometimes they are responding to threat.

For any project which actually works is threatening. It has to be. If it doesn't change anything it has failed. A scheme like the TVEI is particularly dangerous, because to deliver the TVEI criteria you normally have to change the timetable, alter the option system, give power to people who didn't have any, open up the school to outside scrutiny, cut across the traditional lines of authority and decision-making and allow students to behave in different ways. A school can usually put up with a degree of disruption, especially if systems change is handled sensitively and systematically, but legitimized changes in student behaviour can be personally alarming to some teachers.

When the TVEI is successful, the students get used to contributing to the ways lessons are shaped (Oxfordshire TVEI has student committees who talk regularly to staff about the project) and to being treated as young adults. They expect to be shown the relevance of their work to possible future careers, to comment on how they are doing, to have practical experiences of the world outside school and to operate in a variety of groups for different purposes. When a TVEI student appears in a non-TVEI class, therefore, the teacher may have problems in adjusting to the student's expectations. One can see why, and sympathize. The teacher feels usurped and believes his or her discipline is being undermined. It is. A major failing of innovations is their blindness to the culture of the rest of the school community: they are too busy building roads to worry about the effect on the environment.

Such a failure is critical. If a project attempts to redefine teacher–student relationships but does so only within its own boundaries, the effect on the school community can be negative: a house divided; and nothing divides a school more than disagreements about what constitutes acceptable behaviour, because consequences are sharply felt in classrooms.

Negotiation

It could be argued, however, that differences of opinion about discipline do not simply result from individual personalities and practices, but are symptoms of a philosophical dissent. A useful test case is the way in which teachers respond to the idea of *student negotiation*, because *negotiation* is, I think, a touchstone for the success or otherwise of the TVEI, or any scheme that claims to place the personal effectiveness of students at the heart of its manifesto. It may be worth examining the concept. Negotiation is one of the current words of power in education and like most magical words it often carries symbolic rather than actual meaning. It tends to mate with terms such as *active learning*, *experiential learning* and *participatory learning*, phrases often used interchangeably.

The term appears to have come into school jargon from two sources; the writings of the Further Education Unit (FEU) who have struggled to support college staff dealing with the *new* FE programmes (YOPS, YTS, PICKUP, NCVQ etc.); and the development of Records of Achievement, in particular of students' personal profiling. In its most Romantic form, negotiation implies an equal partnership between teacher and learner, with the student choosing his or her personal learning objectives based upon a recognition of current abilities and future needs. In this ideal relationship the teacher acts as consultant or counsellor, helping the student to analyze present skills, knowledge and experience, pointing out possibilities and limitations of particular courses of action, and assisting in the construction of learning programmes. The assumptions are that curriculum can be customized, that students know what they want and that teachers have the skills, time and resources to meet the student's needs. The promising developments in Open Learning and Supported Self-Study extend the organizational possibilities available to teachers interested in negotiation.

The realities of negotiation are of course rather more complicated. The frames within which decisions are taken are almost always set by the teacher and the student's choices are restricted by the nature of the course of studies he or she is taking, by the requirements of assessment and by the availability of resources. Furthermore, one can recognise the value of negotiating a work-experience placement or a statement for a record of achievement, or a personal target for homework in English, but one cannot negotiate whether an experiment was correctly conducted or whether one should study mathematics. Negotiation is, we might say, one of a number of strategies for conducting a formal relationship, and an entitlement within limits. Nevertheless, intelligently used, it is highly motivating and, perhaps more importantly, is an open recognition of the autonomy of the learner. It is, I believe, a fundamentally democratic procedure. Tacit negotiation goes on continually in any relationship of teacher and learner, about power and authority, accepted levels and rates of work and so on, but Negotiation with a capital N is a statement of belief in student rights.

That is why issues of discipline are actually issues of philosophy; and why, despite the fears that TVEI might be too narrowly utilitarian, its acceptance of negotiation with students is a guarantee of its liberality. You cannot negotiate if you do not accept the equal rights of the other party, despite their immaturity, their inexperience and their status (for equal status and equal rights are not necessarily synonomous). Most teachers, in my experience, are prepared to extend the right to reply of students, but they are sensible of the limits and aware of the dangers to established rules of behaviour. The fact that our students are indeed young and sometimes confused and awkward at having to talk personally with teachers means we have to be extremely skilful and sensitive; it doesn't mean it isn't worth doing.

Conclusion

I would like to conclude this essay by pursuing briefly the way in which avowedly innovative schemes such as the TVEI fit (or do not fit) into the whole school community. You cannot introduce a concept such as *student* negotiation in one part of a school without very careful *staff* negotiation, and the evolution of new styles of working throughout a school takes careful management and time. Projects such as the TVEI, however, tend to rush at change (they are time-limited, the teachers are enthusiastic and the purseholders are hungry to appease Questions in Parliament) which increases the possibility of fracturing a school's communal identity by applying too much pressure at one point only.

There are real difficulties in whole-school change, largely because we cannot close down operations while we reorganize. Indeed, our learning can only take place through doing. Schools try to accommodate new methods of working in two major ways: they start with one or more departments and spread out over time; or the whole school considers one issue (such as Equal Opportunities) and works on it together before moving on to the next issue. The TVEI Pilot Schemes tend to use the former strategy, the TVEI Extension the latter. Neither method guarantees total success, however, because of the natural instinct of institutions to resist any change which threatens status, territory, work-patterns or relationships.

We might in fact venture a dismal proposition: the more radical the innovation, the greater the community's resistance. A school tends to respond to a project much as flesh heals around a wound. The project is seen to be the sole responsibility of those staff who have been chosen to run it, systems are put in place which are believed to be necessary but temporary: teacher teams, co-ordinators, budgets; the project is perceived as an activity limited in scope and time, bringing useful resources into school. Timetablers minimize potential fabric damage by compromising ('Can't give you a halfday but I can offer a double period'). Project teams are not located within the senior management structure, co-ordinators are appointed who are keen but junior in status. The school organization acts to surround and normalize the project.

These things aren't necessarily deliberate. Sometimes the school management is simply not capable of effecting the necessary modifications, sometimes it argues that complex structures cannot be changed for the benefit of a minority of students. Whatever the reasons, the effect is the same. The funding ceases, the project ends; a few courses are in place, some equipment survives, teams disband, leaving teachers to carry on alone with their new insights.

There are ways around the problem of resistance to change within a school, but none of them are easy. In an ideal world (where one area of change is operating within an otherwise stable framework) it may be sufficient for senior management to persuade the whole staff that the new innovation is in everyone's interest, to consult and disseminate widely, tie the new scheme firmly into the school's management structures, systematically induct colleagues into the project, and spread the benefits as widely as possible from the beginning. Indeed, one of the undoubted benefits of the TVEI Extension is the way schools are encouraged to think in terms of the whole curriculum, though still, naively, starting with fourteen year olds, and to work closely with other schools and colleges for mutual support.

Such mechanisms for integrating trials and pilots into a school community are essential, but made difficult by the obvious fact that the rest of the school is not standing still. At the time of writing, schools are still struggling to implement GCSE courses, which will undoubtedly be rethought in line with a TGAT (Task Group on Assessment and Testing) Report which will determine ways in which an imperfectly formulated National Curriculum is taught, a curriculum package which looks at this stage very unlike that encouraged by TVEI, and in an uncertain relationship to an out of date 'A' level system of certification which most people want to change; while the Local Management of Schools, devolving greater financial and decision making to schools, is in potential conflict with the Training Agency's desire to encourage inter-institutional co-operation through formal *consortia* management structures. At the same time LEAs themselves are rapidly calculating the different roles and responsibilities being thrust upon them by a hasty government.

Interesting dramas wait to be played

The TVEI Extension is coming onto this scene at a fascinating period of educational history. No one is sure yet if it arrives as hero, villain or supporting player to be killed off in the first act. Some people believe it is in the wrong play.

The TVEI Extension is going to have to compete or co-operate: it cannot be seen as just another project — nobody can stand the thought of yet another one-off project; but if it competes it will lose. The only answer is to use the TVEI as a means of co-ordination; paradoxically, perhaps, as a radical mechanism for stabilizing a system in upheaval. LEAs aware of the possible disarray that may result from poor co-ordination of too many half-thought out plans for changing schools are using the money and management structures of the TVEI Extension, which will affect all secondary schools and colleges, as part of a much bigger planning operation. The TVEI, for them, is part of their strategy for coming to terms with an evolving National Curriculum.

We seem to have come a long way from the initial discussion of TVEI and discipline, via the nature of projects and the difficulties of managing large scale institutional change. The issues seem, to me at least, to be closely related, so I hope you will forgive a peroration. If we are to safely steer our educational system through the next ten difficult years, we need a vision. The vision of students working within more adult relationships, upon tasks which are essential to personal understanding and social health, that belief in the integrity of students as learners which underlies the TVEI and all the major curriculum initiatives of the last twenty years, can be the blood that makes the National Curriculum live. If such a belief informs the ways we construct our curriculum, train our teachers, assess our children, and manage our schools, we may reach a better land; the TVEI and all the other initials will in due time fade and fall away, but whether they have acted as rocket boosters or unwanted baggage is up to us.

13
Project Work on Pupil Achievement: the LAP Programme

Eileen Baglin

Introduction

The Lower Attaining Pupil Programme was announced in July 1982 by the Secretary of State, Sir Keith Joseph. His purpose was to provide a more effective form of education for fourth and fifth year pupils who would not be expected to take national examinations like CSE and GCE. This lower achieving group was estimated to cater for some 40 per cent of pupils in each of the age groups targeted. Some 13 LEAs joined the Programme for a three year period 1983–6: and there was a partial extension of funding for dissemination until 1987–88. The LAP Programme was the beginning of a period when central government, through the DES, would directly fund a curriculum initiative projected through LEAs.

In Oxfordshire the Programme was renamed the New Learning Initiative — a correction that was necessary in view of the fact that among low attaining 4th and 5th year pupils are many who are disaffected with their experience of schooling and what they have achieved. The Programme was, therefore, a challenge to schools to take up the critical issue of how to plan and execute an effective curriculum for pupils of possibly low motivation, poor self-esteem, and whose expectations for gaining meaningful employment on leaving school were low. It was not expected that pupils in their last two years of schooling would suddenly make up for what would be for many pupils a wasted time in school. To achieve improved motivation this meant developing schemes that would not challenge too abrasively areas that had been unfulfilling and demoralizing. Furthermore, pupils would need to see the relevance of what they were doing, both in interest terms as well as related to prospects for when they would leave school.

Although the LAP Programme was an initiative that joined others in trying to provide a relevant curriculum for this group of pupils, it differed significantly in that (a) it was a national initiative directly funded by Central Government, and it was a programme that contributed a great deal to the debate on issues related to attainment and differentiation for all pupils taking courses in the 14–16 curriculum (Weston, 1987). In 1984 a national evaluation team was commissioned by the DES and was based at the National Foundation for Educational Research. In July 1988 the Team produced a series of documents covering various aspects of the national evaluation.

In Part Two of the series report called *The Search for Success*, Penelope Weston cautions that in carrying out an evaluation 'it is important to be sure to what extent the new practice has actually been implemented, on the ground'. This is even more important she says when implementation involved 'changing attitudes and teaching methods'. She also draws attention to the 'intrinsic difficulties for the evaluator in measuring pupils' progress' bearing in mind that there were no clear baselines provided by the government as to how to assess progress. Furthermore, 'some schools — anxious to develop new opportunities for success in order to remotivate pupils — tended to see conventional tests or other baseline measures as either irrelevant to new approaches or as demotivating for the pupils'. The evaluation team had to listen carefully to what teachers, pupils, parents and project staff had to say about their respective projects, bearing in mind that at the time many projects had to develop their own criteria for assessment 'for approaches and skills not hitherto recognised in the 14–16 curriculum'.

In this chapter we shall first look at how the LAP Programme was developed in Oxfordshire. We shall then look at the evaluation carried out in relation to the Oxfordshire Project, which from now onwards we shall refer to as the New Learning Initiative (NLI). In conclusion, we shall describe the projected work of the Achievement Project in Oxfordshire (AP), which in essence capitalizes on the considerable ground work already established in this course of piloting and running of the LAP Programme. Finally, we shall consider the link between the NLI project and pupil behaviour.

The New Learning Initiative in Oxfordshire

The LAP Programme was in the vanguard of curriculum development projects which can also be seen as efforts by the government to solve the increasing problems of disruption and disaffection shown in the behaviour of pupils at the upper end of the secondary school. Also to involve schools in more vocational forms of education. By targeting the Programme so specifically (it was to focus on the bottom 40 per cent of the 14–16 age range) teachers' hands were tied. Many felt that the seeds of low attainment which would so frequently manifest themselves in disturbed behaviour patterns, were sown much earlier than age 14. A pupil does not suddenly become a low attainer, unlikely to reach the standards of which he or she is capable. Nevertheless the LAP Programme offered welcome resources especially in the light of striking examination failure on the part of significant numbers of pupils. The GCE and the CSE were still then the targets offered to pupils, many of whom, teachers suspected, were following courses in which they had scarcely any hope of success from the start. Thus there was a considerable degree of enthusiasm to tackle the challenge set by Sir Keith Joseph as the project began. The aim stated by Sir Keith Joseph was to 'shift education away from narrowly conceived courses and teaching styles and to prepare young people better for adult life and the world of work'.

In Oxfordshire, teachers began by attempting to identify the characteristics which may be observed in pupils whom they would see as low attaining. Long check lists were devised, using evidence gathered from discussions with pupils, from teacher observations, from test and examination results, and from discussions with parents. Such lists were not intended to provide standard criteria but to indicate areas of particular difficulty. These could be summarized as relating to motivation, behaviour, aptitude and performance. However, it was frequently difficult to separate one strand from another and teachers soon realised that these areas are inextricably woven together. Pupils' motivation, behaviour, aptitude and performance occur as a result of exposure to a variety of influences. Who can decide easily, for example, whether a pupil who is unmotivated in class and who does not produce work of an acceptable level is responding to peer pressures, or has a generally negative attitude to school or has a poor ability to learn from past mistakes?

These are complex and difficult questions. Aspects of personal and social development cannot be overlooked, nor the issue of pupil–teacher relationships. The poor self-image of many of the pupils identified in the earlier cohorts of pupils was very evident. It was accepted by teachers concerned that it would be important to find ways of increasing pupils' self-confidence and self-esteem. It was expected that this would result in improvements in the areas of behaviour, motivation and performance allowing pupils to reach their potential, and to experience success.

In the early months of the project the discussions centred strongly on the need for teachers to find ways to change pupils. Pupils' attitudes and responses to the curriculum on offer, were seen as being at fault. Schools worked in different ways but the majority first sought to identify their lower attaining pupils and then set about providing different, alternative curricula for them. In some places this seemed to emphasize the lack of achievement of particular groups of pupils and confirm their low opinion of themselves — sometimes other people's opinions too. Such experimention, very similar to that of Newsom or ROSLA groups, may have provided some worthwhile and enjoyable experiences for individual pupils, but it did not ensure that this curriculum change was seen as the responsibility of all staff nor did this approach really challenge teachers', parents' and pupils', fixed notions of ability and achievement. Several such groups became notorious as 'sink' groups of badly behaved pupils and the impact of the way in which pupils were organized in groups were evident in their attitude and behaviour.

An examination of the fortunes of one such group may serve to illustrate the problems. In an effort to cover topics which would be useful to the pupils, the group was studying services in the community. This was a topic chosen by the teacher without reference to the pupils. A visit to the local sewage farm had been arranged which became a nightmare for the teacher, embarrassing for the hosts and because of the total lack of involvement of the pupils, a complete waste of time for all involved. Some pupils refused to leave the bus, others sought attention by shouting and calling out rude remarks, and the force of the group dynamics was such that any pupil who might have been prepared to give the visit a chance, was carried along by the most vocal members of the group. The trip ended in chaos. This exercise, conceived with good intentions by the teacher and arranged at considerable cost, became a challenge to his authority and, during the ensuing discussions and recriminations, a means by which the group could question the whole rationale behind the special course which they were so unwillingly following.

This instance was an uncomfortable one for all concerned, but it brought doubts to a head amongst staff involved and created an opportunity for the school to review its policy. The bad behaviour of these pupils and their lack of achievement called for an answer. At this particular school wisdom prevailed and the decision was to abandon the discrete grouping which was causing so much anxiety and feelings of low status amongst pupils. In subsequent years the curriculum was drawn up in a less divisive manner and often changes were made to allow pupils more choice and involvement in decisions about courses. The ability to learn from experience, to listen to pupils and to be prepared to make changes is not always evident as schools tackle the problems of providing an appropriate curriculum for the whole range of pupils. It is significant to note, however, that the first batch of GCSE results from the school mentioned above were considerably better than those of other project schools. Even allowing for other variables of catchment area, parental expectations etc., there are issues here that merit discussion.

The development and changes made which have been detailed above did not take place overnight. Curriculum change is generally a painful and slow process. In the NLI project, the processes were considerably helped by the team of community link tutors and the co-ordinator of evaluation who had a strong influence in moving the thinking of the project ahead.

Because Project teachers were encouraged to use wider contexts of learning than the classroom, and because the emphasis shifted from seeing the pupil as being in some way deficient to an acknowledgement that the curriculum and its organization was less than perfect, some real changes of the kind already referred to began to take place. There was also an emphasis in the project on residential education which encouraged re-assessment of the way in which pupils learn best. These developments were greatly strengthened by the third aim where there was a focus for the project on cognitive skills development. The thinking skills programmes and the training which gives teachers the skills to be involved in these, led to some radical re-thinking about approaches to teaching and learning and to a recognition that a more individual and precise appreciation of pupils' progress in learning is necessary. Among other ways used by teachers to promote more creative and conducive contexts for learning, seen as relevant and purposeful by pupils, were work experience and links with further education colleges.

The work of the LAP Programme in Oxfordshire was taking place alongside other developments, which were also recognising that active learning and problem solving approaches to learning could bring benefits to all pupils. The development of Records of Achievement, which seek to help pupils record and review their own achievements was influential in helping teachers to find ways of recognising and recording successes which bring with them gains in terms of pupil motivation, behaviour and general attitude. In some situations, discrete grouping, which gathers together its pupils identified by the project can provide some answers. One headteacher accustomed to a series of embarrassing silences and rather difficult interviews when he made his personal farewells to the lower attaining fifth years as they left school, was surprised and delighted by the way in which the latter group responded to him. Their pride in the work they had completed and in the Record of Achievement which described and celebrated it was clear. These young people were leaving school in a confident and hopeful frame of mind, able to communicate with adults and with a record of skills gained and used. The comment was made that these pupils appeared more equipped for life after school than many of their more academically able pupils. Again, the reasons for the success noted by the head-teacher were complex.

However, some instances can be drawn from the incident. The project, in seeking to identify and disseminate good practice has spent time attempting to understand good practice, which produces the kind of positive results with pupils noted above. Perhaps the most important reason for peoples' positive attitudes is that they (and we all) respond to being valued. This means the schools have to create real areas in which pupils can be successful and deserve praise and recognition for their achievements. In practice, this often meant finding ways for pupils to work in small group situations, where the contributions of individuals can be fully understood and recognised. Such situations may not be within the traditional classroom based activities of schools. Community links of an enormous variety have helped many pupils to develop greater self awareness, to make sense of their experience of life as a whole and to understand, cope in and make a contribution to society.

The kind of situations in which pupils find themselves, both during community links and during residential experiences demand a clear response from pupils and expect participation. The LAP Programme has taught us that such direct experiences bring better motivation, increase self awareness and self-esteem.

All pupils need to perceive themselves as having worthwhile and important contributions to make to the life of the school, and where the school's definition of success is broadened beyond academic achievement, it is more likely that more people will succeed. One pupil from a project school who had a bad attendance record, a bad image of herself: 'I'm nothing', and who could be very troublesome to teachers when she found herself out of her depth because of fragmentary appearance in class, was asked to help at the local old peoples' day centre during a community links course. Here, under the guidance of sympathetic adults ('they treat me as if I am responsible' a cry frequently spoken during the project and illuminating the image some pupils have of their relationship with their teachers) she became an indispensable organizer of the bingo sessions. The adolescent who could behave so badly in school was transformed. The real purpose of the experience, the clear value of her contribution and the relevance of the task were perhaps some of the reasons for the success for this youngster.

Such lessons are perhaps easier to recognize in situations, such as the example quoted, outside the classroom. There are of course good reasons for ensuring that all pupils have access to what might be seen as more intense or exciting opportunities for learning of the kind created by residential experience. However, these general principles also need to be applied to matters of school and curriculum organization and practice. There is a clear need to find nationally validated certification of all pupils, which is not perceived as indicating failure for some. The GCSE has only gone part of the way of providing an assessment system for all pupils and there are still some subject areas which find the current syllabuses are often meagre in meeting the needs of the full ability range. Teachers working with the project found that modular approaches to the curriculum which can offer short-term, attainable goals with explicit learning targets can be successful and thus improve attitudes, but such approaches are not available in all subject areas.

Perhaps one of the most important lessons that the LAP Programme has taught teachers is the need to have a much more precise awareness of the individual needs of the pupils. Individualized learning targets can meet pupils' specific needs, arouse interest more effectively, and remind teachers that pupils have different needs at different times and in different areas of the curriculum. Too frequently in the past, schools were ready to define pupils as of *low ability* and assume that a pupil with difficulty in one area would have equal difficulty in all areas. It is interesting and encouraging to note that in Oxfordshire the term *low ability*, as a generalized statement about a pupil, has virtually disappeared. It is much more common to hear a teacher talking of lower attainers in a subject or under achievers in a particular area. The challenge there must be to accept these attitudes can be made easier by encouraging teachers to work together in cross-curriculum groups if possible and really address the problem of underachievement and low attainment. The cross fertilization of ideas between teachers in their own school, and between groups of teachers from different schools, has been instrumental in encouraging project developments.

This kind of curriculum change and the influence it has on pupil behaviour has implications for the management and organization of schools which cannot be overlooked, for example, how to promote the practical experiences within the community which can be so valuable and frequently difficult to organize within a conventional timetable framework. If the pupil has to miss other classes in order to fulfil a commitment to community links, this can either imply that the other subjects are less important, or the child has little chance of success anyway. Can all pupils miss classes to undertake community links? Unless a school has considered all these facets of the issue and resolved problems before offering opportunities to pupils, the negative results could be more significant than the gains. In general, the structures of many schools are not enabling ones and most find difficulty in accommodating the needs of individuals.

Similarly, several schools in the project have come to understand the need for policies for residential education. Difficult to staff *and* to organize in term time because it is frequently imposed on top of existing rigid structures, the residential experience offered to many pupils seems likely to be haphazard. Little progression can be built in and there is not always a determination to weave residential work into the curriculum. Problems of this kind can only be solved when timetables and staffing arrangements can be made more flexible. The timetable should be an aid to good practice: not a barrier against it. Perhaps the strongest factor in all this is teacher expectations and attitudes. For this reason, inservice training has been a strong feature of the NLI project. At times one was tempted to view the project as a teacher-development exercise far more than as an attempt to improve the education for particular pupils.

Monitoring and evaluation procedures, of a formative nature, became a very important facet of the project's work. Building on the notion that self-evaluation was the best and most effective approach, schools and teachers were encouraged to be constantly aware of what they were doing and the effects that the project was having. Community tutors wrote regular reports to review progress and set targets and these were discussed with the project evaluator who was part of the central team. Schools gained valuable experience, in fact, in preparation for the monitoring and evaluation procedures which will be expected as part of the 1988 Educational Reform Act. The most ambitious evaluation was that carried out at the end of the five years of full government funding. The next section of this chapter will describe the interesting way in which this evaluation was organized and give an account of what it said.

The Oxfordshire evaluation of the LAP (NLI) programme

At the end of a five year programme of curriculum change and innovation it was important to establish what had been achieved, to understand what worked and what didn't work and the reasons for this, and to make recommendations for the future. The evaluation, planned by the Heads' Monitoring Meeting, was aimed at allowing for individual responses, but managed in a variety of ways within a common structure. The aim, therefore, was to involve as many staff as possible, to be as objective as possible, to concentrate on the outcomes which related to the original aims of the project, and to create a balance between asking schools to discuss issues, yet not being too demanding of staff time and energy. Schools were asked to respond to a broad framework of questions aimed at bringing together a collective view on:

1. How pupils, as a result of being part of the project, came to perceive themselves, and were perceived by others?
2. What aspects of the pupils' attainments were raised?
3. In what way attitudes and self-image had been improved?
4. What staff, directly involved and staff as a whole, learnt from the experience of being involved with the LAP Project and what lessons would be applied in future planning?

Each school was allocated two 'critical friends' (one central team member and one community link tutor) to act in that capacity in whatever ways the school felt to be appropriate. For example, in some schools the critical friends met groups of teachers (the project team or heads of departments); in others they talked to individual staff or to staff in twos and threes. The role was to ask questions which would help schools to undertake this evaluation exercise profitably. Each of the original eleven schools produces an evaluation document.

Initially the NLI project was set up to focus on and develop:

1. School-community Links
2. Residential Education
3. Instrumental Enrichment

as means by which the curriculum could be made more flexible, practical, motivating and accessible for lower attaining pupils. These three main areas were intended to service and support the curriculum rather than be discrete activities within it. There was a whole-curriculum aspect to the project's original aims, and these areas were pegs upon which to hang the more specific objectives of developing active experiential learning, increasing pupil choice and motivation, and providing more opportunity for success and achievement. The project set out to make school a positive experience for the pupils whose typical experience was characterized by failure and disaffection.

Instrumental Enrichment, and then the Oxfordshire Skills Programme (both Thinking Skills Programmes), were discrete activities for which time was needed on the curriculum and pupils had to be selected. The teachers were specially trained for Instrumental Enrichment, the programme had its own philosophy and methods, and was offered, as a new and different *course* for low-attaining pupils. In this sense it was the most clearly defined focus for the project, initially, and the most visible during the first year.

The School-community links aspect of the project was conceived with the general aim of developing community schooling. This was thought about in terms of opening the school up to adults in the community, as a resource for them, as a means of using their skills in classroom alongside teachers, as well as in terms of facilitating pupils' learning out in the community. It was evident, well into the project, that the aims of school-community links were being interpreted differently by the participating schools, and this was due to the lack of overall specific objectives and targets, common to all schools in this area at the initiation of the project.

The third focus for the project, Residential Education, aimed to provide pupils with active experiential learning in various residential contexts. It had most of the project's resources, and was targeted at more pupils than others areas and was the most immediately accessible project activity. It had a seconded teacher to evaluate its impact for two years of the project's life.

The NLI project set out to be pervasive in curriculum terms, and to focus on *process* issues in pupils' experience of schooling i.e., on contexts for learning, on the nature of the learning experience, on allowing pupils a new start with new and different kinds of activity, on changing pupil attitudes and increasing motivation. The three areas, Thinking Skills, School-community Links and Residential Education, were in that sense not about specific courses or curriculum slots, although there was clearly a large personal and social element, an implicit practical emphasis, and very quickly as the project was implemented, a focus on pre-vocational learning.

To assist the project leader in the running and development of the project, a number of staff were appointed centrally; a support teacher for science and technology, a project evaluator and a team of eight school-community link tutors to serve the eleven project schools.

An important aim of the NLI project team was that school should *work from strength* and although three particular areas were identified for development, an interesting feature of the NLI has been that schools have responded in a variety of ways. There have been differences in curriculum provision, in kinds of accreditation offered and in the impact and effect of being involved in the NLI project. In some schools, the problems of low-attainment were already a live issue being addressed by teachers, in others a particular area (e.g. community links) had already been developed. The task of the county project was to find ways to support and encourage developments which were already in hand, to find ways of inspiring others and to make the channels of communication between schools as useful and helpful as possible.

Community-links tutors

The concept of a community-links tutor's post, which involves schools using teachers in an enabling, supportive non-teaching role was an unfamiliar one at the beginning of the NLI project. This produced challenges for the schools, for the authority and the community tutors themselves and some problems occurred at the beginning of the project for a variety of reasons: roles were unclear; there were some failures of communication; some community-links tutors faced credibility problems within their schools; and the general process of exploration of objectives, methods and purposes was difficult for all. A critical factor in the extent to which schools now have organized and curriculum based community programmes for pupils has been their interpretation of the community-links tutor post. As the project developed it became clear that the factors which influenced the way in which the community-links tutors worked within their schools, and how much credibility they possess, have continued to be powerful determinants of how much the post could achieve.

Project networks

The identification of these areas of focus made the *development of county networks* more straightforward. These have been an important outcome of the project. Not only have they facilitated the curriculum development taking place under the aegis of the NLI but they have, in some measure, paved the way for teachers working together on subsequent initiatives. The networks can be represented thus:

Figure 13.1

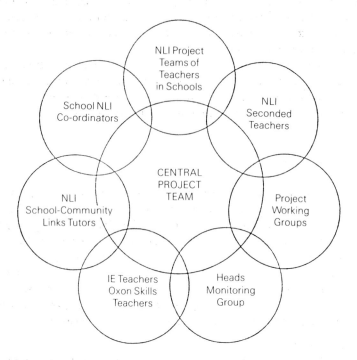

In formal and informal ways, the networks between schools in the county and between the central team and schools have been powerful agents in influencing curriculum developments of the project. One important task of the authority, which has been the responsibility of the central team, was to encourage and sustain such links and, as the time progressed, to make and maintain links with other county initiatives.

The national perspective

It has been important to remember that this project was part of a national attempt to address the problems of under-achievement and with this in mind, an emphasis on the national perspective has been made whenever possible. Reports have been circulated following the various LAPP network conferences, ideas from them have been discussed and tried out and teachers have fairly frequently been reminded of the wider concern about the success of the project by visits from NFER evaluators and from numerous HMI. In the early days of the project, schools often felt very tentative about exposing their pupils and teachers to visitors who would ask searching questions and there was anxiety about disrupting timetables or interfering with school organization. The national evaluators have become in general, however, useful and helpful sounding boards — people who can bring a national perspective and the NFER project leader in particular has fulfilled an important function in drawing together project staff from the LAPP authorities. It seems a pity that the usefulness of such a forum for dialogue was not foreseen by the DES when the project was established.

Contact with the DES was sporadic and usually related to funding. It is a matter of anxiety that this project, like many of pupils it was set up to help, seems to be of low status and little interest now, heavily overshadowed by the National Curriculum and issues related to the Education Reform Bill.

Inservice provision

Inservice provision has taken a variety of forms and involved a large number of teachers across the project schools. A secondment programme, regular summer conferences, school-based inservice events, Thinking Skills training programmes, and a series of linked workshops on various topics have all featured. As the project progressed it became increasingly clear that inservice training was central and critical to the work of the project in a way that had not been envisaged at the beginning. There were changes in the way this was managed as a result of lessons that emerged, and an increase in opportunities provided, partly as a result of devolved funding. Some examples of inservice provision include:

1. *Secondments*

   Initially a number of one year full-time secondments were arranged which allowed individual teachers to pursue areas of interest. Their work was not always as firmly rooted in school developments as it could have been and has not therefore been fully used by schools in some cases. As the project progressed better negotiation has taken place between all concerned to ensure that clear tasks and objectives have been established, regularly reviewed and followed up.

   During the last two years of full national funding, teams of teachers have been seconded on a day-a-week basis, working together to develop schemes of work and assessment. This has been a successful piece of collaborative curriculum development, the NLI project having worked in co-operation with the Oxfordshire Examination Syndicate (a modular GCSE initiative) and other initiatives, although some difficulties have been experienced in releasing teachers.

2. *Summer conferences and workshops*

   These have been held regularly throughout the project and have been extended in the dissemination phase of the project to draw together groups of teachers from all of the project schools and beyond. They have taken both a subject-abased approach and a broader focus on cross-curricular issues of under-achievement. Shared experience and positive relationships between teachers from different schools have been established as a result.

3. *Thinking skills training courses*

These have been important since the outset of the project in establishing networks of teachers and have been a powerful instrument in encouraging teachers to examine their practice. It is a measure of the success of the thinking skills courses that they have been taken up by large numbers of schools in Oxfordshire and beyond. From September 1986 the Oxfordshire Skills Programme was established as a project reaching beyond the LAPP schools and age/ability limits. From September 1988 it has been resourced by the LEA.

4. *School-based INSET*

One of the most successful and expanding areas of development has been the provision of INSET for teams of NLI teachers or larger staff groups, mounted either in school or in pleasant surroundings away from school premises. These have given opportunities for planning, preparation and review, as well as a sharing of the wider issues of the project.

5. *Evaluation and Dissemination*

It is important to note that the project has, throughout, emphasised very strongly that its work would only continue and develop properly if there were regular evaluation and review. Similarly the need to disseminate the ideas of the project and to share these with as wide an audience as possible has been at the forefront of the central team's mind during the latter years of the project and has been accepted as a priority during the forthcoming two years of dissemination funding by the project schools.

The emphasis has been on self-evaluation, to raise understanding and awareness of what has been achieved and to set targets and objectives for the future. Some examples of how evaluation and dissemination have been approached are:

— Regular reports written by the project staff;
— Meetings to discuss these between the writers and members of the central team and/or senior staff in schools;
— Meetings between groups and the evaluators (e.g. community links co-ordinators and evaluators, central team and evaluators);
— Seminars and workshops;
— Evaluation process planned by the Heads' Monitoring meeting, using *critical friends* to support a major evaluation exercise, culminating in a report to mark the end of the five years of full government funding for this project;
— Publication of Occasional Papers and Newsletters.

Outcomes of the project

This part of the paper is a summary of responses to the evaluation exercise undertaken towards the end of the five years of the full funding. The NLI project in general terms has influenced changes made in schools during the past five years. It has raised awareness about a number of issues and changed staff attitudes. It has given schools valuable resources which have been used in a variety of ways to try out and evaluate more active methods of teaching. It has also led the way as far as this model of curriculum change is concerned, which seeks to combine central co-ordination at the same time as promoting individual school developments.

Examples cited of changes made in schools related to organization of the curriculum suggest that in several cases the NLI experience has contributed to a more flexible curriculum structure. Use has been made, for example, of blocked timetabling, longer periods and modular frameworks, as a means of enabling the provision of opportunities for community-based learning, work experience, extended projects, and greater pupil choice. In many cases changes in the curriculum structure meant that pupils were able to spend longer periods of time with a smaller number of staff and therefore to develop stronger relationships both with staff and with other pupils.

The need for clarity and sharing of aims and objectives at the beginning of the project (and reviewed throughout the project) was stressed by schools. It was felt that the lack of these led to problems such as the identification and selection of the pupil target group. A fundamental problem has been the false premises of there being *a bottom 40 per cent*, that low attainment is confined to that group and that disaffection can be isolated in the 14–16 age group. There has, therefore, been a continuing dilemma because of the need to balance the central (government) demands, aims and objectives with those of each institution. Lack of clarity from the DES and the reluctance of schools against the background of GCE and CSE to apply the programme to enough pupils (in only one school was 40 per cent taken as the measure) resulted in unclear local targets and the provision of special courses for small numbers of pupils. This militated against staff development for the whole staff. In several project schools the NLI work has been the preserve of a small group of staff and, although their efforts may have been viewed with tolerance or even with gratitude because they were producing curricula for pupils seen as difficult by other staff, in general the project cannot claim that its aims and objectives were clearly understood nor shared by the majority of staff. This has reduced its impact and effectiveness in some places.

Where schools used the planning year creatively, identified and communicated the roles of the co-ordinator and community-links tutor and organized the way in which the resources were to be used and managed, it seems that they dealt with some of the factors which influenced the success or otherwise of the project. Many schools raised the difficulty of ensuring that all staff had opportunities to consider the issues of the LAP project especially if they were not directly concerned with what the school was providing and had other priorities and responsibilities. The danger of the project being associated with one person only was mentioned. This can lead to isolation within the school group of staff. However, the way in which cross-curricular teams of teachers had worked successfully together was also commented on as a positive achievement of the project.

The question of whether NLI pupils should be identified and then taught as a discrete group or whether they should be integrated into the mainstream curriculum is one which has been raised in most schools. The claimed advantages of a discrete group include the possibility of providing curriculum experiences which really do meet individual needs; the provision of a secure framework in which to learn; the increased possibility of good pupil–teacher/pupil–pupil relationships; the possibility of providing courses with appropriate targets taught by teachers who are (usually) fully committed to their tasks. On the other hand the discrete course can be in danger of promoting a separate, divisive curriculum, with limited horizons. Narrow courses can be offered, and the effect on pupils' self-esteem can be bad. Partial integration has therefore operated in many of the schools, with pupils involved in separate NLI provision for varying percentages of their curriculum time.

What kind of provision to make is a subject for continuing debate. It is closely connected to matters of status. Several schools have recognised that the issue is not whether all pupils would have the same curriculum offer but that there should not be a divisive offer made. Each group of pupils should be offered a curriculum that is valued by all and therefore has status. Problems of how to manage the curriculum so that this can be true are being approached by different schools in different ways, although once a particular pattern has been established, changing it is difficult. It is perhaps a measure of the success of this project that schools now seem able to approach this flexibly — at present several are abandoning discrete grouping and trying to provide appropriate opportunities for all within GCSE provision, others are introducing pre-vocational courses. The challenge being met by these schools is of finding ways to broaden the range of the vocational field and thus ensure acceptance of these courses as having status equal to other courses. This move is part of the national trend towards greater vocationalism and a practical emphasis in the curriculum.

In some ways the LAP project itself can be said to have been tinkering at the edges and trying to treat symptoms not causes. One important lesson that has been learnt is the unwisdom of this. Having experimented with the provision of alternative curricula for small groups, several schools are now recognising that the real need is to change attitudes and teaching approaches for all staff. Such radical change needs to take place within the context of whole-school developments. The NLI project has made a significant contribution alongside other initiatives (e.g. OCEA, TVEI, GCSE) to whole-school curriculum review. It has shown that the kind of provision that a school makes for its low-attaining pupils has implications for the whole curriculum. Identification and action is needed in schools to address the root causes of low-attainment.

Some features of the successful practice which has been investigated and used during the project and which schools seek to continue include:

1. *Active Learning*: interactive learning and teaching processes have been identified by most project schools as important features of their provision and as means of improving pupil motivation, although there are

implications here for the need for enabling structures and for Inset to allow teachers time to examine their pedagogy and methodology.

2. *Small Group Size*: Various strategies have been explored to find ways of reducing class size in the recognition that this can make teaching and learning more effective. These include flexibility in groupings, using group work, using adults other than teachers to support teachers.

3. *The Use of Modular Approaches*: which can facilitate greater achievement. They necessitate clear aims and objectives with notions of progression addressed and built in. At their best they can offer pupils choice, variety, differentiated targets, more flexibility and individualized pathways. The challenge has been to make them also coherent and rigorous.

4. *Community Links*: to provide pupils with different and more motivating contexts for learning, have been one of the outstanding successes of the NLI project. All schools involved are seeking to maintain the community links tutor post as the full funding comes to an end and the pioneering work of the team of tutors as enablers and facilitators for teachers, and as course developers has been very important.

Examples of community links experiences which involve pupils going from the school into the community includes:

1. Placements in primary schools, special schools, play-groups, hospitals, old peoples' centres, community centres, libraries, training centres, charity shops, Meals on Wheels assistance;

2. Projects in conservation, painting and decorating, designing and making toys, conducting surveys, organizing entertainments for groups in the community, producing community newsletters, local history projects, and fundraising.

Examples of community links experiences which involve adults and groups coming into the school include:

Various speakers and adults prepared to share their skills in the classrooms, careers officers, youth workers, first aid course leaders, parents, further education representatives, artists in residence, school based crèches, special events/entertainments for community groups. specialist courses run by adult volunteers etc.

The success of these has been very evident as shown by the following examples of pupil comments on what they have learnt from their community experiences:-

'Now I can get on better with people, I have more confidence in myself, I talk to other people more freely and listen to other peoples "problems better''. To be trusted on my own with other people and not to argue with them. To help me understand my friends better and to trust them'.

'Sense of satisfaction, more belief in my ability'.

'From going over to the crèche the thing I learned was patience because I haven't got any and you can't be impatient with children because it just doesn't work. You learn how to be patient and to consider other people'.

'My Mum thinks it's good because she said you learn to use your own initiative because she didn't think I had any'.

'You feel you're achieving something because you're actually doing it, not like in other lessons when you look up in a book or something, you've actually done this, you've taken part in it and it's yours'.

5. *Skills-based Approaches to Learning*: have been developed through the original involvement with Instrumental Enrichment and subsequently with the Oxfordshire Skills Programme. In addition to the special courses offered the approach and philosophy have been extended in some schools to other areas of the curriculum for example, Maths and English. Greater understanding of the cross-curricular skills of learning has been developed and from the small beginning within the NLI project, another major county project has been established.

   Ten of the project schools continue to use a Thinking Skills Programme with the target pupils, (in all but one of the cases the Oxfordshire Skills programme), and two of the remaining schools plan to use the programme next year. This aspect of the project has also extended considerably beyond the target group and more than thirty-five schools in Oxfordshire now use the programme in one of its two forms. Two of the target schools are extending the programme so that it becomes incorporated into the other curricular experience of NLI pupils.

6. *Residential Education*: especially for lower-attaining pupils, has been greatly enhanced because of the NLI project. Several schools are developing policies for residential education and the way in which residential work has enriched and extended the curriculum has been praised by HMI and national evaluators.

   All NLI target pupils have been offered opportunities for residential education as part of their curricular provision. Examples of opportunities offered include: outdoor pursuits and adventure, camping, youth hostelling, problem solving and decision making courses, arts residentials, outdoor survival, field studies, personal and social education courses, sailing, cycling, conservation courses, thinking skills course, sports courses, community projects courses, overseas visits, study courses and induction courses.

   Pupils comments concerning the value of residential education include the following:

   'I do more for myself and others'.
   'I have learned to be more confident and not to be scared to do things I have not done before'.

'I get on with people more and I help out'.

'I've learned that I'm not the only person with problems'.

'I've learned how to cope with snoring and small spaces'.

'How surprised I was at myself for getting along with other people who I haven't paid much attention to before'.

'I learned that when faced with a problem I can cope'.

'Not everybody can be perfect'.

'If I get on with people they get on with me'.

7. *Home School Links*: several project schools point to the importance of their work in this area and to the range of ways in which better relationships have been sought. Examples of home school links developed through the project include: home visiting schemes, parents' involved in visiting pupils on placements, volunteer parents running short courses, parents assisting in classroom work, revamped parents' evenings, exhibitions and presentations for parents following residential courses, parents attending residential courses and parental involvement in profiling systems.

8. *Assessment and Accreditation*: are also issues which have occupied much staff discussion time, especially as this project has been working against the background of the change to GCSE. There is much anxiety from schools that GCSE is not meeting the needs of low-attainers and although there is great interest in county modular GCSE developments, these are as yet for the future. Meanwhile practice in the project varies from offering GCSE to all pupils to offering a range of other kinds of accreditation. There are examples of RSA and City and Guilds/B.Tech prevocational programmes. The tension between examinations and interest-led curricula has been keenly felt and continues to be explored. (It is interesting to note that the majority of target pupils from schools have secured employment without reference to examination qualifications).

Many new courses of great variety have been developed as a result of schools' involvement in the NLI project. These include: Integrated Humanities, Community Studies, Community Projects, Communications, Numeracy, First Aid, Creative Arts courses, Vocational Preparation courses, Computer courses, Residential courses, Outdoor Survival, SMP Maths, Lifesaving, Science and Technology courses and Thinking Skills courses.

Teams of teachers have worked on the development of modular GCSE courses which cater for the full ability range, e.g. in English, Community Studies, Media Studies, and seek to incorporate the good practice of the NLI project. It is hoped these will be approved in the future. Schools have also developed their own forms of certification and profiling to credit pupils' achievements in, for example, residential education, community links work, work experience, practical projects, etc. Profiling systems — OCEA, City and Guilds B/Tech, or R.S.A. have been an important feature of most school developments.

Outcomes for pupils

During the four years of the classroom phase of the project, over 2,000 pupils have been directly involved in NLI provision for varying percentages of their time in school. This section outlines some of the positive changes that have occurred in these pupils' attitudes and performance as a result of the project.

In general it was felt that the attitudes of pupils identified for the purposes of the project have become more positive — both towards what they do in school, and towards their teachers and one another — as a result of changes in curriculum and classroom practice. Pupils now left school with a sense of achievement and increased confidence. Typical comments from teachers include:

> 'Most of the group I had for two years increased their own self-confidence and felt they had *achieved* something from their last two years of schooling. They did not generally consider themselves *failures* and if asked most would say they enjoyed the course, saw it as more relevant than options and left better prepared for work and adult life'.

> '. . . there is no question that there was considerable rise in self-confidence during the course. This might have been as the result of students having to rely on themselves, e.g. on Work Experience, more than they would have otherwise or it might simply have been part of the maturing process. Small groups also meant that individuals could have more attention than would otherwise have been possible'.

It was also felt that better pupil–teacher relationships have resulted from a more co-operative approach to teaching and learning, and from the increased individual attention and dialogue possible in smaller groups. Greater continuity of staffing and improved pastoral provision have been important features of many integrated courses. Relationships have been strengthened particularly during residential courses. Similarly pupil/pupil relationships have improved as a result of more emphasis on group work and collaboration.

Changes in attitude and relationships were largely ascribed to the fact that pupils have been able to see the relevance of new courses and activities and take a more responsible role in the planning and evaluation of their own learning. The provision of opportunities for learning in the community and in the new environments has increased their motivation and enjoyment. Pupils have responded well to being trusted and to being included in the decision-making process. More variety in the kinds of learning available and a wide view of what constitutes achievement has meant that their successes have been recognised and valued. Self-esteem has therefore improved significantly for many pupils.

In many cases attendance has also improved notably, with few instances of persistent non-attendance, and a decline in the number of referrals for poor behaviour has been observed. Selective attendance and behaviour in favour of project activities has also been an indicator of the success of these in relation to the rest of pupils' school experience. However, negative behaviour has sometimes been reinforced in situations where disruptive and poorly motivated pupils have been grouped separately.

It should be noted that where groups of pupils have perceived themselves as low status, and their work as peripheral to that of the school as a whole, the effect on attitudes, confidence and behaviour has sometimes been counter-productive:

> For a few, attitudes and self-image have moved in a positive direction. However due to the high concentration of poorly motivated pupils who have a limited range of social skills many pupils' self image has moved in a negative direction. They see the group as a *sink group* and have developed a sink mentality (a teacher).

Several organizational factors have been critical in determining the status of project provision within school and therefore affecting pupils' perceptions of themselves and how they are perceived by others.

The criteria used for identifying and selecting pupils for project involvement have been especially influential. In schools where pupil selection has been based upon individual needs and interests in specific areas of attainment, rather than generalized and negative criteria such as poor behaviour, the perceptions of all concerned have been more positive.

The extent to which the pupils have had open access to project provision, or have been heavily guided, has had a significant impact on pupils' attitudes. In cases where pupils feel they did not exercise genuine choice, there has sometimes been resentment both on the part of the pupils involved in project activities and on the part of the pupils who have been excluded. Negative labelling has been more likely to occur and the provision has tended to assume low status in the eyes of the school as a whole. When groups have been largely self-selecting, however, this has not happened in the same way. A relevant pupil comment is:

> 'If you choose what you want to do and you don't enjoy it, then it's your fault, but if the teachers tell you what to do and you don't enjoy it, then it's their fault'.

Perceptions have also depended on the number of pupils involved in the project. Whilst few schools have been able to address the intended 40 per cent target population, the problem of labelling has been overcome where project activities have been available to a substantial proportion of pupils, or where a whole school approach has been adopted. Small, discrete courses occupying a large percentage of pupils' time have most difficulty in raising their status and the perceptions of others.

The nature of the divide between project provision and non-project provision has been a contributing factor in influencing staff and pupil attitudes generally. Tensions have existed when the contrast was such that identified NLI groups were perceived either as an elite with privileges and greater opportunities, or as a *sink group*. Alternative approaches which are seen to function in opposition to mainstream provision can exacerbate the problem, and it has been important to avoid establishing a separate ethos.

The location of the project classroom within the school, the positioning of NLI courses in the options booklet and other such factors have also been instrumental in enhancing or diminishing perceptions of staff and pupils and have also reflected the value placed on project activities by the school.

In general terms the extent of the ownership and understanding of the aims of the project within schools has been crucial, as has the provision of valid forms of accreditation for NLI courses and the availability of those to a wide group of pupils.

Schools concentrated initially on establishing changes in pupils' attitudes and motivation as a necessary foundation to raising levels of attainment. It was felt to be important to broaden definitions of achievement and to increase the opportunities available to pupils to perform in areas other than the traditionally academic. Greater success was therefore possible in the sense that a wider range of skills were being assessed and properly accredited.

In particular, gains in personal and social skills have been observed as a result of increased group work and collaboration in classes. Pupils have demonstrated their ability to take responsibility, make decisions, solve problems, act independently and co-operate within a group context. Parents, teacher and pupils have all commented on the improvements in confidence in these areas. Typical comments include:

'My Mum thinks its good because she said you learn to use your own initiative, because she didn't think I had any. She didn't think I could be punctual, she didn't think I could be confident! Before I was really quiet, I was shy and sort of nervous, but I've relaxed now because I'm used to it'.

Particular emphasis has been placed throughout the project on extending opportunities for pupils to develop their skills of communication. Some examples of how the NLI project has attempted to enhance pupils' communication skills are as follows:

— More discussion work, e.g. planning and organizing residential experience and whole group discussion in Thinking Skills lessons;
— More contact with adults in the community, e.g. placements, work experience, interviewing, hosting visitors;
— Use of video and tape recorders in and out of the classroom;
— Use of the telephone;
— More group work, e.g. problem solving activities. More one-to-one dialogue and decision-making, e.g. pastoral, careers, curriculum choices, negotiation;
— More teacher/pupil and pupil/pupil profiling sessions.

Pupils' oral competence has improved noticeably with the emphasis in project work on interaction and discussion, both in the classroom and in different social situations. Many teachers have noted significant increases in oral confidence and skill:

'I think the main improvements in attainment in my 365 group were in the oral skills of students. Some of the students came into the courses with an ability to speak well although it wasn't always a skill that had been valued in school previously, e.g. the ability to describe vividly a fight at a disco or to tell a good joke. By using much more talk than would normally occur in a classroom the oral skills did improve in all of the students'.

In terms of literacy, pupils' resistance to writing has decreased and purposeful reading sessions have become possible in cases where they had not been previously. The use of word processing facilities has allowed pupils with writing difficulties to express themselves and practice skills, and to have pride in their work. The provision of real purposes and outcomes for pupils' talk and writing, particularly through community links work, has increased motivation and enjoyment in both these areas. Some examples of ways in which real purposes and audiences for pupils' talk and writing have been provided include: writing childrens' books for use with primary school classes, interviewing members of the community about local history, making arrangements for field trips, residential courses, visiting speakers, writing letters of invitation and thanks, compiling and conducting questionnaires and surveys, writing and producing a play for broadcast on the local radio service, producing a school or community newsletter and plays and other entertainments for groups in the community.

The Thinking Skills Programmes (I.E. and O.S.P.) appear to have had a positive impact on pupils' sense of achievement, both within the curriculum and in other aspects of their lives. Teachers, pupils and parents have commented on increases in confidence and performance that appear to have resulted from the Thinking Skills input. Examples of comments from pupils include:

> 'It has helped me with my job in the market, dealing with customers and customers' complaints. I am not so embarrassed with customers, I know exactly what to say to them and can deal with customers who argue'.

A geography teacher remarked that pupils who did the Thinking Skills course appeared to think more effectively and were able to apply an *intelligent* approach to problems. They seem better able to identify the cause of difficulty rather than making a general statement such as *I can't do this*.

Maths and English seem to have benefitted particularly in that pupils are more able to approach the task, analyze the problem and formulate their own responses. Teachers of these and other subjects have noted that pupils' organizational ability has in many cases improved dramatically, as well as the ability to think about problems in a more exploratory and creative way. Pupils claim that they feel more able to communicate effectively in class, and to respond to questions. They are better able to cope with interview situations and to understand what is required of them in examination papers. For example:

> 'It makes you read through the instructions until you understand them and you read things properly and don't rush into them. It gives you more self-confidence'.

In the areas of numeracy, more pupils were able to gain a qualification than was previously the case as a result of new courses and forms of accreditation offered. Practical projects, such as budgeting and shopping for residential courses, has been an important feature of numeracy courses offered to target pupils and instrumental in increasing pupils' confidence and skills.

Pupils have also been able to acquire a variety of vocational and manual skills through college link courses, work experience, and workshop opportunities, which have better prepared them for working life than they would have been before the project. Courses in retailing, computer awareness, electronics, and workshop technology have been available through school/FE links. The extension of industrial links has meant that there have been more opportunities for work experience and structured day release schemes. For example, experience has been offered in local shops, factories, farms, garages, vets, surgeries, hospitals, with building firms, local council offices, parks and garden centres, sports centres, schools, and pre-school groups.

In general levels of attainment across a broad range of skills have been most effectively raised when high expectations have prevailed and courses have not become too narrowly vocational in focus or lacking in rigour in terms of the assessment and monitoring of pupils' progress. However, where the perceptions of other pupils and teachers have been of a *sink group* provision, low attainment has persisted in many cases.

It should be noted that many pupils who, prior to the project, would have left school with few or no qualifications have left, as a result of their involvement in project activities, with various forms of certification and detailed profiles. In addition, many teachers consider that more of the target population have gained good jobs or training following their schooling than would previously have been the case, and that more pupils have gone on to some form of further education. Very few pupils remained unemployed for long after leaving school. Many pupils gained jobs as a direct result of their work experience.

Outcomes for the teachers

Staff perceptions

Responses to this section emphasized the importance of staff really *owning* the project. Schools which did not achieve this later experienced difficulties in terms of staff involvement and project development. It also proved difficult to change teachers' understanding of the implications of the project once it had become established in a particular way.

It has been pointed out that those involved in such a project should realise that the ground rules will and must change as development takes place. Accommodation of staff to this has best been brought about through continuous feedback of evaluation information so that staff are kept informed of the changes which take place. For constructive development to take place ongoing evaluation needed to be communicated widely and to involve enough people. Experience suggests that changes take place in those who are supportive and willing to adapt. It is widely recognised that for the project to have status, *high status* staff must be actively involved and this seems to have a clear bearing on the way in which the project is viewed within the school. This, however, needs to be linked with real and active participation of staff.

Professional skills and development

The NLI project sought to make staff much more aware of what is meant by a *positive and appropriate* curriculum and is concerned with changing perceptions of the role of teacher. In order to make the teacher not simply a disseminator of information, but, rather, one who focuses on the skills and processes that enable the pupil to learn how to learn, the project depends upon professional skills and existing expertise.

Appropriate use of INSET has been seen in many schools to be of great value in not only supporting staff directly involved but also in spreading interest and involvement across the curriculum and amongst the whole staff. Lack of INSET seems directly linked to limited staff involvement and project effect.

The project has invested considerable resources in Inservice Training and tremendous numbers of teachers in project schools have taken advantage of opportunities offered. The project has also made a significant contribution in that teachers have considerable expertize, gained from their NLI involvement which can now be exploited, e.g. assessment, profiling, residential work, and modular approaches. The point must be made, however, that the staff who were involved were generally encouraged by the project and claim that it gave their work status, presented opportunities for innovation and made them part of team.

They also felt that various aspects of their classroom practice had changed and improved as a result of being involved in the project, in particular, sensitivity to the needs of individual pupils, better relationships and understanding and more individual attention. Teachers pointed out too that they had in many areas become more professionally aware of exactly what they want to achieve from their groups and how they might be able to do so. The abilities of low-achievers were seen to have been under-estimated in the past, in many cases, and the more thorough and rigorous approach adopted by some schools within the project led to very positive results.

It may be helpful to include a list of what appear to have been the benefits of the NLI for the professional development of teachers during the years of the project.

1. Greater awareness of the organisation of their own school, and the possibilities for change.
2. The acquisition of new skills and techniques in the sphere of team work, interpersonal relationships, cross-curricular work and participating in

curriculum development in an open-ended, flexible and collaborative way.

3. Increased self-confidence to initiate change, identify key issues and problems, disseminate ideas, influence other colleagues and generate discussion. This confidence manifests itself in terms of a key role to play in the school's development, new knowledge of curriculum theory, and the needs of low-attaining pupils.

4. A greater awareness that the individual teacher to a certain extent, and the school, has the power and capacity to change and develop, by creating more team and cross-curricular approaches, which focus on curriculum-wide change.

5. A less defensive, more collaborative atmosphere among teachers, who are more prepared to question and be questioned about what they do and how they do it. This means an increased ability to self-evaluate and relate theory and policy to actual practice.

6. More emphasis on the needs and problems of pupils, a greater insight into *how* pupils learn.

7. The creation of a more open, critical, questioning climate in some schools, among some teachers, who respond to ideas from inside and outside the school and who look for ways to assimilate them into current practice.

8. An appreciation of the ways new ideas can be accommodated and assimilated in the school's environment, i.e. by building up relationships, providing the mechanisms for discussion and action, by establishing the means for support and by identifying the factors which inhibit change.

9. A greater realization for teachers that they already possess a great deal of the experience and skills needed for curriculum development, and that they can initiate and manage a process of change in their schools.

10. Changed attitudes to teaching — a greater emphasis on being a teacher of children, a manager of learning, as opposed to being a teacher of a specific subject. Thinking about classroom practice and teaching styles is now more focused on active-learning approaches and skills-based learning.

The achievement project in Oxfordshire

As a direct result of the good practice engendered by the NLI Project and in recognition of the work which there was still to do in raising pupils' attainments and aspirations, the Oxfordshire County Council have agreed to fund a permanent project, to be known as the Achievement Project, which is the successor to the NLI project. Whilst building on the positive outcomes of the NLI project it has the possibility of a broader focus than the lower attainers of the 14–16 age group.

Working closely with a limited number of schools who are encouraged to form networks to exchange experience, the Achievement Project challenges teachers to identify areas of underachievement and then to develop strategies to overcome them. The emphasis is on school-based curriculum development. The project is being run as a partnership between the small central team of two, the teachers in the schools and four Community Link tutors. Attached to a particular school for 0.5 of a week, the community tutor posts are available to provide schools with the benefit of a facilitator for project activities who is extra to the establishment staffing ratio.

The Achievement Project is running for the first two years concurrent with the dissemination phase of the NLI project. This is creating many opportunities for shared work directed towards improving the achievements of significant numbers of pupils and working alongside other curriculum initiatives. By directing itself to issues connected with the management of pupils' learning and the implications for teaching style and pedagogy, the Achievement Project is making an important contribution to current curriculum developments and providing some of the resources necessary for them to happen.

The first year of this new project which ensures that there is a clear focus on the issues of underachievement in the Authority is already under way and a great variety of activities taking place in project schools with enthusiastic support from many teachers. We view the future of the project with optimism, expecting that it will play its part in improving achievement and attainment, broaden the criteria by which success is measured in schools, extend the range of contexts for learning offered to pupils and improve motivation, involvement, self-esteem and confidence. The LAPP Programme was possibly the first major attempt by government to address the problem of disaffection, and hence all the problems associated with this (including misbehaviour and discipline), and the reports now available indicate clearly that in many schools there has been a major shift both in attitudes and practice towards this issue. The benefits of the work carried out under the LAP Programme are now becoming evident. Perhaps of greatest importance is that a population of school pupils from where often problems of truancy, vandalism, and underachievement emerged, have become conscious of the fact that their school experience could have a relevance according to their needs and abilities. Already in train, therefore, was a major programme of reform aimed at meeting individual pupil needs but in reality having a much wider impact in terms of pupil self-esteem, learning and accomplishment, and consequently having something to say about behaviour and discipline in schools. Here was an area of curriculum development that could well have been researched in relation to the preoccupations of the Elton Committee. Clearly, if pupils feel they are valued and succeeding, and there is a legitimate place for their particular skills and knowledge, then it would seem likely that such pupils would be unlikely to behave in such ways that have caused such concern to teacher unions in recent years. The LAP Programme was only a beginning, but an important start, to looking at how schools could make an effective *curriculum* response to certain pupils within a framework of a whole-school policy. So already, the government has to hand a way forward, through ordinary curriculum development, of improving the quality of education for all pupils, and at the same time, meeting individual needs where these are not met and result in disaffection or alienation. It has yet to be seen whether the government, in its pre-occupation with the provisions of the 1988 Education Act, can capitalise on the work already carried out through the LAP Programme, and can re-address the issue of school discipline as a question of effective school management and appropriate curriculum, rather than in strategies that in outcome marginalize yet even more pupils in our schools.

Reference

WESTON, P. (1987) *The Search for Success*, LAPP National Evaluation, No 1 Slough, NFER.

Acknowledgement

The section of this chapter which deals with the evaluation of the NLI Project at the end of year 5, draws heavily on the evaluation document produced in Oxfordshire in July 1988. The way in which the evaluation was carried out is described fully. It involved many hours of teacher time and the final document is a tribute to the commitment of all involved. I am pleased to take this opportunity to disseminate some parts of it in a more public arena, but am anxious to make clear the collaborative nature of the work involved.

Publications on the Oxfordshire LAP Programme

A   Newsletters Nos. 1–16
B   Occasional Papers:

   No. 1 Issues for Development and Dissemination
   No. 2 In-service Training and Staff Development
   No. 3 A Focus On: Open and Interactive Learning
   No. 4 School-Community Links and Experiential Learning
   No. 5 A Focus On: School-Community Links
   No. 6 Identifying Lower Attaining Pupils
   No. 7 Teaching Cognitive Skills
   No. 8 Residential Education

C   Residential Education: A Seminar, 10 March 1988
D   Self Evaluation After Five Years
E   Report of National Seminar, July 12, 1988

The above publications may be obtained from:

   Eileen Baglin
   The Education Unit
   Littleworth Road
   Wheatley,
   Oxfordshire.
   Telephone: Wheatley 3989

14
Curriculum and Pupil Behaviour: One School's Experience

Howard Green

Introduction

It is with some reluctance that a headteacher puts pen to paper for a book like this. Does a contribution imply exemplary practice and perfect discipline? Certainly not! My own school is typical of many. It is a mixed comprehensive (group 11, 11–18) in a small Shire-county town with a fairly typical intake. Founded in 1660, Henry Box School was reorganised as a comprehensive school (from grammar) in 1968. Its greatest asset is a team of relatively young, energetic and talented staff. Our twin aims are firstly to achieve the highest standards from all pupils in all that we do and, secondly, to make education an enjoyable experience for pupils and staff alike. Again, these are not particularly exceptional.

What we have done over the last five or six years (1983–8) is to carry out a planned programme of whole school review underpinned by a deliberate strategy for staff development and appraisal. One purpose of the review, which is ongoing, was to ensure that all pupils were well-motivated and realising their potential. The review has allowed us to integrate a significant amount of change (national, LEA and school stimulated) into *our* order of priorities. The acid test of all this endeavour is to look for improvements in the inter-related areas of teaching and learning, pupil attainment and behaviour and job satisfaction for staff.

We believe that school management, the curriculum, and pupil behaviour have a direct relationship. Management is interpreted in the broadest sense to include issues of detail like the management of classroom practice and specific projects (e.g., introducing SMP maths) to holistic issues like the management of whole school ethos, the curriculum and initial teacher-training. Unfortunately, too many teachers still believe that management is only about drawing up staff duty rotas or attending the occasional course to improve one's *curriculum vitae* and the prospects of promotion. Put simply, we understand management to be a deliberate and planned attempt to achieve positive outcomes from education. The curriculum is probably the crucial area where planning must be effective and one important positive outcome should be good pupil behaviour. Tattum (1988) in a recent book expressed it thus:

'Too much of our thinking about discipline has started from the wrong end, that is with questions as to how young offenders might be identified, punished and contained rather than how to create learning environments that might encourage productive pupil behaviour'.

In what follows I shall discuss six areas of our work at Henry Box School which have helped to create such a positive learning environment:

— School ethos
— Curriculum
— Learning support
— Low Attaining Pupils' Project
— Flexi-School Project
— Internship Scheme of initial teacher-training

School ethos

Explicit values and expectations

It is vital that a school has a clearly articulated and explicit set of values. In 1983 the whole school review began with a re-examination of our published aims and objectives. These had been a part of the school prospectus for several years. Pupils, parents, governors and staff were given the opportunity to comment on a fundamental question: what should Henry Box School stand for? or put another way, what should be our basic principles, and the practices to achieve these principles, as we enter the next decade? Contrary to a popular misconception that in a multi-cultural, pluralistic society, one can never reach agreement about basic values, we found a remarkable similarity in the views of each group that contributed to our debate. It was agreed that our four guiding principles should be that we:

— Value all our pupils equally;
— Stand for the successful education of the whole person;
— Want to contribute to the development of mature adults;
— Try to heal rather than increase the divisions in society.

It was also decided that there should follow a series of statements indicating how these principles will be achieved through more detailed practices. The complete statement of principles and practices takes just over two sides of A4 in the new prospectus. For example, under the *equal value* principle are the following practices:

— To ensure that our educational provision does not discriminate between pupils on the grounds of race, religion, sex or social background;
— To have a clear picture of the potential and progress of every pupil.

Under the *mature adult* principle:

— To help our pupils to possess a right self-esteem, acknowledging personal strengths and weaknesses, responding to the needs of others and resulting in stable personal development.

Finally, under the *healing society* principle:

— To establish a successful comprehensive school;
— To create an atmosphere which is purposeful, disciplined and constructive and where pupils and staff gain satisfaction and success from their work.

There is a separate section about Discipline in the prospectus which starts from a positive position:

Our aim is to achieve a situation where good discipline comes from a natural attitude of self-control and removes the need for punishment and detailed rules. However, we do have clear expectations of our pupils and our rules are regularly emphasized at assemblies and by form tutors. There is a system of rewards and punishments to underpin our discipline. *First and foremost we wish to encourage and give praise.*

The section goes on to explain a few basic rules for behaviour in the classroom and about the school and the punishments if these rules are broken. It seems to us that positively presented, clearly explained and consistently applied rules, are essential for a well-disciplined school.

Clearly, if such ambitious principles and practices are to be effective in establishing an ethos for the school, even partially, then they must be regularly re-emphasized and reviewed. This we try to do. But at least the school's value system with its emphasis on the *equal value* of all pupils, the importance of a right self-esteem and the expectation of a purposeful and disciplined environment is made quite explicit.

A strong pastoral system

The effective form (tutor) group is central to achieving many of our purposes. Without a strong pastoral system the principles and practices that we have nailed to the mast will be worth little more than the paper that they are written on. For example, under the *healing society* principle there is the following practice to 'develop a commitment to the tutor-group, the year and the School, by sharing in group tasks and activities, not out of compulsion, but out of a sense of belonging'. This is a demanding and yet a crucial practice to be implemented.

At Henry Box School we have a year system with a team of Senior Year Tutors and usually six form tutors taking their groups through from year 1 to year 5. There is a separate team for the 6th form. As head I take great care to appoint strong and committed Senior Year Tutors who are established and successful teachers. Several of them also have departmental responsibilities which helps to reduce the pastoral/academic divide. The new system of (Baker) allowances has been used to raise the status of several Senior Year Tutors and give the pastoral structure parity with the departmental structure. The pastoral system is certainly not seen as a way of moving less competent teachers sideways or rewarding those unlikely to be promoted through the departmental structure. Most of the staff take their roles as tutor and as subject teacher equally seriously.

The year teams have two key tasks. Firstly, to know their pupils very well as individuals, and secondly, to monitor their progress effectively. The school has a well-established and extensive programme of residential activities, including the 1st year going away for a week in the summer term. We have developed active tutorial work and pupil profiling. There is now a whole school policy and programme for monitoring pupil progress which is implemented by the Senior Year Tutors. Every form has a log book where details of classwork, homework and behaviour are recorded lesson by lesson throughout the week. The log is regularly reviewed by the form tutor who also checks each pupil's homework diary on a weekly basis. In these, and other ways, the pastoral system supports and enhances the work of the departments in maintaining high expectations of work and behaviour for all pupils.

High expectations bear fruit

Where is the evidence that such explicit values backed by a strong pastoral system are bearing fruit? How do we know that our expectations for high standards of work and behaviour are being met by the majority of pupils? Firstly, attendance rates are good and normally around 95 per cent. Secondly, the unsolicited comments from a regular stream of visitors including parents, governors, LEA officers and HMI are that the school is, with very few exceptions, orderly and well-disciplined. There are frequent remarks about the relaxed but hard-working atmosphere, the positive relationships between pupils and staff, a polite attitude to visitors, and the high quality of undamaged pupils' work on display. There is very little deliberate vandalism and an absence of graffiti. We have few pupil exclusions: about two or three short-term exclusions each term and only two permanent exclusions in the last seven years. Corporal punishment has not been used since 1981. Thirdly, nearly all 5th year pupils are entered for public examinations, and most of these take eight subjects. Results are normally above the national averages and in many subjects they are outstanding. However, what delights us as much as strong results at the top end is the small proportion of pupils with ungraded results or very low grades of pass. Fourthly, employers' reports from 4th year work experience are, with very few exceptions, excellent and all our school leavers who want jobs get them. There is also a high staying-on rate for education post-16. Finally, the graded system of merits, weekly from teachers and tutors, half-termly from the head and annually at presentation evenings, is used to reward the widest possible range of achievement. The aim is that every pupil will at least receive a weekly merit mark on several occasions during their first three years at Henry Box. This is usually fulfilled without having to invent reasons to award them and the merit system does help to enhance pupil motivation in the early years. Even the most difficult pupils possess all sorts of skills and talents that can be rewarded, if only we are willing to set aside our prejudices and take some risks. For example, a very disturbed 14-year-old who had been expelled from two previous schools has been kept on the rails by skilled teaching and tutoring but also because his excellent work on the lighting for the school play resulted in public recognition. His self-esteem rose several points up the *Freud-Scale* overnight! Half-termly head's merits have been used to recognise outstanding academic work at *all* levels of ability, extra-curricular achievement and personal/social qualities. Most human beings will flourish in an environment where there are clear expectations, where other people notice their attainments, and where there is a system of rewards for achievement.

The curriculum

The successful management of the curriculum, the way in which it is reviewed, planned and delivered to pupils, is also vital for ensuring a positive response from all pupils. Our experience of curriculum development over the past few years will not differ greatly from the experiences of many other comprehensive schools. Therefore, in this section, I shall only make some general comments about issues relating to the curriculum. The three sections that follow, learning support, low attainers and the Flexi-school Project, will examine in more detail specific aspects of the curriculum that are relevant to pupil behaviour.

The context of the curriculum

Another important aspect of the school ethos is what might be called the context of the curriculum — how the school approaches its central task of curriculum planning and the organisation of learning.

Curriculum debate and curriculum change is open to all staff, with the opportunity for inputs from pupils (via the School Council), parents (via regular curriculum evenings and open days), and governors, through a carefully planned programme of working parties and management meetings. There is, therefore, a broadly-based sense of ownership of the curriculum. Change has never had to be imposed by the senior management team or, worse, the head acting alone.

Cross-curricular awareness is still a very weak area in many secondary schools despite moves towards *faculty structures* and the *homogeneous blocking* of 4th and 5th year option subjects i.e., similar subjects timetabled together, both of which may end up by being merely cosmetic. The key questions are whether the experiences of education hang together for pupils, and if the whole more than the sum of the parts for the insights and understanding that it brings. Current curriculum jargon would call this *balance* and *coherence*. We have approached the issue of cross-curricular awareness in a number of ways with staff: by ensuring that all departments have published schemes of work with a wide circulation; by establishing working parties with representatives from all departments to address important whole school issues like information technology, pupil assessment, personal and social education and general curriculum development; by involvement with national projects, e.g., *Arts in Schools*, which can have an integrating function; by using school-based INSET for cross-curricular topics like active learning.

Staff commitment to all pupils. Every department is expected to take the education of all pupils equally seriously and all staff are expected to teach across the full ranges of age and ability. The evidence from recent curriculum development and staff timetables suggest that these expectations are being fulfilled.

Pupil grouping within the framework of some general staff debate is left to individual departments to decide how they will group pupils. In practice there is mixed ability teaching, in form groups, throughout the 1st year, setting by ability for Maths and Modern Languages in the 2nd year with the addition of setting for English, Geography, History and Science by the 3rd year. The latter pattern of grouping is generally maintained in the 4th and 5th years. Much of the setting by ability is fairly loose often with one top set and then several mixed sets. It is our view that the equal value principle does not necessitate mixed ability teaching in all subjects right through to the 5th year, provided that setting is conducted openly and flexibly and that the general ethos of the school in all other ways supports the ideal of equal value. Certainly our experience is that we do not have the *sink teaching groups* now that the school had several years ago when there was streaming from the 1st year and all the concomitant behaviour problems.

'Equal value' must mean 'equal access' to all areas of the curriculum

If pupils are to feel equally valued and so develop a right self-esteem then they must have equal access to all areas of the curriculum. This may seem an obvious point to make but it does merit some deeper analysis. For example, what about access to the learning of modern languages? We now have the situation where all pupils study two modern languages, French and German, during the first three years. This policy has resulted in large numbers opting for both French and German in the 4th and 5th years. Even the small minority of pupils who need learning support during modern languages' lessons retain contact with these subjects. Motivation is helped by regular graded assessment of basic language skills.

Then there is the problem of the gradual drift of girls away from subjects like physical science and technology and of boys away from modern languages as they move through the school. Does equal access mean equal levels of achievement by boys and girls across the curriculum? Experience suggests that the answer is *No*. On the basis of our own experience and some research evidence we have tried single-sex setting in Modern Languages and Science. Single-sex setting in 3rd year Science has produced the most marked results and we have seen a substantial increase in the numbers of girls opting for chemistry and physics in the 4th and 5th years. The move towards Balanced Science for all pupils to 16 should, on paper at least, remedy the traditional imbalance in option choices but we shall still need to watch the levels of achievement by boys and girls on different parts of the Balanced Science courses, particularly where courses do not integrate the separate sciences effectively.

Differentiation

In the first three years of an 11–18 (or 11–16) comprehensive school differentiation of educational experience is normally limited to modern languages, where only a minority of pupils usually start a second language, and perhaps the withdrawal of a small proportion of a year group from certain lessons for additional learning support or peripatetic music lessons. However, by the 4th and 5th years differentiation frequently becomes more extensive and is formalized in the option system. This is also the stage, perhaps not coincidentally, when behaviour problems may become more widespread and more serious. Some differentiation is clearly desirable to reflect the varied strengths and aspirations of older pupils. How have we faced the issue of differentiation in the 4th and 5th year curriculum?

At present we expect all pupils to continue with English, Mathematics, P.E., Personal and Social Education, including Religious Studies, a science, a humanities and a practical/creative subject. The last three subjects are chosen from within a six-option system. This pattern will need review and some modification to fit the National Curriculum.

The GCSE English course is followed by all pupils, but the weakest are also entered for a City and Guilds Communications course. SMP Mathematics is increasingly accessible to the full ability range and for less numerate pupils there is now a scheme of short term, modular assessment. We offer about twenty-five options which are freely available to all pupils. Most lead on to a GCSE examination but we include in the list a Child Development option, from the National Association of Maternal and Child Welfare, several school-certificated courses e.g., Outdoor Pursuits, Community Placements, and a number of link courses at the local technical college, e.g., Business Studies and Engineering. We find that this breadth of offer caters for all our pupils without the need for separate streams, course-packages for the less able or similar patterns of organization which can so easily result in a substantial group of pupils feeling that they are second-class citizens and behaving accordingly. Nearly all 5th year pupils take some public examinations and this will range right across the spectrum from eight or more GCSEs to perhaps two GCSEs, one City and Guilds and an NAMCW examination. Public examination entry helps to enhance self-esteem, brings a sense of normality to the 5th year and the recognition from a wider audience that secondary education has been successfully completed, even if the grades at the end of the day are not brilliant! The majority of 16 year olds believe this implicitly, even if they would not proclaim it publicly, perhaps because it is such an essential part of the culture of British education.

The School has been directly involved with the national Lower Attaining Pupils Project and TVEI extension. In both cases we insisted that what was good in these initiatives was good for all pupils and, despite some pressure from outside the school to do otherwise, we refused to bolt on to the 4th and 5th year curriculum special courses for lower attainers or those with so-called technical inclination. The common threads that have emerged from the LAPP, TVEI and GCSE like active learning, setting shorter term goals for assessment, modular courses, supported self-study and making education more relevant to life after school, should be particularly helpful for many pupils who have become disaffected in the past. This assumes, of course, that the early criticisms that GCSE courses favour pupils from more literate, middle-class backgrounds are either unfounded or speedily resolved.

I must conclude this section with a note of caution to the reader. As a result of the general approach to the curriculum outlined above, we do not have 100 per cent highly-motivated, hardworking, happy and successful pupils through to the end of the 5th year! Like all schools we do have a few pupils who become disaffected in various ways and who leave at Easter without taking public examinations. However small that number may be, it is unacceptable and we are constantly seeking strategies to reduce it. The next three sections look at some of the ways in which we have been tackling disaffection, often, but not always associated with poor behaviour, through specific aspects of the curriculum.

Learning support

Many and perhaps the majority of pupils will need learning support at some time during their secondary years. Such support has usually been provided for a small minority of pupils with learning problems by *remedial* or *special needs* teachers/departments. Although colleagues teaching in this area have often done excellent work the very titles *remedial* or *special needs* have unfortunate connotations and can encourage a low self-image and poor pupil behaviour. For example, 'I go to the remedial department some of the week so I must be a *thicko*, so I'll lark about in Music'.

What's in a name?

In September, 1985, the Special Needs Department at Henry Box School, which consisted of one full-time teacher plus occasional part-time support and operated mainly on a pupil withdrawal system, was reorganised as the Learning Support Department (LSD). Names are important as they can convey hidden messages. The LSD now has four teachers, who contribute about three and a half full-time timetables between them, plus the equivalent of one full-time non-teaching classroom assistant. Their brief has been extended to cover the following main areas of learning support:

— Withdrawal and classroom support for pupils with learning problems;
— Extended projects with the most able;
— Residential work with categories (i) and (ii);
— Co-ordination of standardised testing;
— Monitoring the progress of low-attainers particularly in the 4th and 5th years;
— Co-ordinating and teaching cognitive (thinking) skills, (see the next section on the Low-Attaining Pupils' Project);
— Developing supported self-study for all pupils.

One can appreciate from this list that at some time all pupils may indeed receive support from the Learning Support Department.

Cognitive skills and supported self-study are being developed across the age and ability range so that our least able pupils who have learning problems can no longer feel that they are somehow different in working with LSD teachers. We have no empirical evidence, but plenty of anecdotal evidence, that these pupils who frequently showed behaviour problems by the 4th and 5th years in the past, are now much better integrated into the general life of the school and much less likely to behave badly. It also seems to be true that the bright and disaffected are a dying breed.

Management of learning support

Central to these changes has been the management of the transition from a special needs to a learning support department within the context of the whole staff. The Head of LSD is a quiet but innovative and persistent colleague who has successfully led her team into much closer co-operation with other departments. LSD teachers frequently work with other teachers in normal lessons; each department has appointed a link-teacher with the LSD and LSD teachers also attend other department meetings; the LSD has produced a wide range of teaching material, for the full ability range, in co-operation with and for the use of other departments; the LSD has been at the forefront of whole-school developments like information technology, pupil assessment and personal and social education. It is also important that the senior management team has made this area a high priority motivated by the belief that learning support has a particular part to play in ensuring that every pupil realises his or her potential. As a result pupils should experience success, enjoy their education, and so be far less likely to become disaffected.

Lower Attaining Pupil's Project (LAPP)

Oxfordshire made a successful bid to be a part of the LAPP from its inception in 1983 but called their version the New Learning Initiative. Henry Box School joined the Oxfordshire programme and from the outset was committed to the view that, as low attainment may be apparent in all pupils, LAPP developments must be broadly-based within the curriculum. Some of our work was focused on the bottom 40 per cent of the ability range in the 4th and 5th years, (the original target group for this government-funded Project) but most innovations were aimed at the full ability range. In reality the Project has had effects on the whole school.

LAPP at Henry Box School

Four areas became the foci for County intitiatives: community links; courses for low attainers in the 4th and 5th years; residential education and the teaching of cognitive (thinking) skills. The school was involved with all four and I shall say something about each of them but more about the teaching of cognitive skills which has been an extremely powerful means of raising the achievement of low attainers with the undoubted knock-on effect of improved behaviour.

Community links

We were able to appoint an additional full-time member of staff for five years (1983–88) as Community Tutor. This turned out to be an invaluable resource as it created time to undertake the hundred and one tasks, make the innumerable contacts, and oil the works which facilitate extensive and effective school-community links. Among many new initiatives in this area I will mention only two: a Community Club was established for all pupils and eventually provided opportunities for over 100 young people of all ages to take part in a wide range of community service. Secondly, a Community Placements option was offered as an additional option in the 4th and 5th years. Pupils spend two hours each week on a regular placement in the local community returning to school from time to time to review progress and maintain their log books. At the end of the 5th year they receive a school certificate listing the placements and providing a profile of their achievements. Although this option attracted pupils of all abilities, a number of them, who were likely to cause behaviour problems or become school-refusers, have flourished in this rather different context for learning about themselves and other adults. It is also encouraging that improvements in attitude and behaviour on the Community Placements option have been carried over to other subjects.

Work with lower attainers

We decided not to bolt on special courses for low attainers in the 4th and 5th years although most other LAPP schools in Oxfordshire offered the City and Guilds 365 programme to one or more groups. We took the monitoring of pupil progress seriously following LAPP developments and, in particular, spent time interviewing and recording the progress of our low attainers. For us *lower attainment* was measured in several ways, including ability at various school subjects. The monitoring was carried out discreetly and undoubtedly kept the pressure on many who would have begun to drift downhill by the end of the 4th year. It also allowed senior year tutors and subject teachers to counsel pupils with much more background knowledge and it gave early warnings of potential problems which might have escalated into behavioural difficulties. The whole process allowed our counselling to have a more constructive, preventative focus, rather than being curative and crisis-orientated. With the departure of the Community Tutor in 1988, who undertook much of this counselling, we have revised our management structure to ensure that the work will continue under the auspices of the Learning Support Department.

Residential education

Residential education has been extensively developed at Henry Box School for many years but the LAPP gave us the opportunity to provide some further residential trips and to review our procedures. One such innovation, referred to above, was a series of residential trips for more able pupils who, despite their ability, may still be attaining below their potential. Another new venture was urban residential courses for low attainers. Usually residential courses are held in rural areas but many of our pupils live in the countryside and so we decided to take them to live in a large city for a week. One exercise involved finding their way to a venue using public transport, which is virtually non-existent in many rural areas. This urban trip proved to be highly successful and has since been repeated.

Our assessment of residential education was reviewed. This was a relatively easy task as we had been recording very little about the performance of pupils on residential trips. How often do we overhear conversations in the staffroom like this: 'You should have seen John (usually a *pain* in school) on the field course — he was brilliant'. But how rarely is that good performance recorded and placed in the pupil's record or profile. We now assess residential education much more thoroughly and have formalized the assessment as an integral part of the pupil profiles. This can only be of help to the 'Johns' of the world.

Cognitive skills

When one looks back over the history of teaching children with learning problems in the normal school it is surprising that the main focus has always been on reinforcing basic skills like literacy and numeracy rather than teaching children how to think. Certainly my experience is that one can batter away for the first three years of secondary education trying to help so-called slow learners to read, write and do simple arithmetic. They often make little progress and enter the 4th year pretty bored with school and then make a nuisance of themselves. The really irritating fact is that one often knows that they have plenty of brain power and, of course, they normally do very well in adult life! One of the great successes of the LAPP has been the introduction of classes on cognitive (thinking) skills to help pupils with learning problems and poor motivation.

The initial material for teaching cognitive skills was produced in Israel and called Instrumental Enrichment. The theoretical framework had been devised by Feuerstein who undertook the immensely important task of trying to find ways of helping Jewish children and young people to switch back on to learning after the traumatic experiences of the Holocaust during the Second World War. The *instruments* were simple exercises, frequently based on drawings and patterns, to teach cognitive skills like perception, memory, comparison, classification, orientation, analysis, hypothesis and synthesis. The essential aim was to teach children how to think clearly and so learn more effectively.

From September 1984 we introduced Cognitive Skills as a new 4th year option taught by staff who had undertaken a week's training in the use of Instrumental Enrichment materials. Althouth the option was freely available to all pupils we carefully selected a target group of low attainers. Most of this group decided to take the course following full discussion with both the pupils and their parents. Some did so with reservations. Since September 1984 we have been running one or two Cognitive Skills groups each year with between 15 and 20 pupils in each group. A growing number of staff have been trained to use the materials and, with the ending of the LAPP, the co-ordination of Cognitive Skills teaching has been taken over by the Learning Support Department.

It takes two or three months before pupils become aware of their own progress on the Cognitive Skills course. During the early weeks it is not uncommon to hear the comment 'I am not learning anything in this subject'. Such a reaction is hardly surprising as the Cognitive Skills materials have little subject content and the teacher rarely gives a pupil a right or wrong response to an answer. However, gradually pupils come to realise that they are acquiring skills to help them with the *process* of learning rather than a specific product. For many teachers who have been directly or indirectly involved with Cognitive Skills it has been a very exciting innovation, particularly for low attainers. Almost without exception pupils and parents are now convinced about the benefits of the course.

As Cognitive Skills was introduced under the umbrella of a national project it has been subject to exhaustive evaluation by our own teachers, County LAPP staff, HMI and independent evaluators from the National Foundation for Educational Research. All agree that the effect on most pupils has been significant and in some cases profound. Many have shown a tremendous increase in self-confidence. For the first time they have understood that divergent views are to be expected on controversial issues. Pupils can now consider various arguments critically and have acquired the ability to disagree in a precise and reasoned way. Individuals have overcome their impulsive behaviour and can now work out what a task or problem requires before rushing to an (often wrong) answer. They learn to express their ideas more clearly and use more accurate language. Pupils show an increased willingness to ask questions and, so important, to listen to other people which often increases respect for their peers. Many are better organized as they are encouraged to develop

their own strategy to cope with a problem and then compare it with the strategies ·
chosen by other pupils. They must devise procedures for checking their work and so
come to understand the importance of evaluation in the learning process.

There has been much unsolicited feed-back from pupils. For example, 'I had
better results in the (5th year) mocks than I have had before because now I read
questions several times and work out what is asked for. I divide the question into
parts and tick off each part when it is completed'; 'My golf handicap has improved
because I now choose the golf clubs more carefully, work out the distances and take
more time making my shots'. Parents have also noticed the difference in their
children. One couple commented on the very full and descriptive postcard sent
home by their son from a school trip and the clear, interesting way in which he
talked to them about his photographs on returning home. Previously their son had
found it difficult to communicate to them using monosyllables and grunts!

Staff have commented that pupils following the Cognitive Skills course
completed projects more effectively and cover topics more systematically. Visiting
HMI showed considerable enthusiasm for the Cognitive Skills course after initial
scepticism and having followed a group from the 4th year through into the 5th year.

If this all sounds like the next best thing after sliced bread it probably is! At last
we have teaching methods available and materials to hand which address the *process* of learning. Undoubtedly many pupils who have followed the Cognitive Skills
course have become more higly motivated across the curriculum and would have
shown behavioural problems by the 5th year without it. In many cases it has
provided the key to unlock the grey matter and get the brain working. It has also
had a beneficial effect on teachers, particularly those who have undertaken the Cognitive Skills training.

Certainly, Oxfordshire is directing more resources into Cognitive Skills. An
LEA team is now producing an Oxfordshire version of the Instrumental Enrichment
materials and it is being extended from the 4th and 5th years down into the first
three years of secondary school and up into the 6th form.

Flexi-School Project

Despite all the effort and enterprise mentioned thus far to try and ensure that every
pupil realises his or her potential and continues to be well motivated to 16, some
will fall through this carefully constructed net. Traditionally pupil behaviour problems that can become more acute and less containable during the 4th and 5th years
are dealt with by a combination of withdrawal in school, temporary or permanent
exclusion and extended work experience. In 1987 the LEA took the enterprising
step of giving each secondary school about £2,000 over two years to use as they
thought best to help with the problems of disaffection. It was a relatively modest
sum of money to try and help those of whom it could be said, 'they and school just
don't get on'!

This money has been used to fund a Flexi-School Project. Individual pupils
have been identified, usually during the 4th year, because their behaviour or school

attendance is deteriorating. A careful review of their timetable is undertaken by a deputy head, who has overall responsibility for Flexi-school, working with pastoral staff, subject teachers, parents and the pupil. Flexi-school is not offered as a reward for bad behaviour or attendance. It is based on a positive contract with the pupil to maintain an acceptable standard of work and behaviour across most of the curriculum but to be allowed certain alternative activities.

Two examples will illustrate how Flexi-school has been used. N. was a very shy and withdrawn 4th year pupil who was increasingly absent from school. His one real interest was art. Using the Flexi-school budget, we employed an art therapist to work with N. The results have been most encouraging. His attendance improved, and therefore his work in all subjects; the quality of his art improved considerably so that we were able to mount a display of his work in the school foyer which did wonders for his self-esteem. The art therapist took N. on several visits, including his first trip to London, which boosted his confidence, e.g., he became much more willing to engage in conversation with other adults.

Secondly, two 4th year girls were becoming increasingly disruptive in school — on this occasion the sort who are rarely absent! They both had an interest in horses. Using the Flexi-school contract they were given the opportunity to work at a local riding school for several hours each week. Their time in school became much more productive and they have both successfully completed Pony Society examinations.

The experience of Flexi-school suggests that a process like this can be used productively with disaffected pupils without encouraging other pupils to misbehave so that they too can get the special treatment. It may also be less expensive for an LEA to fund a scheme like Flexi-schol than to pay for officers' and home tutors' time in coping with long-term exclusions.

Internship scheme of initial teacher training

A fundamental way of dealing with the problems of disaffection and poor behaviour is to increase the range of skills and strategies for coping with all pupils through the in-service and initial training of teachers. I have mentioned in the section on the Low Attaining Pupils Project how INSET related to the new Cognitive Skills course at Henry Box School has helped teachers to broaden their teaching techniques and to look at pupil disaffection from the viewpoint of how we teach rather than what we teach.

The new pattern of PGCE training at the Oxford University Department of Educational Studies has been an exciting and valuable development for initial training. Called the internship scheme, the student teachers, or *interns*, spend much more time in schools rather than in the University Education Department. Also most of their tutoring is now undertaken by experienced teachers in the school, called *mentors*. Interns spend their early weeks attached to classes working as members of a teaching team and preparing materials for small groups.

Three immediate and positive benefits for the interns have been the acquisition of a larger armoury of teaching skills than would be provided by more tradition

PGCE courses with a relatively limited block practice; secondly, a deeper insight into problems of pupil behaviour and how they are handled by experienced teachers; thirdly, more opportunities to share teaching successes and problems with other interns as each school now hosts between 8 and 12 interns.

Benefits for the school include the fact that interns can be used to work with more difficult pupils on a one-to-one basis or to teach the class while their normal teacher works with individuals. Interns usually bring a welcome enthusiasm and freshness to the classroom.

Closer contact with day-to-day practice in schools must make initial training more relevant to the actual demands of the classroom including the challenge of disaffected pupils. Certainly involvement with the internships scheme at Henry Box School suggests that this is happening and the responses from the interns confirms our view.

Conclusions

In this chapter I have recounted the experiences of one school trying to ensure that its management and curriculum are directed towards positive pupil outcomes and minimize poor behaviour. However, in conclusion I should share two salutary tales. The first relates to Denise, one of those figures from the past that become seared on the memory. I am sure all of us in teaching have them! Denise was in many ways a bright and likeable girl but one who often caused havoc in classes and ploughed a very lone furrow. For example, the school had a flexible but definitive code of dress which Denise would often flout in the most outrageous manner. I remember taking an American visitor round the School passing hundreds of well turned out youngsters. Suddenly Denise crashed through a doorway full of laughter and replete with shaved head, Union Jack T-shirt, skin-tight calf-length jeans and Dr. Martins! Continuing on our tour I was making rather embarrassed and apologetic noises about Denise to our guest. His response gave me much to reflect on as he compared the rather boring image portrayed by our average product with the obvious vitality and individuality of Denise. Where pupil behaviour is concerned one person's sign of disaffection may be another person's sign of life.

The second tale, again from a previous school, is about my experience of a quite sincere, but disastrous, attempt to make the curriculum more relevant and interesting for pupils who were more likely to become disaffected. I am sure that many readers will remember that in the wake of the last raising of the school leaving age the Schools Council supported a number of curriculum development projects. Several of them were aimed at low attainers and the bottom of the ability range. At the time I was tutoring a group of 4th and 5th year pupils among whom several were following the Schools Council Humanities project — famous for its emphasis on the teacher as *neutral chairman* which was a very avant-garde concept in the late 1960s and early 70s. Some of the pupils loved it, while others found it utterly boring and, from the frequent complaints that I received, were obviously a nuisance in the lessons. On further investigation it turned out that these two reactions were linked to two separate classes with different teachers. The material was the same — incidentally my impression was that in much of the Humanities project the resources were most unsuitable for the apparent target group, with numbers of extracts from newspapers and journals like the *Guardian*, *The Observer* and *New Society* that demanded a high reading age. However, the use of the material was quite different.

One teacher set most of the published resources aside and in an imaginative and skilled way had absorbed the spirit of the project. The pupils responded positively and were obviously learning a lot. The other colleague slavishly worked through the prescribed packages of material in a most uninspiring, didactic manner. The pupils responded accordingly and were becoming increasingly difficult to control. Where teaching all pupils, but particularly the disaffected, is concerned the process is far more important than the content. An old truth perhaps but one that is worth reiterating.

We still seem to stumble into the trap that attractively presented packages of new teaching material will magically motivate a class with little change on our part. It is also possible to teach well with good material and yet still find that many pupils are not actually learning very much. As I have pointed out in a previous section, the great strength of the Cognitive Skills course at Henry Box is that it has successfully addressed the inter-related issues of teaching style and learning processes. Frequently we focus too much on the processes of teaching and too little on how children learn.

A positive approach to school management and the curriculum which focuses on the learning needs of all pupils and seeks to promote high standards and enjoyment should reduce serious pupil misbehaviour to a minimal level. However, it is a fact that we shall not win them all, but despite this we should not give up! A positive approach must be shown by all the partners in education — central government through the DES, local authories, teacher trainers and schools. In sharing one school's experience of this approach I hope that I have indicated that it can work. Without a positive attitude from the DES we would not have had LAPP; without a supportive LEA we would not have had Flexi-school or the development of our Learning Support Department; without a forward looking education department at Oxford University we would not have had the internship scheme, and above all, without skilled, hardworking teachers who were open to change, we would have had none of the developments at Henry Box School. If any of these partners had shirked their responsibilities to work for improvements in teaching and learning our pupils would have been the losers and that would not have been acceptable.

Reference

TATTUM, D. and LANE, D. (eds) (1988) *Bullying in Schools*, London, Trentham Books.

15
The Psychology of Schooling:
Supporting the Curriculum

Neville Jones

Introduction

In a book about pupil behaviour and discipline the view taken in this chapter is that the most relevant way of approaching this issue is through effective school management, skilled and innovatory teaching, developing an appropriate curriculum for the needs of all individual pupils, and for this to take place in a context of values which enhance staff and pupil esteem and the process of learning. This provides the *whole school context* in which all who are concerned and spend their time working in schools can have an objective for their professional skills and energies. The term 'curriculum' in the title of this paper refers to all these activities: a recognition that all that happens in a school, the formal as well as the informal or hidden curriculum, the resources in terms of human qualities as well as educational equipment, the quality of relationships between all who work in a school, are of direct relevance to how both pupils and adults behave and conduct themselves. The starting point in considering issues about behaviour and discipline is in this inter-relatedness of aims and purposes throughout a school community, the outcome of which is the behaviour of individuals and the self discipline of all.

It is not an uncommon practice to tackle behaviour problems as if they existed in isolation from all other aspects of an individual's corporate life. To do this is to trivialize an individual, whether child or adult, and it also trivializes the coming together of individuals to learn in a variety of one-to-one and group settings. But there has always been common support throughout society (in Britain) for a system of coercion and physical punishment as the one and only response to children and young people misbehaving. This has been the case, historically, irrespective of whether the behaviour has been intentional or not.

If schools and their curriculum represent a 'slice of the culture' in which they exist, then it is not surprising if schools, and those who work in them, reflect these values about how to tackle matters of behaviour which are seen in one respect or other as being a question of indiscipline or deviancy. It has been equally logical, therefore, that educational psychologists have had a child-centred approach to their

229

work. Much of the early research into child behaviour in schools was geared to identifying areas of inadequacy which could then be justified for placing children in segregated special education or in special classes in ordinary schools. The child and his problems has been a central plank for much of the work carried out both by the Psychoanalytic and Behavioural schools of thought for much of this century. Although this traditional medical model of approach to a child's problems is one from which educational psychologists have tried to distance themselves in recent years, there is still very strong pressure from teachers, parents, and within the educational psychology fraternity, to tackle behaviour and learning difficulties as if they were independent of the context in which they appear and develop. But in spite of this, teachers are aware that isolating behaviour in this way is not to tackle the 'problem' which is more complex. From a management point of view it is useful to question whether misbehaviour seen as a 'problem within the child' is a useful way of looking at the matter and whether it gives rise to useful strategies and methods of remediation. Certainly it has a short term value in the sense that it quickly relieves immediate concern and stress if a pupil can be referred and seen by an educational psychologist, or there are administrative structures whereby such pupils can be either marginalized or actually segregated from ordinary classroom activity. Many teachers recognize that the behaviour of a child is an effective way of signalling that something is going wrong and some children can only do this because of an inability to verbalize their anxiety and stress. It is often from the group of children who do have problems with communication that behaviour problems arise and to remove the only method of signalling discontent or distress, is to place such pupils in an even more vulnerable position. Equally, some educational psychologists also work on a basis that it is important not to extinguish the signal that says 'help me' but to keep the signal bright so as to alert as many people as possible that something is going wrong. Clearly, the aim is not to approve and sustain misbehaviour, but to recognize that misbehaviour needs a response that is both meaningful to the child and to the teacher, and that where behaviour is ignored then the door opens for the child to express his or her discontent in other, and maybe, more extreme ways.

Behaviour signals, therefore, need to be kept in place, alerting and calling for a response, sometimes by teachers and other pupils, sometimes by parents, or both in negotiation with the pupil. To approach behaviour problems in this way is to tackle them as part of a complex system of relationships, of values and experiences, and which embrace or engage all who work in schools. It is in this context that the notion of a whole-school policy approach in schools begins to be fleshed out in practice which represents the ethos and values of the school (Hargreaves *et al.*, 1988). This brings about responses which are both meaningful to staff and individual pupils. An implication of this is that not only should all those who work in schools daily be involved, but equally all those who work in schools from a position of consultancy or support. If it is a task of educational psychologists to participate in the work of schools in general, and in relation to behaviour problems in particular, then if we ask questions about all those who work and have their being in schools day by day, and this is seen as appropriate as a first time response to behaviour difficulties, we have to ask the same questions of those who advise and intervene. If schools are required to examine carefully their management structures, their teaching styles and the nature of their curriculum (and whether it meets adequately the needs of all pupils in the school), and not least to examine the value system of those who work in a particular school, then it is also incumbent on those who participate in school activities, to look at their management structures, the philosophy of the interventions which are offered, and the value systems which they introduce by virtue of being participants. This would include those who work as educational psychologists, educational social workers, LEA advisory services, and those teams who support learning in one way or another through remedial approaches.

The aim in this chapter is to explore how far an effective psychology of schooling can be developed, that in outcome will support those school communities which are aiming towards whole-school styles of management, and what the implications of this would be for psychological practice in an important area, that of pupil misbehaviour. We shall first consider some aspects of the notion of whole-school policies and what this could mean for school psychological services. We then need to consider briefly some of the problems that occur when we try to build a bridge, in terms of a working structure, between a psychology that has its own in-built theory and values and an education system where management and classroom practice may be geared to quite different objectives. We shall then consider what is entailed in a psychology of education that takes as its starting point the school, and all that happens within its walls and jurisdiction. This leads to a consideration of why there is still a credibility gap between present-day educational psychology and present-day school practice. We can examine how solutions have been sought to this issue and the reasons why many of the problems seem to perpetuate themselves. From this we can then look at a particular approach to this issue under a title of a *Psychology of Schooling* and whether this promises a better solution and a way forward so that psychologists have a greater relevance and make a more significant contribution to education services in the future. In exploring these ideas it would be foolish to ignore the impact that recent government policies may have on school practice, the changes that may occur as a consequence of the 1988 Education Act, and how this will provide a different context within which educational psychologists will have to work. Finally, we can look at how a more effective management of pupils with discipline problems can be handled when located within, not only a changing educational scene, but possibly a changing style and approach of an educational psychology which is firmly rooted in day-to-day school practice.

Whole-school policies

Where there is the intention to pursue a whole-school policy then it would be expected that *all* those engaged in work in such a school would become involved in such policies. This would apply to all support services no matter how minimal their interventions if these interventions are aimed to change in any way the thinking and behaviour of adults and children who work daily in the schools. School Psychological Services would need to consider their management policies and practices, not as 'in-house' exercises, but in collaboration with the staff of schools they support. Equally, headteachers in planning whole-school policies, would need to consider what role and function those with psychological expertise could play in a new form of co-operative management, involving directly all those who work in peripatetic support services. It is clearly an opportune time for educational psychologists to look again at their own professional accountability and add a voice to the debate: not waiting for government legislation, like the 1988 Education Act (through its local school finance provision), to bring about the debate and decision making.

Secondly, as schools move forward to styles of managing the curriculum that will take greater account of student interests, through such mechanisms as modular learning, it is necessary for educational psychologists to examine closely the nature and context of the psychology that dictates EP practice, and those aspects which make for a lack of credibility between educational psychologists and teachers.

Headteachers have a particular problem if they want to draw upon the discipline of psychology, among other disciplines, to address their managerial planning of whole-school policies. Here we are talking about matters like personnel selection, group relations (for staff as well as pupils), reconciling individual and group values and conflicts, the management of stress, staff development and staff appraisal issues, the relationship between the physical environment and effective learning, for example. At the moment heads may recruit a member of staff who is qualified in psychology, and this person may teach 'A' level academic psychology, where this is a school option. But apart from this there is little scope for this graduate in psychology to work as a psychologist/teacher in the same way that graduates of other disciplines — maths, sciences, humanities, PSE and physical education — capitalize on their basic knowledge and specialization. A headteacher has to look for 'expertise' from someone who is likely to be in school not more than once a week, and whose role is already prescribed by the employer (the LEA) and expected by parents, being that of a trouble-shooter for particular pupils. But the expertise of present day EPs, lies not in those areas that address the wider issues of school management, but derives from time given to a very small group of pupils whose needs are seen as special.

Research into effective schools has isolated a number of factors which together, and applied in context for each individual school, determine a pupils' experience of schooling and hence has something to say about how pupils respond to that experience. This material has been reviewed by Reynolds (1982), Rutter (1983) and Mortimore *et al.*, (1988). Some of these factors relate to value systems, both of individuals who work in schools and institutional values, and are linked very closely to issues about discipline and behaviour, rewards and privileges, leadership, school ethos, and personal relationships. Much of this is not subject to precise evaluation and categorization, but has to be taken into account where pupil behaviour is concerned. This is another area where educational psychologists find themselves at a disadvantage in not being part of the community where such values are held, developed and practiced. For the *outside school* consultant, this area is part of the hidden 'curriculum' of a whole-school policy: for the EP consultant it is hidden most of the time. In spite of its importance, many EPs practice a theory of psychology that assumes that such inter-personal matters are known and accounted for within whatever scheme or style of psychotherapy they introduce. Furthermore, as participant in the life of a school, albeit a small part, but touching on individuals who sometimes make a great impact, EPs all the time bring to each contact and meeting with others their own set of values. Seldom is there an opportunity for this aspect of psychological intervention to be examined: the list of pupils waiting to be seen is too long.

Psychology and education

Teachers are conscious of the fact that educational psychology, in the form in which it is presented in schools at the moment, is a discipline that has its own internal contradictions, and often offers a theory of practice that is not relevant to what happens in schools. It is a theory of practice that becomes more relevant the more a child is removed from the centre of normalizing and learning promoting influences i.e. the ordinary effective classroom. Educational psychologists, by tradition, offer a service based on problems being child-focused, determined by procedures of testing using psychological tests, the introduction of one or more of a series of strategies or remedial programmes, and where the maintenance of the intervention is usually left to teachers. This stereotype of the traditional EP is made complete when he/she works within a peripatetic delivery service and is accountable to an official of the LEA. It is a stereotype that many EPs would like to abandon, but find it difficult to give up such attitudes and most practices which secure the stereotype in its place in education. How far is the stereotype a true one in the 1980s and how far have EPs in practice been able to move away to other styles of working? If there is a serious intent on the part of the EPs to move towards a more central role in education, to be participants in a meaningful way in schools that are pursuing whole-school policies, then each and all of the following issues have to be tackled:

1. the service is still fundamentally a testing agency;
2. its existence for the most part is in relation to pupils who are failing in their schooling;
3. the focus of much of its intervention work is in the treatment/remediation of the pupil;
4. it is seen as a marginal service by schools because of the frequency in which school visits are made;
5. it is a peripatetic service and not school-centred;
6. it has an accountability away from schools i.e., the LEA.

Educational psychologists may reject partially, or wholly, this description of their role and function. It is interesting, however, to look at what advice the government was offered in drawing up its management plans for the 1988 Education Act.

The Coopers and Lybrand, 1988 Report (Local Management of Schools: A Report to the Department of Education and Science) illustrates the central problem. In para 2.64 the Report, in its opening statement on educational psychology, school welfare and school health services, states the following:

> For these three services the primary client is the individual pupil, particularly for educational psychology which operates on a case-work basis.

The 'primary client' was the individual pupil way back in 1913, when the first school psychologist Cyril Burt was appointed, and the purpose of the new appointments were for the testing of children's needs and abilities for their exclusion or otherwise out of mainstream schooling and into special education, usually in segregated schools. This view of the central task of the educational psychologist has persisted down to the present day. It is a view held by employers (the LEAs), by parents, and for most part teachers. It is also a role and function that attracts certain individual psychologists into the work itself inspite of the fact that some EPs will, from time to time, protest that this is an exceedingly limited and restrictive view of their activities. It is here that EPs have to remind themselves, that the testing and assessment role is a brief they have as employees: everything else is a matter of local negotiation between an EP and individual heads in context where EPs have organized their time and energy for other pursuits. There is considerable uncertainty within the educational psychology fraternity about his matter: nowhere is there a statement of policy and aims, nowhere an active decision to abandon the psychological testing of children. Research to date suggests that the majority of EPs still cling tenaciously to their test equipment and use tests of one kind or another as the basis for their assessment work with children referred to them in schools (Quicke, 1980, 1983). Presumably, before writing their Report, the Coopers and Lybrand team took soundings from psychologists, or those that represent their interests, and were advised on this matter that individual pupils and their needs are the focal point of EP work. Of course, school psychologists have never been actively discouraged to think otherwise. The pupil population with whom they have contact, though very small in numbers, are for the most part those who are failing to learn as defined in the 1981 Education Act. Educational psychologists have been recognised as the 'experts in learning failure' though the psychological and remedial solutions developed and practised have not always given support to the *expert* notion.

In the early discussion leading up to the 1981 Education Act, educational psychologists offered the government little advice on this issue, but rather clamoured for recognition of the legal role of the EP in the testing of pupils with learning disabilities. This recognition was given. Where before EPs were 'free' to decide the extent to which formal testing and assessment of pupils were part of their work, now the 1981 Education Act, in its *statementing* procedures, has made much of this work a legal responsibility. Furthermore, some LEA psychological services not only offer psychological time and expertise to these statementing procedures, but have actively moved into the area of LEA administration and taken over the paper work involved in the compiling of the various reports and statements. In recent years educational psychologists have tended to take up and respond to almost every problem that is raised in schools and this arises partly from uncertainties about both theory and practice of EP work. It is a feature, discussed eloquently by Neil Bolton (1989), whereby educational psychology, not having a recognized and agreed theoretical rationale for work, grasps at any innovation or theory and translates it into yet another *therapeutic* intention and activity in schools.

In spite of these and other difficulties, educational psychologists, even when working in a peripatetic and centralized LEA service, have had opportunities to change their role and function quite dramatically. Possibly the first opportunity came with the integration movement: for pupils with special needs to remain in their ordinary schools or for segregated pupils to become part of ordinary school management structures. It is here in the area of integration that educational psychologists could have made a positive contribution to a future management of ordinary schools, especially those pursuing comprehensive and whole-school policies. Educational psychologists might well have developed the managerial expertise that was required to bring the very significant change in the way we educate a proportion of our pupils and to have been in a position to share this expertise with heads and staff of ordinary schools. Much of the initiative for the management of integration schemes that have taken place have come from heads of special and ordinary schools, who together, and with an occasional support from an adviser or LEA official, brought about the new management structures that were necessary. This is not, in any way, to denigrate the special imagination of a few individual educational psychologists who have worked hard in this field to bring about change and opportunities for certain pupils (Dessent, 1987).

A second opportunity for educational psychologists to lead from the front, not only in their own professional interests, came with the post-Warnock debates and the 1981 Education Act. But educational psychologists did not campaign against the continuation of dividing school pupils into two categories, those special and those normal. The legislation was passed with the provision that some pupils would continue to be regarded other than normal (those to be *statemented* under the 1981 Act) and those pupils who would continue to be regarded as normal learners (those *not statmented*) with all the benefits that accrues from not being categorized and classified in this way. There are, of course, other and better ways of providing positive discrimination in education than through legal procedures which have an element of confrontation and which in the end marginalize individual pupils. Once the legislation was passed then educational psychologists had a legal responsibility to be part of the system of sustaining, and working with, a segregated minority of pupils with specified learning needs. As mentioned above, in some LEAs the EPs have set aside their psychological skills and duties in order to take over the administrative functions of the statementing procedures!

Although it is clear that not all educational psychologists want to abandon their 'scientific' testing of pupils, and the management of problems in a mechanistic way, there is a growing body of psychologists who are turning to more humanistic ways of working in schools. To do this they have had to look to other areas of psychological enquiry, particularly social psychology, and to be prepared to work in areas such as moral values. Many psychologists have sought ways of humanizing 'professional help' and to engage in much more of a partnership role with parents. Others have moved very specifically into areas which involve self-growth and the development of communication skills, all of which is an important body of knowledge to be passed on to teachers (Clarke, 1989). So far, in EP training courses, little attention seems to have been given to areas of self-realization, and this has been due in part to educational psychology thinking of itself as a scientific activity, with EPs behaving like behavioural scientists, and consequently distancing themselves from such matters.

A third approach to the future work of educational psychologists is that set out by Neil Bolton (1989) where he sees the need for a broader approach, not just within the discipline of psychology itself, but in a more effective linking up between the foundation disciplines of education. Bolton (1989) summarises his views in the following way:

> Educational Psychology presents as a discipline divided within itself. It has failed to reconcile its two purposes: to build educational practice on a theoretical understanding of the developing child, and to assist as an applied discipline with the management of individuals and groups in educational settings. For the academic study of child development relates only weakly to what actually occurs in classrooms, and those who are professionally committed to the application of psychology have their roles defined for them largely by whatever problems the system throws at them. In short, there is no unity of theoretical and practical understanding.

Bolton sees this failure not simply due to undergraduate psychology but incoherence in educational theory and what he calls the 'multiplicity of therapeutic intentions'. The main problem is that 'the major foundational disciplines of education, by which I mean Psychology, Philosophy and Sociology, have failed to relate to one another'. Furthermore, that because such disciplines do not come together in a coherence that determine practice in schools, we are left with a vast range of styles of working and methods of intervention which, when not confusing the educational psychologist, complexes the teacher. At the end of the day these interventions are very individualistic and sometimes idiosyncratic.

The 1988 Education Act presents now a new opportunity for educational psychologists to work more closely with schools in so far that schools in the future will decide what support help they will purchase. There is a danger, however, that schools will only buy in psychological expertise to use this facility in order to have certain pupils removed from the school because of behaviour or learning difficulties. A second danger lies in the government looking to educational psychologists to underpin the national system of testing pupils at 7, 11, 14 and 16 years. Where this happens the educational psychology service will be back with Burt. The 1988 Education Act does, however, provide an opportunity for individual psychologists to come forward and open up a dialogue with heads and teachers to work out a different psychology of schooling that could be developed. The nature of this psychology has yet to be worked out but some work has already taken place.

The Psychology of Schooling

In 1986 a group of headteachers, psychologists, administrators and those in research and teaching, met together to explore issues that were common to those in the field of school management and the discipline of psychology. These seminars, held at regular intervals throughout the year, at the London University Education Management Unit, focused essentially on the effective management of schools and in identifying what skills and perceptions of psychology could be utilized to contribute to good educational practice. In November of 1986 a writing workshop was held at Halifax House, Oxford University, and initial draft papers were presented in preparation for a volume to address the issue of *Management and the Psychology of Schooling* (Jones and Sayer, 1987). The first volume on the Psychology of Schooling explored a number of avenues where psychology could be a contribution to the practice of schooling. Areas like values, classroom management, curriculum, community links, school climate and ethos, and pastoral systems all came under scrutiny. These were but a few of the topics discussed during the seminars and detailed at the Oxford meeting. Additionally, it was possible to look at areas of school activity where psychologists might offer a more intensive input for the benefit of the work of teachers and their pupils. The issues looked at were communication skills, managing groups, professional development, pupil learning, work with parents, consultancy work with teachers, in-service and advisory activities.

At the initial meetings it was quite difficult to find common ground that would provide a starting point to advance thinking and planning. For headteachers, a visit to a school by educational psychologist was only part of a wide range of people who throughout a day, or week, would pass through the gates of the institution. Fom the heads' point of view, and from a management standpoint, the visit was for purposes of identifying the nature of the needs of individual pupils and to bring about remediation. This was basically a *service* activity, carried out usually once a fortnight, and restricted to influencing the behaviour of a minority of pupils who were misbehaving or under-achieving. This only marginally touched upon the other concerns of the headteacher which related to questions of leadership, decision making, organizing resources, managing change, curriculum planning, managing a work force of teachers and paraprofessionals, liaison with a variety of support agencies, with parents and industry, and the management of self and others in a variety of one-to-one and group settings. For the psychologists it was difficult for them to 'centre' themselves in the position of a headteacher. Psychological practice, with its service to as many as forty or more schools, units, clinics, parents and other agencies, provided almost a completely different set of aims and objectives for planning work and therapeutic interventions. Of all the activities that went on in the life of a school it soon became apparent that the psychological contribution, with its link to behaviour problems and learning failure, was offering only a minimum considering that the discipline of psychology preoccupies itself, elsewhere in the community, with whatever interests and occupies human beings. Schools were not capitalizing on this knowledge and expertise partly because of the restricted brief educational psychologists have for their intervention in school activities.

The aim of the seminars was not to examine present-day educational psychology in its scientific stance, nor to question the place of academic psychology vis-a-vis other disciplines: all this has its own rules and legitimacy. What was being considered was the fact that many educationalists were aware that in a wide range of managerial aspects of running a school, like with personnel selection, management of staff, appraisal and review activities, for example, there was much that the base discipline of psychology could offer. Unfortunately, for schools, much of this expertise is syphoned off into other areas of the community, into industry, commerce and government agencies. The central question was how much of this knowledge and expertise could be garnered for the benefit of the educational service, and through what kind of delivery agency?

The basic problem is not a new one and educational psychologists have frequently examined the implications of new roles and areas of work. Perhaps the first intention of the London seminars was to broaden the dialogue: to date much of the discussion has been 'in-house', and yet a way forward involve others, especially as changes will affect significantly the work of others working in schools. Nowhere, of course, at the moment, do educational psychologists have licence to practice other than what has been expected of them over the past seventy years. Alternative work has only been possible where individual psychologists have been able to create a space for themselves, to explore and carry out other ways of working, and to do this in partnership with heads.

The general concept of a *Psychology of Schooling* is not an easy one: the thinking to date has shown this. Some colleagues have approached this in an evolutionary spirit seeing a psychological practice emerge having grown on from old ways of thinking and working. Others, knowing how easily new change becomes old practice with new titles, look to a *paradigm shift* in the way we have to think, and practice our psychology in education. Yet others look to progress, and a way forward, in a combination of approaches. This would entail a change in practice arising from looking to other areas of the discipline of psychology, to abandoning scientific pretentions in the process, and to defining ways of developing and practising new styles of working while at the same time abandoning or resolving all problems. But there is also the need to change the perception we have of the work — a shift in the way we think about what tasks to take on and how we go about tackling these.

Finally, there are those who, while recognising some of the present day problems, look to a role that is completely centred on good school practice in terms of effective management, skilled and innovatory teaching, developing an appropriate curriculum for all pupils irrespective of age, ability and aptitude. This is a *Psychology of Schooling* that starts at the positive end of pupil self-esteem, achievement, and the recognition of positive educational goals for all. The slow-learning pupil, the maladjusted, less-able, disaffected etc. are no longer a target group for the exercise of psychological skills because where the school management, teaching, and curriculum planning takes place in a context of positive values and practices, such categorized pupils do not exist. We only have pupils, all with personal needs, all needing support and the opportunity to engage fully in learning (and the making of mistakes), coming together where the appropriate management structures support a positive education. Educational psychologists could, and should, make their contribution appropriately to this positive education, and heads would welcome this.

A positive aspect of the 1988 Education Act is that headteachers, what with local management of schools, now have it in their hands to offer to educational psychologists a place in this partnership: some heads will want something different from what has been offered in educational psychology in the past — some undoubtedly, will want EPs to remain *testers* of the system for ever — but here is an opportunity for educational psychologists, from whatever organizational base, to offer schools a comparable response.

In the discussion and publications to date on a *Psychology of Schooling* there has been some determined effort to identify ways forward. The dialogue extends and widens, and by nature of what is entailed, has to encompass many others beyond those working directly in school psychological services. In a second volume (Jones and Frederickson, 1989), a further set of areas of work are examined, and these include chapters on individual pupil learning, future work with parents, approaches to pupil behaviour, the need for better communication skills, and impact of working and learning in groups, consultancy roles in schools, the issues of teacher stress, EPs as leaders with teacher in-service training, systems work and theory, links between psychological theory and educational practice in a context of political change, and a role for psychologists in new innovations.

To summarise

It has been argued in this chapter that to facilitate a new Psychology of Schooling educational psychologists will need to find ways of abandoning their role as *testing agents*, and to do this as a matter of professional intention. They will need to free themselves of the *legal restaints*, acquired through legislation since 1980, where dubious legislation, (like the 1981 Education Act) places a straitjacket on good psychological practice, and determines EP roles and functions in ways in which the profession needs to abandon. There is a need for EP services to acquire a new status and a new role: on which addresses itself to helping schools develop in positive ways, and to make schools more effective places of learning, to help pupils secure a better sense of self-esteem and achievement. The avenues for this work are through the *ordinary* channels of effective school management, inspiring teaching, developing appropriate curriculum, and the development of appropriate value systems. This requires a gradual withdrawal from areas of work linked to pupils who are seen by teachers and others as failing, or have failed, in their learning while at school. There would be a need for EPs to distance themselves from things *special* in education and any activity, which in outcome, marginalizes a pupil from ordinary school experiences.

The changing context

In recent years we have seen a strong move by government to determine and control what is taught in schools: determined through the national curriculum and controlled through a combined system of pupil testing and teacher appraisal systems. To this extent the government is shifting its control on how resources are used and the methods aimed to develop a more efficient, and skilled teaching force. This begins to force out the range of alternatives that can be developed in schools to meet individual needs, and the participation of educational psychologists in those alternative strategies.

On the other hand, we can observe contra moves to place more authority in the hands of headteachers, in terms of financial control of their schools, and this in turn places the educational psychologist, for the first time, in competition with others in LEA support services, in social work and in learning support facilities, for areas of work where there is much overlap in the skills offered and the support provided.

Clearly, LEA support services will, in the future, work to some form of contract system, and skilled help will be *bought in* by individual schools. This could have the effect of linking more closely the school and the EP, or a consortium of schools with a psychologist working in a consultancy or prescribed way, as determined jointly by heads and EPs. Some educational psychologists would welcome this: others might well want to preserve what they would regard as a professional autonomy, offering a service to schools, but from a base in the LEA or private practice. Apart from the competition with other support agencies there might well be a re-defining of the role of an educational psychologist in his or her work in school, and this would be to reinforce the role of the educational psychologist as the person who comes in to oversee some of the testing of pupils at different stages of their education as part of the provisions of the 1988 Education Act.

Bolton (1989) summarizes these points in the following way:

> We are confronted here with an all-embracing framework which effectively prohibits any radical alternative. The management philosophy is clear: centralize to control quality and the best use of resources; decentralize to allow a form of individual freedom that will challenge the system, and focus attention upon the shop floor as the locus of problems and solutions.

What cannot be judged at this moment is how this system of running an education system will finally determine what work and function there is for the educational psychologist in schools. Some aspects of the changing model may be welcomed, as with the greater participation of parents, the greater freedom for schools to determine their own local management, and some would claim, the opportunity of schools to be free of LEA control. Some educational psychologists are confident that the good working relationships they have with their schools will ensure a continuity and call upon their services. This is now uncertain because with local school management, the LEA will have to consider seriously its own financial priorities, and whether running a school psychological service will, in time, be justified considering other claims to what will be limited financial resources.

In the Coopers and Lybrand report it was recommended that services like educational psychology should remain a centralized service of the LEA and this places EP services in the *market place* in which there will be future claims on LEA funds for a variety of services and functions. It is yet to be seen whether, in the financial formula allocation for the running of schools, they will be set aside finance whereby schools can buy in the LEA psychological services. For schools where there is little uptake and regard for psychological help it would be too easy to circumvent this issue by simply ensuring that within the school there are no pupils who require psychological help. This would be the case if educational psychologists continue to see their work in relation to pupils who are failing to learn. If educational psychologists are prepared to draw on other areas of their discipline (other than those needed in order to practise deficit-model testing and assessments) and address themselves to a range of issues in schools which are the daily pre-occupation of all headteachers and their teaching staff, on matters of daily management, then heads might well welcome an opportunity to use their financial resources for purchasing psychological expertise that they see as relevant to their task of managing schools. A closer link between educational psychologists *and their schools* might well bring about a better understanding of why some pupils fail.

A psychology of schooling and pupil behaviour

The above account raises many of the central issues of how educational psychologists go about their work and points to a direction for future work of EPs in schools. This book is about pupil behaviour and discipline in schools. This chapter suggests that a way forward in dealing with pupil disruption, disaffection, or with aggravating discipline problems, is not through individual strategies aimed at irradicating inappropriate behaviour of pupils. Rather than a deficit-model approach to human behaviour, it proposes an approach through *the complete management of schools*. Much of the evidence to the Elton Committee draws attention to the fact that serious pupil disruption and behaviour is but a symptom of a malaise in the area of schools management in total, in teaching and planning curriculum in particular, and in a breakdowm of relationships where appropriate value systems have not been worked out, or are not working well. Some of the analysis applied to educational psychology services could also be employed in understanding why some schools carry a burden of disciplinary issues with consequent bad behaviour of pupils.

At the moment there are some educational psychologists who wish to move away completely from old ways of working, particularly in the area of learning failure. There are many heads who are trying to establish a school ethos of achievement and success for all, staff and pupils. Where educational psychologists have moved towards working in schools where already heads have a positive management stance, then both members of the teaching staff and members of the support services, like educational psychologists, work together for an even more enhanced results. The areas of school management and practice so far identified for more attention and action are those set out in the two volumes on the *Psychology of Schooling* (Jones and Sayer, 1987: Jones and Frederickson, 1989). Educational psychologists might well consider which of these particular areas they could offer to a school, based on a very specialized knowledge of that area, and where it would be recognized by all members of staff that this is the school resource for that kind of knowledge and skills. This would suggest that, for the most part, educational psychologists in the future will be highly trained specialists in areas of school management indicated above, which take up a good deal of the time and energy of headteachers in the running of their schools.

We can conclude this chapter on educational psychology services, and their contribution to schools on pupil behaviour, by drawing attention to what HMI recommended in their recent publication *Good Behaviour and Discipline in Schools* (DES, 1987). The HMI report focuses attention on areas of school practice that would, from their surveys, enquiries and consultations, indicate how discipline matters should best be tackled. These areas are complementary to those being looked at and studied as appropriate work areas for educational psychologists interested in a *Psychology of Schooling*. If there is a priority in all this it has to be the issue of school management: if there is a priority for educational psychologists it is that they too concentrate on how, and in what way, they can in consultative or other styles of working, maximally assist heads in facilitating *effective management* of their schools. Issues like discipline then become and end result, varied among many matters of management style, and not a beginning for provocation or even the setting up of government committees of enquiry.

References

BOLTON, N. (1989) 'Educational psychology and the politics and practice of education', in JONES, N. and FREDERICKSON, N. (eds.) *Refocusing Educational Psychology*, Lewes, Falmer Press.

CLARKE, C. S. (1989) 'Skill, Problem Solving and the Reflexive EP', in JONES, N. and FREDERICKSON, N. (eds.) *Refocusing Educational Psychology*, Lewes, Falmer Press.

COOPERS and LYBRAND (1989) *Local Management of Schools*, A Report to the Department of Education and Science, London, HMSO.

DEPARTMENT OF EDUCATION AND SCIENCE (1987) *Good Behaviour and Discipline in Schools*, Education Observed 5, Report of HM Inspectors, London, DES.

DESSENT, T. (1987) *Making the Ordinary School Special*, Lewes, Falmer Press.

HARGREAVES, A., BAGLIN, E., HENDERSON, P., LEESON, P., and TOSSELL, T. (1988) *Personal and Social Education: Choices and Challenges*, Oxford, Basil Blackwell.

JONES, N. and SAYER, J. (1988) *Management and the Psychology of Schooling*, Lewes, Falmer Press.

JONES, N. and FREDERICKSON, N. (1989) *Refocusing Educational Psychology*, Lewes, Falmer Press (in press).

MORTIMORE, P., SAMMONS, P., ECOB, R. and STOLL, L. (1988) *School Matters: The Junior Years*, Salisbury, Open Books.

QUICKE, J. C. (1980) *The Cautious Expert: an emperically grounded critique of the practice of local authority educational psychologists*, Ph.D thesis, Sheffield University.

QUICKE, J. C. (1983) *The Cautious Expert: An analysis of developments in the practice of educational psychology*, Milton Keynes, Open University Press.

REYNOLDS, D. (1982) 'The search for effective schools', *School Organisation*, Vol. 2, No. 3, pp. 215–237.

RUTTER, M. (1983) 'School effects on pupil progress — findings and policy implications', *Child Development*, Vol. 54, No. 1, pp. 1–29.

16
School Discipline and the Elton Report

Neville Jones

Introduction

This book has been compiled during the period the Elton Committe was carrying out its enquiries. The HMI Survey Report *Behaviour and Discipline in School* (Education Observed 5) (DES, 1987) was the basis for an HMI Invitation Conference to LEAs held at Newman College, Birmingham in December 1987 and was the initial inspiration for a publication. The HMI Survey put into perspective a view about violence and disruption in schools. The independent research over many years into this area of schooling had consistently come up with the conclusion that violence was of very small dimensions in our schools, was often specific to particular schools, or particular geographic areas such as inner-city urban conglomerates.

The HMI Survey was a very positive document, contrary to expectations on the part of government and some teacher unions, establishing the consistency with which violence was a limited phenomenon in schools. The Survey became, therefore, a document on good practice in schools, outlining a whole range of areas and strategies to bring about improved discipline in schools. The Survey was very much an 'ideas' document, avoiding detailed prescriptions in the knowledge that every school has its own starting point on matters of morals and discipline. It attempted to concentrate on areas where schools might draw strengths and power to meet indiscipline needs should and where they occur. Because of this emphasis the Survey has been and is being used by LEAs as a base training document for in-service work and in providing guidelines for individual headteachers. The findings of the HMI Survey were given general support by LEA representatives at the HMI Invitation Conference in Birmingham and the specific detailed recommendations of the HMI Survey and the Birmingham conference are given below, partly because of their general importance in the debate about school violence, but also because many of the recommendations have been touched upon by contributors to this book.

The evidence of limited violence in schools seemed to contrast with what was being published by some teacher unions arising out of their internal membership surveys. It was, perhaps, unfortunate that in one of the surveys the media were specifically active and involved in circulating and commenting in the usual sensational way on the data being produced; data which on later analysis showed that less than 1 per cent of the union membership was concerned about violent acts in schools (see Rosenbaum, Chapter 6, this volume). A further problem was that any violent incident was reported as if violence was happening in schools in general. This meant that the majority of state schools were being besmirched with the brush of incompetence and indiscipline. But the majority of teachers at this time were silent on the issue of school violence. Large numbers of teachers did not complete their union surveys, and a proportion of those who did said that violence was not a problem. It was not until the publication of the Elton Report, in March 1989, that some understanding of this reluctance of teachers to speak out about these over-exaggerated claims for violence began to emerge.

As already mentioned, the HMI Survey was one in a long series of investigations into school discipline and confirmed yet again the findings of independently researched investigations. Possbily there was a need for the various studies to be collated, analysed, and evaluated. This could easily have been done by a DES statistician or the task put out to one of the many reputable research centres we have in this country. Government funding for additional research into behaviour and discipline was already out to tender, but was withdrawn, and instead the government set up its own Committee of Enquiry under the chairmanship of Lord Elton. Clearly, political considerations were having a greater influence on action to be taken about violence and discipline in schools than could be derived from independent research. Something more than systematic research was required and there was the necessity for the Enquiry to be headed by a distinguished member of the government. It has to be recalled that the bruising confrontation between teachers and the government, involving the teachers in strike action, was for the majority of teachers a recent and still painful experience.

The 'violence' issue provided the government with a golden opportunity to offer a conciliatory hand to teachers, bearing in mind that the 'violence issue' was a teacher union-led concern being promulgated through the media. Equally, the violence issue was one which also was preoccupying the government on the question of increased community hooliganism. Already the blame for hooliganism at football matches was being laid at the doors of the teaching profession. The HMI Survey had 'failed' to make this link simply because the link was not there to be made. It is of interest that the HMI Survey, with its positive findings and recommendations, was not well received by government nor by some of the teacher unions. In the setting up of the Elton Committee the government was achieving for itself two aims: first, it was showing a willingness to make a response to the violence issue which some teacher unions were claiming to be an issue endemic throughout our schools. Secondly, there was still an outside chance that a link could be made between educational philosophies of recent years, in terms of a greater freedom of pupils to determine their own learning needs, for example, and the growing concern of government and the general public about the increasing breakdown of law and order in some parts of society, particularly in our large cities. If the school — violence link could be established then the government would be well pleased that youth unemployment was now off the political agenda as a cause of urban violence. Perhaps the greatest value the Elton Committee has contributed to the education service is that in considering the evidence in a balanced way, it can be shown that we cannot connect community violence in general with problems of indiscipline in schools. What has been staved off is the risk that teachers and schools will yet again be used as the 'whipping boy' for the ills of society at large.

It must be said that during the time these claims and counter-claims for violence in schools were taking place, and the teachers seemingly going along with the general premise that schools were places of chaos, teachers found themselves in both a professional and sometimes personal dilemma. Changes taking place in schools over the decade or so were causing teachers much concern, over-preoccupation, and for some, damaging stress. The causes of this concern were, and are, various and affect teachers in a differentiating way. For some teachers the expection to relate to pupils as individuals, recognizing and responding to a variety of personal needs, and not just to imparting knowledge from a syllabus, created a conflict of role of personal identity with that of duty. Such teachers felt they were not doing their job as well as they wanted, or were trained for, in formal terms of teaching. As some schools grew in size, members of staff became conscious that top managment was not trained in the management of large institutions, and they were required to work in schools which were managerially inefficient. At times there were serious shortages in books and equipment and in some schools this became an important source of disaffection for pupils, let alone their teachers. New ideas were being introduced into some schools but in extreme forms: the majority of teachers were not themselves educated or trained in schools where the school ethos was extremely directive on the one hand or *laissez-faire* on the other; or where over-emphasis was placed on such matters as sexism, racism or competition. Some of these matters could have been dealt with by teachers extending their basic teaching knowledge and skills, or informing themselves better on matters which had to be coped with in the staffroom, through school or LEA in-service training. But it is a paradox that where problems are worst so is the intransigence of heads or LEAs to take a lead in resolving conflict and disillusionment. These problems are not new and many teachers just cope or see the teaching task as one of being resilient to such demands and finding ways for personal and professional recoupment of energies.

Perhaps it is the case that we should never have heard about the 'violence issue', nor an Elton Committee, had not changes occurred that brought into being the 1988 Education Act with all its superimposed obligations and duties on teachers. The increasing shift of control regarding classroom practice and curriculum innovation to external agencies set up by government, has compounded the feeling of many teachers that teaching is no longer a worthwhile job and their status in the community, locally and nationally, is much diminished. Had the government used its legislative powers to bring about changes that would enhance the role of the teacher — and the opportunity to do this was present during the teachers' strike — then the current disillusionment in the teaching profession would already by 1989 have shown some significant resolution.

Teachers then had but one response from the government about their concerns, some of which are mentioned above, and this was only in relation to the question of school discipline and violence. The majority of teachers knew that their real concerns lay elsewhere, and indicated so in their silent responses to their union surveys, but it has been necessary for the 'violent' schools issue to be seen through to its conclusion. What has been achieved is that during this time of government enquiry and reporting there has been more open debate about life in schools and what makes for effective and meaningful education for all pupils: the kind of education which, when it is achieved, makes teachers' work rewarding. What the Elton Report has pinpointed is that many problems that now exist in schools, while in themselves of moderate dimension and capable of resolution by most skilled teachers, are present and persistent day-to-day and seemingly are not resolved by virtue of teachers calling upon their repertoire of teaching skills. An example given by teachers to the Elton Committee was the constant and unremitting noise that occurs in some classrooms and corridors *every* day and without let-up.

There is now, and has been all along, the danger that just as schools are likely to be blamed for problems elsewhere in the community, so it is that discipline issues are regarded as the source of so much discontent within a school, and that it is the discipline question that is central and has to be addressed. This does not mean that discipline codes and sanctions are not part of the general ethos and working of the school, and that where discipline matters have not been carefully thought out and put into practice, the school communities are soon in trouble. But it does mean that the issue of discipline, when it arises, should in all cases alert teachers to things going wrong elsewhere in the school, and where individual needs for adults as well as pupils are not being met.

Good discipline is the outcome of an effective school, where learning takes place in the context of individual pupil needs, and where there is the opportunity for *all* to gain and secure a sense of achievement and personal worth. Herein lies a danger with the recommendations of the Elton Committee. If the recommendation, 'that all initial teacher training courses should include specific practical training in ways of motivating and managing groups of pupils, and dealing with those who challenge authority', is followed up by the introduction of simplistic techniques to eradicate inappropriate behaviour, without taking into account the context in which that behaviour occurs, i.e. pupil and teacher, learning group, school and its ethos, then we shall see introduced irrelevant strategies for teachers to use. In outcome these tend not to be lasting, are of little meaning to the pupils, and isolate the 'discipline' behaviour as a separate area of pupil behaviour, that can be de-conditioned. Many of the psychological strategies put forward for eliminating deviant or unacceptable behaviour in schools today have a basis in these rather trite and irrelevant intervention models that depersonalize the pupils and take away personal responsibility and accountability. If the emphasis in the recommendation is on finding ways of motivating pupils to learn, or on discovering how well we are versed in the management of learning in groups, then recommendations of this kind are welcome. The same arguments and cautions apply equally to the Secretary of State's proposal that the management of pupil behaviour should become a national priority in the Local Education Authority Teaching Grants Scheme for in-service training of teachers in 1990–91. Perhaps the safeguard here is that all matters of training and skills related to classroom and school pracitce, promulgated at both initial teacher training as well as in-service post-professional development, should be specifically in the hands of *teachers* who are currently practising their craft, and not left to the idiosyncracies of other professional groups who for the most part take little responsibility for the outcomes of their interventions in this area of schooling.

The rest of this chapter will serve as a reminder of the recommendations of the HMI Survey into Behaviour and Discipline; indicate the main responses that were made by LEA delegates to the HMI Invitation Conference at Newman College, Birmingham; and finally make some initial comments on the Elton Committee Report itself.

HMI Report: Behaviour and Discipline in Schools, Education Observed 5.

This report (DES 1987), was compiled from HMI reports on visits to schools where good practice had been observed and recorded since January 1983. Additional evidence was secured from all HMI visits to schools, for whatever purpose, during the summer term of 1986, and where behaviour and discipline matters were given particular attention. In such schools, judgements were sought on which factors were considered to be contributory to good practice. Also, a review of HMI reports was carried out to identify schools where high standards of behaviour were noted and HMI carried out a small number of specific visits. Note was also taken in the preparation of the Report of the extensive research that has been carried out into issues related to behaviour and discipline in schools, and the wealth of recommendations in the literature which is now available to advise those who work in schols or have responsibility for their management.

In the Introduction to their Report, HMI make the following observations:

- Good behaviour is a necessary condition for effective teaching and learning to take place, and an important outcome of education which society rightly expects.
- A school requires generally accepted codes of conduct and rules of procedure by which the school community abides.
- Schools are not places set aside from the world. Their teachers and pupils live their daily lives in the wider community, and are influenced by its standards and values. Schools' attempts to set boundaries of acceptable behaviour, to develop patterns of rewards and sanctions, and to establish constructive relationships take place within the world as it is.
- The most important of these external influences is that of the parents and home. The majority of parents take their responsibilities to develop standards of decent behaviour in their children seriously. Some parents, however, appear to opt out of their obligations . . . prove unequal to discharging them; a very few seem consciously to encourage standards of behaviour quite opposed to those of schools and of society.
- Society at large does not consistently exemplify high standards of behav-

iour, and there is no longer the same sense of security in shared values as perhaps there was at one time.

- Society has high expectations of its schools, not least that they will by example both set and encourage good standards of behaviour, standards which are perhaps higher than society would insist on for adults.
- Over the past few years, many schools have been adversely affected, directly or indirectly, by the increase in unemployment, particularly among young people.
- The teachers' pay dispute has led to widespread and large scale disruption of schooling affecting pupils, teachers and parents and the relationships between them.
- Some schools, for whatever reasons, have more than their fair share of reluctant, disaffected or disturbed and disturbing children.
- Teaching today is a much more difficult job than it was because:
  - i. Teachers do not always get the support they need from society.
  - ii. It is not easy for teachers to achieve consensus on standards they should set, nor on the most appropriate means of encouraging good behaviour and preventing misbehaviour.
  - iii. Teachers can no longer count on automatic respect as figures of authority and expertise.
  - iv. Teachers have to earn such respect as they can attach by doing their job well: by demonstrating competence in the classroom; by treating pupils, parents and colleagues with respect and fairness; by the example which they set through their own behaviour and attitudes.

Results of research in HMI report: Behaviour and Discipline in Schools.

Factors which emerged as influencing behaviour and discipline in schools were:

- Leadership of the headteacher.
- Opportunities for achievement and success derived from challenging teaching.
- Active involvement of pupils in their own learning and in the wider life of the school.
- Consensus of essential values and norms consistently applied.
- Awareness of the school as a social institution which influences groups and not merely individual pupils and teachers.
- An effective school is effective for all pupils irrespective of ethnic origin, gender and class.

Good behaviour

HMI identified four areas which were found to be associated with good behaviour:

- Good relationships with mutual respect between teachers and pupils.
- Teachers' high expectations of their pupils' academic and social abilities.

- Curriculum and teaching methods well matched to pupils' needs.
- Nurturing of pupils' growing maturity and self-esteem.

In schools were some or all of these conditions were not wholly fulfilled it was found that pupils for the most part behave well. Persistent poor behaviour is most often associated with:

a. Poor relationships.
b. Inappropriate curriculum.
c. Inadequate teaching methods.

The Report then goes on to examine eleven areas where good practices can or should be observed. These are:

1. Aims and policy of a school.
2. Leadership of the headteacher and senior staff.
3. Organization of a school and the way it groups its pupils.
4. Quality of the teaching and learning in individual lessons.
5. Impact on behaviour of the physical environment.
6. Coherence in policies for personal and social development.
7. Arrangement where pastoral care can affect learning.
8. Balance between rewards and sanctions.
9. Need to register disapproval of unacceptable behaviour through sanctions and punishments.
10. Priority required to establish positive links with parents.
11. Centrality of establishing and maintaining a school ethos that in outcome secures high standards of behaviour.

Comments were also made in relation to:

a. the local community
b. the education welfare service and other community support services
c. voluntary bodies
d. employers
e. the training of teachers, and
f. the need for a partnership between all agencies and services in the community.

HMI concluded their investigations by summarizing what they considered were the principles of good practice, namely, that the following areas are those which are given high priority in schools which are successful in achieving and sustaining high standards of behaviour and discipline.

1. *Policies* are explicit to all in the school; they establish clear and defensible principles and set the boundaries of acceptable behaviour; they depend on a carefully developed professional agreement; they provide guidelines for action; they are made explicit to pupils and parents; they are firmly and consistently applied.

2. The focus of such policies is the development of a *positive climate* for the whole school; this is based on a quiet yet firm insistence on high standards of behaviour at all time, and draws its strength from community of purpose, consistent practice and constant vigilance. Within this framework it is expected that a small and changing population of pupils will make extra demands on the time and professional expertise of teachers, and that these demands will be met without prejudice to the over-riding principles by which the school community abides.

3. This climate is affected by *all the school's activities*. Within a well-planned curriculum there is a high quality of teaching and learning, in which purposes are clear to all involved. Pupils as well as being intellectually challenged have opportunities for taking initiatives and for accepting responsibility for their progress. Such learning is supported by a range of activities outside the classroom which also contribute to pupils' personal and social development.

4. There is a range of *rewards and privileges*, with due emphasis on well-merited praise; their use outweighs that of the sanctions available. The sanctions relate to defensible principles; they are applied with flexibility and discrimination. In using them to improve pupils' behaviour, schools also offer teachers support and the opportunity to improve their expertise.

5. The school's *leadership* sets a good example, with clear aims and high expectations which are matched by constant vigilance and a willingness to provide support, to identify in-service training needs and take action to meet them, and to encourage the professional development necessary for the maintenance of high standards.

6. The ethos of the school is grounded in the *quality of relationships* at all levels: between teachers, between teachers and pupils, and between pupils. Such relationships are characterised by mutual respect, by the valuing of pupils, by a willingness to listen and understand and by a positive view of teachers and professionals and pupils as learners. Through good models of adult behaviour, there is constant encouragement to develop self-esteem, self-discipline and autonomous adherence to high standards.

7. The school makes full use of the strengths available to it through the *wider partnership*: its links with parents, with the local community and with the various supporting agencies are all used to enhance the quality of the schools as a community, and to help maintain high expectations.

HMI Invitation Conference: Newman College Birmingham

In December 1987, HMI held a hospitality conference at Newman College, Birmingham, with the 'aim to draw attention of LEAs to ways in which they might make use of the HMI publication'. The conference was attended by representatives of sixty LEAs in England and Wales, plus HMI and a representative from the DES.

This conference provided an opportunity for representatives to express opinions about the Report and the specific matters it contained, drawing on their own experiences. The findings of this conference, summarized below, were circulated to LEAs in February, 1988. The conclusions were as follows:

1. The current position

- The picture of widespread disruption to be inferred from media coverage was seen to be wholly inaccurate.
- The vast majority of schools in the authorities represented at the conference were said to be calm and purposeful institutions going about their work without serious interruption.
- The statement in the HMI Report in paragraph 9–10 was an accurate summary of the situation.
- Where incidents of indiscipline or violence did occur these were spasmodic eruptions condemned by both teachers and pupils.
- Violence which received attention of the national press and media usually had its sources in areas beyond those of the influence of schools.
- Not all incidents were the sole responsibility of the pupil: the school and teachers played a part in creating a climate where such incidents occurred. For example, provision of inappropriate curricular and teaching approaches, or the occasional wrong-footed response by teachers.
- Investigations into incidents of indiscipline need to be fully rounded and take into account the actions of all persons concerned — pupils, teachers, senior management, LEA personnel, parents, and sometimes other agencies.
- LEA representatives reported improvements in the monitoring of exclusions from schools, no overall increase in the numbers of suspensions though suspensions had increased in particular schools (not thought to be related to the abolition of corporal punishment).
- Many schools had altered their practices following the abolition of corporal punishment, governors were taking a great interest in suspensions and exclusions, and implementation of the relevant sections of the 1986 Education Act had made all parties more aware of the need to monitor exclusions and suspensions.
- Some twelve LEAs reported the appointment of working parties to consider policies and practices arising from representations to local educational authorities by a number of teachers' organizations. Aspects being covered included positive and practical ways to improve behaviour, monitoring of exclusions and suspensions, the development of specialist teams of teachers to advise staff in schools, and an examination of the place and value of off-site units.
- Some LEAs reported they were looking at disaffection generally, such as absenteeism and a poor response to education, because it was thought that

this was far more of a problem for most schools. Some LEAs reported they were reviewing the achievement of their pupils, how these were recorded, and using certain central government initiatives such as LAPP and ESGs to assist them. From such reviews it was becoming clear that there was a wide variation in the use of supervision by individual schools.

- Grant related in-service training (GRIST) funds had been used to study discipline and behaviour, records of achievement, unit accreditation, behaviour management, and pastoral and counselling work. LEAs have found GRIST funding useful in these areas and some LEAs were already using the HMI document *Good Behaviour and Discipline in Schools* in positive ways in their in-service courses.

- Many LEA representatives draw attention to the low morale in the teaching profession. Also, LEAs found themselves under pressure from what was described as 'the relentless flood of central government initiatives'. This led to crisis management with fewer opportunities to think out responses and policies.

- Attention was also drawn by conference members to external factors which now affect pupil behaviour: levels of poverty and unemployment, the closure of some social services and DHSS provision, withdrawal or reduction of out-of-county places for behaviourally disturbed pupils, and limited resources to cope with such pupils in ordinary schools.

2. What can Schools do?

- All groups at the conference felt the need for schools to present a *whole school* approach to include a sound curriculum, a sensitive pastoral care and counselling system, and appropriate teaching and learning.

- Schools needed to set clear norms of acceptable and good behaviour.

- The active support of parents and the wider community needed to be gained.

- Concern was expressed that the National Curriculum might put at risk work aimed at pupils' personal development; that tutorial work and PSE might suffer and that elements of the modular curriculum which helped lower attaining pupils might be lost.

- Recognition by teachers and the school of effort by pupils was important — agreement was needed on ways in which a school could recongize and value positive achievement of all kinds.

- Important was the use of school-based INSET to help schools consider their strategies, time for staff to think, support and train each other. All this to encourage team approaches to supporting individual coleages.

- Important value of residential work and off-site work experiences.

- School senior management teams needed to be sensitive managers of plant, resources and personal relations. Cooperative methods of working which enthused pupils and teachers needed to be pursued — this had implications for styles of working and leadership.

- Parents and governors needed to be brought in more fully to the work and life of the school — this helped to create a bank of goodwill when disruptive incidents did occur.
- Absenteeism and truancy in some schools were unacceptably high and were sometimes condoned. Absence in the fourth and fifth years of secondary education had the effect of making success at GCSE much more difficult for some pupils.

3. What can the LEA do?

- The need for more and better directed training in the management of complex institutions was identified for heads and deputy heads.
- Teachers need help and training in the management of stress and in dealing with difficult pupils.
- A number of LEAs reported that they had support teams which offered curriculum initiatives, resources and INSET to support schools.
- LEAs should actively support schools in their work of extending links with parents and local communities.

4. What can Central Government do?

- A positive attempt to tackle the issue of low morale among teachers; to mitigate the effects of the teachers' industrial action; and to remove some of the uncertainties about the future of the education service.
- Remove uncertainties about the final form and content of the national curriculum, the place of personal and social education and the pastoral system, problems of employment and housing.
- Central government action to help deal with the underlying causes of indiscipline and to encourage more focused INSET.

5. Final points

- Important tasks to involve schools in a programme of review and development over policies of behaviour and discipline.
- Good behaviour and discipline cannot be separated from all other aspects of the development of schools which also need to be considered. The national curriculum would bring with it the possibility of changing attitudes to learning and the curriculum — this would form a new context within which schools would have to develop behavioural norms.
- Schools needed to work hard at changing public perceptions — while schools needed informed and critical support it was the responsibility of LEAs and central government to see that they received it.

- Need to retain effective personal and social educational curriculum and other supports which allow children access to, and encourage their engagement in, the curriculum and their own learning.
- A huge communication task was to inform parents and the public at large that most schools are calm and purposeful.
- It was acknowledged that teachers generally feel that pupil behaviour in schools was deteriorating and that it is now more difficult to achieve good educational objectives.

The Elton Enquiry (Discipline in Schools)

The terms of reference of Elton Committee of Enquiry were as follows:

In view of public concern about violence and indiscipline in schools and the problems faced by the teaching profession today, to consider what action can be taken by central government, local authorities, voluntary bodies running schools, governing bodies of schools, headteachers, teachers and parents to secure the orderly atmosphere necessary in schools for effective teaching and learning to take place.

Members of the Committee were:

Lord Elton, Chairman
Dr Roy Bennett, Vice Chairman Derbyshire College of Education
Roy Atkinson, County Education Officer, Northamptonshire
John Phillips, Headteacher, Graveney School, Wandsworth
Linbert Spencer, Chief Executive, Project Fullemploy Ltd, London
Glenda Thomas, Headteacher, Blaencaerau Junior School, Bridgend
Collette Thomson, Teacher, Adlerbrook School, Solihull, West Midlands.

Recommendations: (Summarized in the Times Education Supplement 17.03.89)

A. SCHOOLS

- Headteachers and teachers should, in consultation with governors, develop whole-school behaviour policies which are clearly understood by pupils, parents and other school staff.
- Schools should ensure that their rules are derived from the principles underlying their behaviour policies and are consistent with them.
- Schools should strike a healthy balance between rewards and punishments. Both should be clearly specified.
- Headteachers and teachers should avoid the punishment of whole groups.
- Headteachers and teachers should avoid punishments which humiliate pupils.

- Headteachers and staff should be alert to signs of bullying and racial harassment; deal firmly with all such behaviour; take action based on clear rules which are backed by appropriate sanctions and systems to protect and support victims.
- Schools should not use rigid streaming arrangements to group their pupils by ability.
- Headteachers and staff should adopt comprehensive policies for the care of premises, with responsibilities allocated to specific people, including pupils.
- LEAs and governing bodies with responsibility for buildings should help schools to create a better environment for both staff and pupils by providing soft-floor coverings and other noise-reducing features wherever possible.
- LEAs and governing bodies which employ school staff should ensure that midday supervisors are given adequate training in the management of pupils' behaviour.

B. MANAGEMENT

- Teachers who, after in-service training and other professional support, are unable to control their classes should be dismissed.
- LEAs should set up systems to monitor serious incidents of disruption, based on advice from a national working party to be set up by September.
- Chief police officers and Crown prosecutors should take staff morale into account, as a matter of public interest, when deciding whether or not to prosecute in cases of assault, against teachers and other staff.
- Staff members who are assaulted at school should be entitled to compensation from LEAs or governing bodies, either through insurance cover or ex-gratia payments. Deliberate damage to staff motor vehicles or other belongings on school premises should also qualify for compensation.
- The Secretary of State should commission research to investigate the relationship between school staffing levels, class size, and behaviour.
- The government should systematically monitor for five years the operation of exclusion procedures introduced under the 1986 (No.2) Education Act, and make whatever changes are needed.

C. TEACHERS

- Initial teacher training establishments should give full weight to the personal qualities required for effective classroom management . . . when selecting applicants.

- The development of the ability to relate well to pupils should be a key consideration in assessing a student's overall competence to teach.
- A minimum requirement for regular classroom teaching experience for staff providing training in teaching skills equivalent to one term in every five years should be specified.
- The management of pupil behaviour should become a national priority for funding under the local education authority training grants scheme from 1990/91 until at least 1994/95.
- The Secretaries of State should consider introducing legislation to clarify the legal basis of teachers' authority.
- The Secretaries of State and LEAs should give due weight to the serious implications of any actual or predicted teacher shortages when considering future pay levels and conditions of service for the profession.

D. PUPILS

- Records of achievement should give weight to a wide range of achievements and personal qualities.
- Schools and LEAs should increase cooperation with employers in developing 'compact' schemes.
- Pupils should not have to wait more than six months for statements of special needs. Where waiting lists are longer, LEAs should take on extra educational psychologists.
- Education support grants should be established by the Government to encourage innovative projects for dealing with the most difficult pupils. All LEAs should be eligible to bid for grants for three years.
- LEAs and governing bodies should treat racial harassment of pupils by staff as a disciplinary offence.
- Parents should monitor, and where necesssary, restrict their children's access to network, cable, satellite or video material which transmits violent or anti-social messages.
- The government should consider substantially increased penalties for illegal employment of children during school hours.

E. PARENTS

- Education for parenthood should be fully covered as a cross-curricular theme in the national curriculum. It should also be covered in school personal and social education programmes.
- The possibility of imposing a civil liability on parents for their children's acts in schools should be explored by the Government.

Conclusions

The Elton Committee was established partly because the HMI Report (DES, 1987) was not acceptable to the government, even though it was based on some 15 years of independent research into effective school practice, examples of good practice, 'culled from inspection visits since January 1983', a special study linked to HMI visits to schools during the summer term of 1986, and a small number of 'specific visits to schools where high standards of behaviour were known to exist'. The HMI Report had concluded that:

> The general picture of behaviour within schools which emerges from these publications is that the overwhelming majority of schools are orderly communities in which there are good standards of behaviour and discipline; poor behaviour is unusual, and serious indiscipline a rare occurrence (paragraph 9).

The government, in calling for a report from HMI, were evidently wanting both to point a finger at teachers and schools over public concern on violent crime, hooliganism in sport arenas, the behaviour of young people in overseas holiday resorts and at European football games, and secondly, to make a response to the growing clamour by some teacher unions for some kind of enquiry into disruptive behaviour in schools. The argument, politically, is (as so often) a naive one; namely, that schools are seen as places where young people are cured of their ignorance and taught to be good citizens within the society in which they live. If young people do not conform to the moral standards set in the society (though one might pose the question in reverse and say if young people do conform to a society's standards), and this is unacceptable to those in government, there is but one source of the problems. The schools yet again become the scapegoat for ills in a society which have their beginnings elsewhere than in the education service. No one doubts, for example, the impact on a whole generation of young people, who, during their secondary years at school, were fully aware that there would be no jobs to take up and no careers to pursue.

In 1988, HMI produced a further report called *Secondary Schools: An Appraisal by HMI* (DES, 1988), which also commented on pupil behaviour arising from their work of inspection:

> The behaviour of pupils was often extremely good and they were generally cooperative. In only a small number of schools (5 per cent) were substantial difficulties being experienced in the classroom (paragraph 29).

In this particular Report, HMI made an important connection insofar that they had something very important to say about pastoral care in schools, its development and (by implication) its relevance to the issues of pupil behaviour and discipline:

> There have been moves to simplify the complex and elaborate systems of pastoral care which were established in many schools and to strengthen the place of tutorial work for the individual form or group tutor. At the

same time there has been a growing recognition that pastoral care and the overseeing of pupils' academic progress are inextricably linked. Increasing prominence was given to the planned use of tutorial time for programmes which aim to promote personal and social development and there was a decline in the still common view that pastoral care consisted only of coping with difficulties and reacting to crises (paragraph 1).

This esential connection in a schools' policy between the care and concern aspects of both the staff and pupils, and academic progress and excellence, seems to be a missing ingredient in the government's activities both in relation to school discipline and the planning of a school curriculum. The Elton Committe was given a brief to look at school discipline — and it was only as a spin-off that such an issue was thought to influence other areas of school activity, namely academic progress and the development of social and political responsibility (i.e., to become a good citizen). The news that it is likely that one of the casualties of the cuts in GCSE syllabuses will be a projected course on Citizenship is especially ironic. In Section 1 of the 1988 Education Act schools are required to provide a balanced and broadly based curriculum that 'prepared pupils for the opportunities, responsibilities, and experience of adult life'. This is not to deny that good behaviour is a necessary condition for pupils to achieve, but additionally, pupils must also learn successfully (see Reynolds, Chapter 1, this volume). There are few teachers who do not understand that effective classroom management is closely linked to effective learning and it is imprudent to consider one of these strands (behaviour) in education as separate from another (achievement).

Here there is both a balance that is required and an emphasis. We might argue that to establish the management of discipline in the first place is to ensure that learning will take place. The causal link here is not so simple, and ignores a whole range of issues, not least that of teacher–pupil relationships. Docking (1989) draws attention to the fact that 'good behaviour is not merely a necessary condition for teaching and learning to take place: it is an outcome of an effective education, and means more than superficial classroom conformity'. It is common folklore among the teacher fraternity that at the beginning of one's teaching career the essential task with any class group is to establish the teacher's authority through overtly disciplinarian measures. From this, it is argued, learning will take place and an outcome will be a fraternity of relationships between teachers and pupils. This is not to say that such a causal sequence is not possible, and for some teachers, has not proved unsuccessful. But to start one's teaching career with discipline issues at the forefront on one's teaching practice incurs the risk that, if this is a very successful style of approaching teaching and learning, then it becomes very difficult to abandon something that, even superficially, seems both to work and bring results. What one has to ask is whether, on this point alone, there is a correlation with the numbers of pupils who in secondary schools disrupt, truant, vandalize, or underachieve?

At the same time as the Elton Committee researched the issues of discipline, at government behest, other government activity was targeted towards, seemingly, quite different objectives and with different kinds of criteria. The 1988 Education

Act is based on the government's aim to raise standards across the education scene. To do this we have a change in the control of education — greater central control and by the schools, and diminished LEA power. We have a National Curriculum with specific built-in methods of assessment. Teachers are to be more accountable for what happens in their schools and this accountability is to be more public and to the public. There is too, a significant shift towards the needs of the consumer, in this case parents, with opportunities for a wider choice of where parents should send their children, and to what kind of school. Hargreaves, in the Introduction to this book, has drawn a comparison between the new legislation and the 1944 Education Act. He says, that, the 'underlying philosophy [of the 1988 Education Act] derives from the principles of competitive individualism and consumer rights'. He goes on to say:

> There is nothing to add or enhance our view of schools as moral com-
> munities, educating the young for rational autonomy and social inter-
> dependence, along with academic achievement and preparation for
> working life.

He concludes that the work of the Elton Committee hardly fits into the scope of the 1988 Education Act. In the Reform Act:

> Moral issues are partitioned from the rest of the curriculum and the oper-
> ation of the education system. Pupil conduct and behaviour are treated as
> separate and distinctive issues outside the main thrust of the reforms and
> are, unlike almost everything else on the educational agenda, syphoned
> off to the old-fashioned independent committee . . . .

Perhaps the most significant omission in the government's National Curriculum is that of pastoral care, presumably on the grounds that it is not a subject as such, to be taught and assessed. A challenge to most secondary schools in the immediate future will be, in trying to implement the various aspects of the National Curriculum with its tight time schedule and over-load of follow-up assessments, to protect those aspects of the personal and social curriculum which in many schools (60 per cent say HMI) are already part of their compulsory core curriculum.

One possible reason for the failure of government policy to connect the matter of pupil behaviour and characteristics of schools is that, for the most part, responses to indiscipline are always seen at the level of individual pupil behaviour. Schools obviously have to provide for occasions when individual pupils act violently and the safety of the disruptive pupil and other pupils in the class, or even the teacher's adult or professional dignity, is at risk. But short term responses of this kind, the crisis intervention model beloved of educational psychologists, provides little for future prevention, or long term management of the disruptive pupils' needs. A persistent disruptive pupil simply finds him or herself suspended or excluded from schools, or on occasions transferred to a special unit or school. The kind of knee-jerk reaction frequently taken by government, and geared towards a response specifically to individual pupils (when not to matters of cost effectiveness), is that of the recently established *Special Action Squads* (SAS) to combat school arson and vandalism. The SAS group, established by the DES in December 1988, is chaired by John Butcher, the Education Junior Minister. Although the group is concerned about the effects of arson and vandalism on other pupils — the disruption, demotivation and demoralisation — there seems little doubt that the basic aim is a monetary one. The Minister, when interviewed by a *Times Educational Supplement* correspondent was quoted as saying:

> The setting up of the squad was triggered by the need to cut the costs of vandalism and arson . . . if making a significant dent in the cost of vandalism and arson can release additional resources, that would be a major benefit.

The issue of 'care for the environment' in which individuals have to work and learn is closely linked to how teachers feel about their work place, the expectations of pupils to take an active role in securing clean and attractive premises — coupled with a sense of ownership (difficult when pupils move from room to room every lesson period), and in the way parents are included in schools' activities and helped to feel that the school belongs to them in a shared partnership with others. Already, it is possible to see a move towards a sense of ownership, both from within schools with teachers and pupils, and with parents, in the *whole-school* movement. Here the shift has been, as far as pupil behaviour is concerned, to limit the cost of treating individual pupils — through placements in units or special schools, or the employment of support services like educational psychologists and education social workers — and to recognize that many forms of problem behaviour may be caused by various deficiencies in the schools themselves. The change in policies has been to look at those features of schools that may be causing behavioural problems with some pupils. But there are difficulties here (Ramasut, 1989).

An opportunity to bring about change in a school occurs when a new headteacher is appointed. Falling rolls and the increase in premature retirement have meant a reduced turnover in the number of headteacher positions. Mobility has declined in the education service as a consequence of the uncertainty there now is within teaching, accompanied by a general lowering of teacher morale linked to disputes with the government over pay and conditions of work. This means that new policies, like *whole-school* concepts, have to be introduced into schools as they are now, good, bad or indifferent. It is difficult to look to in-service work as a source of change agent for those teachers who possibly most require it but who are most likely not to recognize it. LEA advisory services are not well-placed to bring about changes in ineffective schools, where the change is focused essentially on management techniques, and where advisers are usually subject specialists.

A second reason for the government wanting to tackle the problem of pupil indiscipline out of context of what else happens in a school is a possible growing concern that schools, particularly comprehensives, are in fact coping better and better with their indiscipline problems. It is an irony that this may have been helped by a government initiative, whereby Sir Keith Joseph introduced into secondary schools the Lower Attaining Pupils Programme in July 1982. The aim was to provide a more effective form of education for fourth- and fifth-year pupils who would not be expected to take national examinations like the then Certificate in Secondary Education (CSE) and General Certificate in Education (GCE). In spite of cautious evaluations of this project, by government (DES, 1986), the National Foundation for Educational Research (1988), and by individual LEAs (Leeson *et al.*, 1988; Baglin, Chapter 13, this volume), the LAP Programme allowed, for the first time, a substantial number of teachers to focus on the educational needs of a group of pupils many of whom become disenchanted with their experience of schooling, disaffected, or actively alienated. An enormous expertise has been built up over the past seven years on how to intervene for individuals with needs in the ordinary school, how to establish and sustain working management networks — linking LEAs with support personnel and teachers, and how to evaluate areas of living and learning and what this entails. What is remarkable, however, is that in the indecent haste to have policies implemented, giving rise to the 1988 Education Act, the government has practically ignored the work carried out through the LAP Programme leaving a substantial number of project teachers disenchanted, and failing to capitalize on an important body of knowledge for future use.

Reynolds (Chapter 1, this volume) has speculated that recent government legislation and policies aimed specifically at the secondary school, i.e., encouraging a return to 'more academic outcomes and concentrating more on the needs of higher ability' . . . may paradoxically have been because comprehensive schools *were* beginning to succeed in generating authentic comprehensive education, not because they are *not*. Reynolds goes on to make the following points:

1. A school's increasing concentration upon the bottom two-thirds of the ability range may already have affected the top third of the ability range and also the traditional six formers . . .
2. A school's increasing concern with social goals, even more marked in other societies with the *common school*, such as Sweden and the United States, was perhaps threatening to open the curriculum and the schooling experience to forms of discourse and interaction much more suited to the expressive culture of lower social class pupils (Bernstein, 1959).
3. The widening of the curriculum to include more relevant and 'new' knowledge may well have been a powerful spur to learning to those of lower ability, who had come to be labelled as culturally disadvantaged because of their non-possession of the cultural capital (Bordieu and Passeron, 1977) necessary to perform well in acquiring the old, traditional curriculum.
4. The hegemony of this traditional, subject-centred curriculum, is being emphasized to reinforce the advantages of these pupils who can acquire it easily, even though this may generate problems for the many pupils not so equipped.
5. Present policies may well generate grammar school-like comprehensive schools which may generate the same range of pupil behavioural problems that have been so notable in the past, problems which the schools themselves deliberately changed to try to avoid. The more relevant curriculum,

the increased concern for social goals, and the increased concern for the lower ability child, were all intended to avoid the problems that conventional comprehensive schooling had generated.

Responses to the Elton Report

The Elton Report received a mixed response from the teacher unions and the media: the government has so far taken up very few of the 138 recommendations put forward in the report. In the government press release, the Secretary of State, Kenneth Baker, said that:

> The government believes that immediate action should be taken to deal with indiscipline in schools and violence, wherever it occurs. It fully supports teachers in their efforts to establish good order in the classroom. It welcomes the contribution which the Committee's report makes to solving these problems.

In Parliament, the Secretary of State said the government would act on the following recommendations in the report:

> I have accepted the Committee's recommendation that in future all initial teacher training courses should include separate, compulsory elements of practical training in how to manage pupil behaviour, and that these skills should be a key factor in assessing a student's performance and competence to teach.
>
> I propose to set a clear national standard for the amount of time which teacher trainers must spend in school, so as to ensure that they have sufficient recent practical experience. I shall take action forward through the review which I am conducting of the criteria for approval of initial teacher training courses.
>
> Subject to the necessary consultation, I propose to accept the committee's recommendation that the management of pupil behaviour should become a national priority in the Local Education Authority Training Grants Scheme for in-service training of teachers in 1990–1991.
>
> I accept the Committee's conclusion that the procedures for excluding pupils from school should be monitored closely. I propose to institute a monitoring scheme for two years, rather than the five years recommended in the report. I will require reports in all cases where a headteacher's decision to exclude a child from a school is over-ruled by either the governing body or the local education authority. At the same time I shall require full details of incidents leading to exclusions, so that we have a national picture. At the end of that period I shall decide on the future of the existing statutory provisions.
>
> Subject to the necessary statutory consultations with the local authority associations, I propose to make an Education Support Grant

available to encourage local education authorities to work up coherent plans to address the problem of difficult pupils, whether on-site or off-site. I also propose to support through Education Support Grants a programme to encourage local education authorities and schools to take positive action to tackle truancy. Both grants would be made available in 1990–91, and would be targeted on inner city areas in the first instance.

I intend to require all Local Education Authorities to introduce teacher appraisal schemes covering all their teachers within the next few years; and I shall expect these schemes to pay close attention to classroom management.

I am asking the School Management Task Force to act on the Committee's recommendation that management training programmes for headteachers and other senior staff should give emphasis to the skills required to motivate and lead staff, and to manage institutional change.

The National Curriculum Council is already considering the place and content of personal and social education in the curriculum. I have asked the Council to report progress to me by the end of March.

The Committee's recommendations are addressed not only to government, but to Local Education Authorities, teachers, governing bodies, parents, the police and others. I look to all those groups to play their part in responding to the report. In particular, I hope that governing bodies and schools will look hard at what they can do to win parents' active support and partnership for their policies on discipline. I hope they will find opportunities to emphasise to parents the key role which they play in promoting good discipline in schools through the example they set and the control and guidance they provide in the home.

If there is a final comment to be made it is that in the Elton Report itself, and in the government's response, there is still an emphasis on the management of misbehaviour in schools being dealt with as a phenomenon isolated from the wider context of the ethos and organization of the school. If there is a consistent theme threaded throughout this book by its contributors it is that good behaviour is one result of an effective school where all pupils are recognized to have value, worth and significance — including those who from time to time transgress the codes of acceptable behaviour.

References

BERNSTEIN, B. (1959) 'Public Language: Some Sociological Determinants of Linguistic Form', *British Journal of Sociology*, Vol. 10 No. 4.

BORDIEU, P. and PASSERON, J. C. (1977) *Reproduction in Education, Society and Culture*, London, Sage.

DEPARTMENT OF EDUCATION AND SCIENCE (1986) *The LAP Project Survey*, London, HMSO.

DEPARTMENT OF EDUCATION AND SCIENCE (1987) *Behaviour and Discipline in Schools*, Education Observed 5, HMI Report, DES, HMSO.

DEPARTMENT OF EDUCATION AND SCIENCE (1988) *Secondary Schools: An Appraisal by HMI*, DES, HMSO.

DEPARTMENT OF EDUCATION AND SCIENCE (1989) *Discipline in Schools*, The Elton Report, DES, HMSO.

DOCKING, J. (1989) 'The Good Behaviour Guide: HMI Observations on School Discipline', in: Jones N. (Ed.) *Special Educational Needs Review*, Vol. 1 Lewes, Falmer Press.

LEESON, P., BAGLIN, E., and OLIVER, L. (1988) *Perspectives on the Lower Attaining Pupil's Programme*, Oxfordshire County Council, Education Unit, Wheatley, Oxfordshire.

NATIONAL FOUNDATION FOR EDUCATIONAL RESEARCH (1988) *National Evaluation of the LAP Programme*, Slough, NFER.

RAMASUT, A. (1989) *Whole School Approaches*, Lewes, Falmer Press.

Notes on Contributors

Roy Atkinson was educated at Bolton County Grammar School and followed graduate and post-graduate studies at the Universities of Leeds, Nottingham and Birmingham. His main studies have been in Psychology and he is a holder of the Diploma in Management Studies.

Following teaching experience at Colne Valley High School, further professional training at Birmingham University and experience in the counties of Durham and Gwent, he became Principal Educational Psychologist to the County of Staffordshire in 1976. During his service with Staffordshire he moved into educational administration, being first Principal Assistant Education Officer for Special Services and then for schools in the northern part of the County. In November 1984 he moved to Northamptonshire to the post of Deputy County Education Officer and succeeded Michael Henley to the post of County Education Officer in September 1986.

Roy Atkinson is a member of the Elton Enquiry into Discipline in Schools and is also the Chairman of the Interim Core Subjects Committee of the National Curriculum Council.

Eileen Baglin is Director of the Achievement Project in Oxfordshire. She trained as a teacher at Westminster College, Oxford, having taught at Henry Fawcett School in ILEA. She taught English and Religious Education at Burford Community College, and became Senior Teacher. It was here that she developed an interest and expertise on the learning needs of less able pupils and became involved in a number of schemes, relating to curriculum change and innovation. This interest was extended on becoming a magistrate in the Witney Petty Sessional Division where she continues to work in both the adult and juvenile courts, and currently the Chairman of the Juvenile Panel. In 1988 she completed a Master of Education Degree at Warwick University making a special study of school reports for the juvenile court, bringing together a joint interest in education and juvenile justice. It is from this basis of interest and expertise about pupils with learning difficulties that she became leader of the Oxfordshire Lower Attaining Pupils Project (LAPP). She is joint author of *Personal and Social Education: Choices and Challenges* (1988) (with A. Hargreaves, P. Leeson, P. Henderson, and T. Tossell).

Tim Brighouse is Professor of Education at Keele University. He graduated from Oxford University and was Head of History at Cavendish Grammar School, Derbyshire. In 1964 he was Deputy Head/Warden of Chepstow Community College and in 1966 moved to Monmouthshire where he was AEO for Sites and Buildings. He was Senior AEO in Buckinghamshire 1969–74 and Under Secretary (Education) for the Association of County Councils until 1977. He then joined the Inner London Education Authority as Deputy Education Officer (Services). He was Chief Education Officer for Oxfordshire for ten years before moving to Keele University in January 1989.

Ron Davie is Director of the National Children's Bureau in London. He graduated in psychology and taught in a variety of schools before taking up a post as educational psychologist in the Isle of Wight. From 1964–73 he was first Senior Research Officer and then Deputy Director (Research) at the National Children's Bureau. He was professor of educational psychology at the Department of Education, University College of Cardiff from 1974–81. He has published *11,000 Seven-Year-Olds*, (with M. Kellmer Pringle and N. R. Butler) (1966); a *Directory of Voluntary Organisations Concerned With Children*, (1969); *Living with Handicap*, (1970); *From Birth to Seven*, (1972); and an *Evaluation of INSET Course on Behaviour Problems: Welsh Office* (with E. Callely and D. Phillips) (1984). He has contributed many chapters in books and papers in scientific and other journals on education, psychology, child care and health. He was Chairman of the Association for Child Psychology and Psychiatry (1972–73); of the Developmental Psychology Section of the British Psychological Society (1975–77); and the Steering Committee of the Child Health and Education Survey, University of Bristol (1979–83). He is currently a Member of the National Curriculum Council.

Jim Docking is Principal Lecturer in Education at Roehampton Institute of Higher Education, London. He has taught in comprehensive schools in Yorkshire and Coventry, the latter as Head of History. His main areas of special interest and expertise are those of pupil behaviour, social and moral education, and parents in education. He has published *Victorian Schools and Scholars* (1967) and *Men and Machines* (1969). In 1980 his book *Control and Discipline in Schools: Perspectives and Approaches* was published and this appeared in a completely revised edition in 1987. He is currently editing a volume on pupil disaffection in primary schools, 7–11 years, which is part of a new series called *Education and Alienation* being published by Falmer Press. He is also completing a book on the role of parents in education.

David Galloway is Lecturer in Educational Research at the School of Education, Lancaster University. He has written and researched extensively on matters relating to pupil absenteeism, pastoral care and counselling, the management of special educational needs in ordinary schools, pupil truancy and disruption. He is a qualified teacher and professionally trained in residential child care and educational psychology. He worked as Senior Educational Psychologist with Sheffield

LEA where he was also responsible for a programme of research into pupil truancy funded by the Department of Education and Science. From 1980 to 1983, he was Senior Lecturer in Education at Victoria University of Wellington, New Zealand. He completed a Ph.D thesis on *A Study of Persistent Absence from School in Sheffield*, in 1980. His publications include *Case Studies in Classroom Management* (1976), *Educating Slow-Learning and Maladjusted Children* (with Carole Goodwin) (1979), *Teaching and Counselling* (1981), *School and Disruptive Pupils* (with D. Bull, D. Blomfield and R. Sneyd) (1982), *School and Persistent Absentees* (1985), *Schools, Pupils and Special Educational Needs* (1985), and *The Education of Disturbed Children* (with Carole Goodwin) (1987). From 1985–87 he was Chairman of the Welsh Branch of the National Association for Pastoral Care in Education.

Howard Green is Headteacher of The Henry Box School, Witney, Oxfordshire. He has wide-ranging educational interests but, in particular, staff development and the links between management and curriculum delivery. He has published a number of monographs on special needs, management training, staff development and curriculum planning. He is a Member of the National Council of the Secondary Heads Association; a Trustee of Schools Partnership Worldwide; a Member of the Institute of Biology; and Governor of a Primary and a Special School.

David H. Hargreaves is Professor of Education at the University of Cambridge. He was educated at Bolton School and Christ's College, Cambridge, where he studied Theology and Psychology. He taught in both in grammar and secondary modern schools before taking up a lectureship in social psychology in the Department of Education at the University of Manchester. He was University Reader in Education and Fellow of Jesus College, Oxford, prior to becoming the Chief Inspector to the Inner London Education Authority. He is well known for his research into social and inter-personal relationships in schools and has published widely in academic journals. He is the author of *Social Relations in A Secondary School* (1967); *Interpersonal Relations and Education* (1972); and the *Challenge for the Comprehensive School* (1982). In February 1983 he was invited to form the Committee on the curriculum and organization of ILEA secondary schools and became its Chairman. The report of this Committee was published in March 1984 under the title *Improving Secondary Schools*.

Neville Jones is Principal Educational Psychologist for Oxfordshire and tutor in the Oxfordshire region for the Open University Courses on Special Educational Needs E241 and Advanced Diploma. He has been a member of the Council and Executive Committee of the National Children's Bureau, member of the Executive Committee of the National Association for Mental Health, and member of the Consultative Committees on the Schools' Council projects on Disturbed Pupils and Gifted Pupils. Currently he is engaged in directing the Oxfordshire Programme on Pupil Disaffection. He has co-edited *Teacher Training and Special Educational Needs* (with J. Sayer), (1985); *Management and Special Needs* (1989) (with

T. Southgate); *Management and Psychology of Schooling* (1988) (with J. Sayer); and is editor of *Special Educational Needs Review No. 1* (1988) and No. 2 (1989).

Chris Lowe is Headteacher of Prince William School, Oundle, Northamptonshire. He has a special interest and expertise in educational law and is Honorary Legal Secretary to the Secondary Heads Association. He is also actively interested in opera in education and is Chairman of the Royal Opera Education Committee. He has published *Selection from English Novelists*, 1968; *The School Governors Legal Guide*, 1988; and *The School Travel Organisers Handbook*, 1988. On behalf of the Secondary Heads Association he has published *The Education Act* 1986; *Implications of School Management*; *The Education Reform Act*, 1988: *Implication for School Management*, 1988 and *The Teacher, The Pupil and The Law*, 1988. His chapter in this book is based on a lecture given in 1988 at the Institute for the Study and Treatment of Delinquency in London.

Peter Mortimore is Professor of Educational Research and Director of the School of Education, University of Lancaster. He has previously worked as a teacher and educational administrator. From 1979–1985 he was Director of Research and Statistics for the Inner Education Authority. His main areas of interest and expertise are those of school effectiveness, pupil behaviour and leadership in schools. He has co-authored *Fifteen Thousand Hours*, 1979; *School Maths*, 1988; *Behaviour Problems in Schools*, 1984; and *Secondary School Examinations* (Bedford Way Papers), 1984. He was a Member of the Economic and Social Research Council from 1981–85: member of the CIPFA/SEO Research Group on Performance Indicators: and Chairman of the DES-funded Advisory Group on the NFER's Study of Parental Involvement.

Richard Pring is Professor of Education at the University of Exeter. In September 1989 he will be taking up the post of Professor of Educational Studies at Oxford University. His particular areas of interest and expertise are those of the philosophy of education, personal and social education, and pre-vocational education. He has published *Knowledge and Schooling*, 1976; *Personal and Social Education in the Curriculum*, 1984; and *Personal, Social and Moral Education* (with J. Thacker and D. Evans). His is editor of the British Journal of Educational Studies.

Ken Reid is Reader and Head of School of In-service Teacher Education, at West Glamorgan Institute of Higher Education. His main areas of special interest and expertise are those of teacher education, disaffection, and educational management. He has published over one hundred and fifty articles and journals and in recent years published the following books. He has written *Truancy and School Absenteeism* (1985); and *Disaffection From School* (1986). He has edited *Combating School Absenteeism* (1987) and *Helping Troubled Pupils in Secondary Schools* Volumes One and Two (1989). He has also co-edited *Re-thinking Teacher Education* (with D. Hopkins) (1985); *Towards the Effective School* (with D. Hopkins and P. Holly) (1987); *An Introduction to Primary School Organisation* (with R. Bullock and S. Howarth) (1988); *Staff Development in Secondary Schools* (with K. Jones and F. O'Sullivan) (1989); *Staff Development in Primary Schools* (with J. Clarke, G. Figy and S. Howarth) (1989). He is the author of *Helping Troubled Pupils in Secondary Schools*, Vols 1 and 2 (1989). As part of his work he is external examiner for graduate and under graduate courses.

David Reynolds is Lecturer in Education at the University College in Wales, Cardiff. His main areas of special interest and expertise are those of school effectiveness and school improvement. He has contributed many articles on these themes and has been author of *Studying School Effectiveness*, 1985; *The Comprehensive Experiment*, 1987; and *Education Policy: Controversies and Critiques*, 1988. He is co-convener of the International Congress for School Effectiveness and he is also editor of the journal *School Effectiveness and School Improvement*.

Delwyn Tattum is Reader in Education at South Glamorgan Institute of Higher Education. He has taught in a variety of schools over a period of fifteen years and has a wide range of interests and expertise relating to pupil welfare in schools. These include problems of deviance, disruption, truancy, bullying, sociological aspects of special needs, school management and indiscipline, pastoral care and social education. His publications include *Disruptive Pupils in School and Units* (1982); *Management of Disruptive Pupil Behaviour in Schools* (1986); and *Bullying in Schools* (with David Lane) 1988.

Martin Rosenbaum works at the Children's Legal Centre where he is particularly involved with education policy. He was previously Education Secretary of the Society of Teachers Opposed to Physical Punishment (STOPP).

Norman Tutt is Professor of Applied Social Studies at the University of Lancaster. His special interest and expertise is the field of Child Care and Juvenile Crime. He has published extensively in the field of Child Care and Juvenile Crime, having edited a volume called *Violence* (1975); *Alternative Strategies for Coping with Crime* (1978); and *A Way of Life for the Handicapped* (with G. J. Jones, 1983). He has co-authored a book called *Children in Custody* (with G. Stewart, 1987). He has also written *Care and Custody* (1975). Among his various responsibilities he is United Kingdom representative on the Council of Europe Select Committee on Juvenile Crime.

Lawrie Walker is Director of the Technical, Vocational and Educational Initiative in Oxfordshire. He was previously Leader of the LAP Programme in Gateshead.

Chris Watkins is Course Tutor in Pastoral Care at the London University Institute of Education and Senior Tutor for In-service work. He is an Executive member of the National Association for Pastoral Care in Education and specialises in pastoral aspects of the curriculum. He has co-authored *School Discipline: A Whole School Practical Approach* (with Patsy Wagner) (1987) and written *Your New School: Tutorial Responses for Year One* (1988).

Name Index

Subject Index